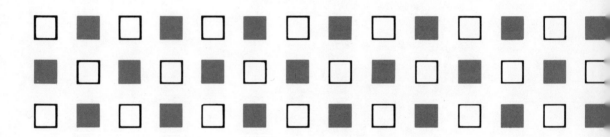

ALSO BY DANNY GOODMAN:

Word Processing on the IBM Personal Computer

A Parents' Guide to Personal Computers and Software

The Simon & Schuster Guide to the TRS-80 Model 100

How to Buy an IBM PC or Compatible Computer
(with the Editors of *PC World*)

Going Places with the New Apple IIc

SUPERMAC

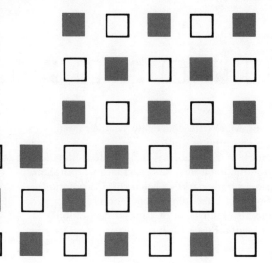

DANNY GOODMAN

MACWORLD BOOKS Published by
COMPUTER BOOK DIVISION Simon & Schuster Inc. *New York*

Published by the Computer Book Division/Simon & Schuster, Inc.
Simon & Schuster Building
Rockefeller Center
1230 Avenue of the Americas
New York, New York 10020

SIMON AND SCHUSTER and colophon are registered trademarks of Simon & Schuster, Inc.
Designed by Irving Perkins Associates
Manufactured in the United States of America

10 9 8 7 6 5 4 3 2 1

Library of Congress Cataloging in Publication Data

Goodman, Danny.
   Supermac.

   1. Macintosh (Computer) I. Title.
QA76.8.M3G65   1985   001.64   85-2065
ISBN: 0-671-49256-X

For JERRY BARINHOLTZ

Form: C

COMO

SAL

SKI

VE

V

ACKNOWLEDGMENTS

OF ALL THE computer books I've written over the past few years, none has had as much of the adventure of exploration as this one. I learned to use the Macintosh along with the rest of the pioneers who purchased the first 70,000 machines. I've listened intently to friends' and colleagues' perceptions of their Macs—their likes and dislikes, their raptures and frustrations. Many of these discussions sent me scurrying to my Mac and mouse in search of better ways, faster ways of doing things. Some of those seeds were planted by Robert Eckhardt, Dan Farber, Andrew Fluegelman, Jeremy Joan Hewes, and Adrian Mello. To my main man at Apple, Guy Kawasaki, I give special thanks for keeping me in the groove before the early days of Macintosh. And my love to Linda, who not only sacrificed hours of playing MacSlots so I could finish the book, but who also ran interference for me in the final, hectic weeks of the project.

CONTENTS

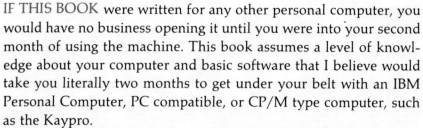

IF THIS BOOK were written for any other personal computer, you would have no business opening it until you were into your second month of using the machine. This book assumes a level of knowledge about your computer and basic software that I believe would take you literally two months to get under your belt with an IBM Personal Computer, PC compatible, or CP/M type computer, such as the Kaypro.

With the Macintosh, however, this book is for your second week.

Having used dozens of microcomputers over the last few years, I've never seen a computer so intelligently designed for the lay user. It is forgiving and encouraging—two qualities one would like to see in the more intimidating types of machines.

By your second week, you're already working on your own—independent of the manuals—exploring and learning new things about how you can use a computer to make you more productive and creative. You probably also have dozens of questions about why certain things work the way they do and how you can speed up some of the procedures. That's why I've assembled this collec-

INTRODUCTION

tion of explanations, performance tips, and techniques that will turn you into a superstar on the Mac.

Throughout this book you'll discover that this superbly designed little computer can be even better, faster, and more powerful than the hardware and software manuals have led you to believe. Armed with a little knowledge of what's going on behind the scenes, you will soon feel in absolute control of your Mac.

What You Need to Know Before You Begin

This book is designed as a *hands on* experience. You will get the most out of it if you have your Mac nearby. You'll be setting up your disk windows and trying all kinds of graphics, word processing, and spreadsheet tricks.

I assume, therefore, that you have been using your Mac for at least one week. In that time, I expect you have learned the basics of selecting icons on the screen by clicking them, and opening icons by double-clicking them. I also hope you have learned the elements of dragging icons around the screen desktop. It will help if you are at least acquainted with the concepts of copying documents by dragging the original icon to the destination of the copy. I expect you to have read the Macintosh and software manuals at least once—even if you didn't absorb it all. As long as the basics of each program sunk in enough for you to try the program out, you're all set.

As you work your way through this book, you will gain valuable experience in these elemental Mac operations mentioned above, so don't worry if you're still a bit unsure about how some of this stuff *really* works. I'll be giving you step-by-step instructions to take you from the simplest operation to some really advanced techniques.

There is one term I use throughout that you won't see in any Apple-supplied manual. It is the name for a feature that Apple calls the selection rectangle. In MacPaint, it's the rectangular icon at the top of the icon palette running down the left margin of the Mac-Paint screen. On the desktop and in MacDraw, it's the box you drag around multiple items to select them. Following a convention begun in *Macworld* magazine, I call this rectangle a *marquee.* When you place a selection rectangle on the MacPaint screen, its dotted line rotates around the area like the marquee lights in front of a theater. It's a most fitting name.

Beyond those few things, there's practically no technical jargon you'll need to know. Anything technical will be explained in full at the proper moment.

Most discussions and exercises are geared for the one disk drive Mac system. If you have a second (external) drive, I still recommend you go through the exercises with the internal drive only. You'll learn the concepts faster, even if it means swapping a few disks. Where operation with a second drive is markedly different, I'll give you special tips.

Chapter 1 starts you off with an in-depth discussion about managing your disks. You'll learn what all those icons in your System Folder mean. The mysterious Finder will no longer be a mystery. Not only will you learn what happens inside the Mac that causes all those disk swaps on a single-drive machine, but you'll also see how to minimize them. In addition, you'll be making truly workable program disks with lots of space on them. At the same time, you'll see how to develop a productive storage disk strategy.

The Mac's onscreen desktop is the target of Chapter 2. There, you'll see how to set up windows for the most effective viewing of your documents. How to name your documents for the most clarity is also covered in some detail. The desktop accessories are discussed at length, including how to make the Control Panel and Key Caps accessories work for you.

In Chapter 3, you'll try your hand at the fine points of MacPaint, many of which are nowhere to be found in the MacPaint manual. You'll also see how to create some striking shapes and images with the program, even if you consider yourself more of a barn painter than skilled artist.

Speeding up your word processing tasks with MacWrite and Microsoft Word is the subject of Chapter 4. Many of the techniques revealed here will also apply to other word processing programs that come along, so this chapter is for everyone.

In Chapter 5, you'll learn the ins and outs of transferring information from program to program. I show you techniques for the most efficient transfers between MacWrite and MacPaint, and how to move Multiplan spreadsheets into MacWrite. I also explain in full detail why MacDraw and MacPaint aren't as compatible as you might like them to be.

Chapter 6 is devoted to those who plan to connect their Macs to accessories and other computers. The full story behind the printer and modem ports is revealed. You'll understand why off-the-shelf printers for other computers don't work with the Mac without special software. And if you're inclined to link your Mac to another personal computer via modem or direct hookup, you'll see how it's done, with MacTerminal. I even supply step-by-step instructions for wiring customized serial cables.

The final chapter, Chapter 7, is required reading for everyone in the market for a new piece of Mac software. Since Mac software requires a different kind of evaluation than software for other computers, I provide several checklists of basic features to look for in every program you see, including tips on how to use the checklists before you buy.

Since I come from an IBM PC environment, I think it only fitting to share with others who are in the same boat the difficulty I had in weaning myself from a more traditional disk-operating system while learning the Mac's operating environment. So if you're going through that withdrawal, perhaps my thoughts, found in the Appendix, will help ease the pain.

Most important of all, I hope you have fun reading this book and experimenting with the tips and tricks I share with you in the following pages. The more you use the book and the Mac together, the more rewarding both should be.

So, grab the book in one hand, the mouse in the other, and get ready to turn your mild-mannered desktop computer into . . . SUPERMAC.

SUPERMAC□

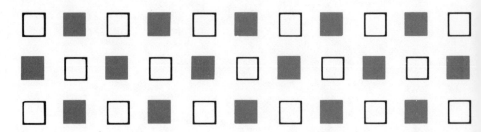

WHILE WE MACINTOSH users think nothing of spending a couple of hours fine tuning a MacPaint picture, painstakingly adjusting each FatBit, we are also the first to grow impatient with maneuvering microdisks in and out of the machine. This is especially true when the Mac we're using is not connected to an external, second disk drive. There are times when disk swapping seems to become a never-ending chore. At other times, the 400 kilobytes of storage on a single-sided disk—a size that it utterly cavernous on other personal computers—dries up, leaving us between the rock of a large document we want to work with, and the hard place of being unable to store it.

In this chapter, I will lay out a blueprint for Mac disk management success. I also intend to help you understand 1) what goes on inside the Mac during disk swaps, 2) why even a dual-drive system does not automatically solve every disk space problem, 3) how to reduce disk swapping on a single-drive system (or at least disguise swaps so you don't notice them as much), and 4) determine whether an external hard disk is a suitable alternative. By the end of this chapter, I'll resolve many of the questions that race through

Efficient Disk Management and Handling

your mind while you sit there anticipating the appearance of that dratted dialog box: "Please insert the disk. . . ."

Rummaging through the System Folder

What makes the Macintosh so much easier to use than other personal computers is the amount of "intelligence" built into it. Intelligence on the Mac encompasses:

- stopping you from doing a potentially disastrous operation
- creating the pictorial desktop environment
- presenting options in easy-to-access, pull-down menus
- keeping track of the time and date
- allowing you to change any of several elements of the Mac environment, including:
  —desktop background pattern
  —beeper volume
  —speed of your double-clicking abilities

The list goes on and on. The primary goal of these features is to make you feel comfortable in front of a computer. The onscreen mysteries of other computers are recognizable pictures and names on the Mac. Unlike on other computers, here *you* are in control of the way your screen looks. And the Mac second-guesses your wanderings from the prescribed path. It stands ready to grab firm hold of you just before you plunge into the abyss. The result is a computer that lets you concentrate more closely on the actual work you're doing, instead of focusing on the tiny details and worries of operating the computer.

What appears to us to be a kind of intelligence working inside the Mac actually comes from three distinct sources: the internal ROM software, the System file, and the Finder. Together, they are the most powerful software triumvirate available on a personal computer under $2500.

◢ ◢ ◢ ◢ ◢ ◢ ROM Software

The Read Only Memory (ROM) circuitry is located on one of the two large circuit boards inside your Mac. Look at the exploded view of your Macintosh in Chapter 2 of the owner's manual. The ROM circuitry is located on the horizontal board at the bottom of the case (in the exploded view, the board with labels for the memory and processor). The Mac's ROM should not be confused with the 128K or 512K of memory listed in the unit's specifications, however. The latter is called Random Access Memory (RAM), and it is where your programs and documents "live" temporarily when you're using the computer. I'll have much to say about RAM throughout the book.

ROM, on the other hand, is a permanent kind of memory, which has been programmed at the factory to contain some very basic instructions for the computer. Each time you turn on the Mac, instructions in ROM tell the Mac to beep, test the disk drive for the presence of a disk, light up the screen, and display the disk icon with a flashing question mark. The rest of the ROM—at 64 kilobytes, it is one of the largest ROMs found in personal computers today—contains many built-in tools, which programmers use to simplify their work. Instead of having to reinvent the wheel every time a new program needs a pull-down menu or dialog box, the programmer only needs to specify where on the screen the menu or box should be located.

This is but one of many built-in shortcuts programmers can find in ROM. Others include aid in quick design of the onscreen pointer and icon designs, easy integration of mouse action into programs, and so on. Most of these processes are invisible to you if you don't do any programming on the Mac. But because they're readily available to programmers, it means that many of the elements linking you to an application—menus, text editing, pointers, etc.—are relatively consistent from program to program. This makes for a computing system that will remain easy to use in the long run, no matter what road software development takes.

▲ ▲ ▲ ▲ ▲ ▲ **System File**

The second unit of the Mac's intelligence, the System file, comes on every program disk and on the System Disk packaged with your Mac. The System file is one of several files found in a Mac desktop folder called the System Folder. The closest you're likely to get to the System file is when you open (double-click) the System Folder. (See the illustration at the top of page 20.)

When viewing this folder's contents by icon, all you see is a row of Macintosh icons, one of which represents the System file. You can't open this icon (try it, and an alert box tells you so), since there's nothing a nonprogrammer can really do with it. Its contents are accessible only by way of a very sophisticated programming procedure.

Viewing the System Folder by size (using the Size option from the View Menu), shows you where a lot of your 400 kilobyte disk goes. (See the illustration at the bottom of page 20.)

As you can see, the System file eats up 192K, or more than one-third of a single-sided disk (the size of your System file may be smaller or larger, depending on the number of fonts you have in the System file—a subject we'll discuss at length later). So what's so special about the System file? you ask.

Two-thirds of the System file holds information the Mac uses to construct the various text fonts available in programs like

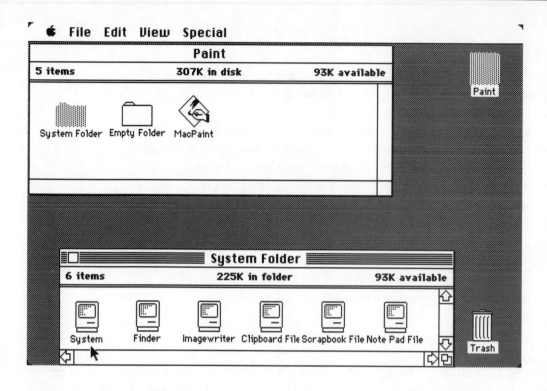

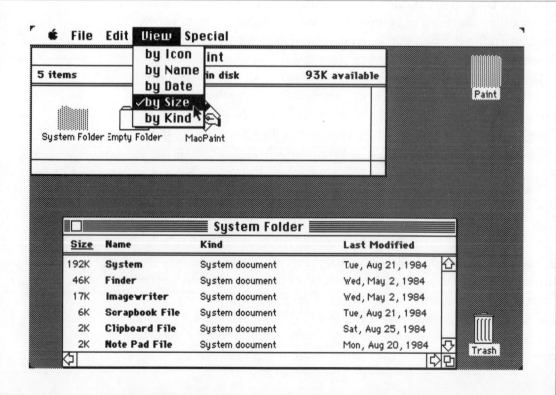

MacWrite and MacPaint. I'll have much more to say about text fonts later in this chapter. But for now, it is important to understand that each font has one or more individual tables for it stored in the System file. Two fonts, New York and Geneva, each have seven different tables, one table for each size (9-, 10-, 12-, 14-, 16-, 18-, and 24-point sizes). Another font, Monaco, has two tables, one each for 9- and 12-point sizes. I'll explain later why these various font sizes are needed.

Let's see exactly how much of the System file each font comprises (they can consume as little as 3K to as much as 8K on a disk).

- Turn on your Mac, and wait for the question mark icon. This assures you that the disk drive is in good working order *before* you entrust your disk to it.
- Insert the System Disk in your Mac.
- Open the disk by double-clicking the System Disk icon.
- In the window is an icon for the Font Mover program. Double-click this icon.

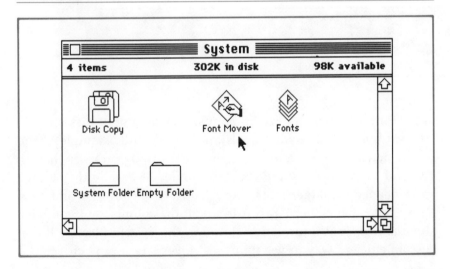

After several seconds, the Font Mover window appears on the screen. On the left is a box with a list of fonts currently contained in the System Folder. On the right is a box listing the fonts held in a separate file called Fonts. Select any font from the System Folder by clicking its name. In the bottom of the window appears a rundown

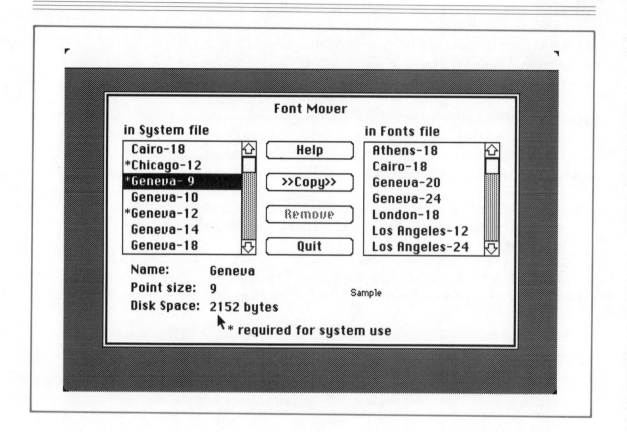

of the font: its name, its size (in points), the amount of disk space it takes in bytes (1024 bytes equals a kilobyte), and a sample of the font in actual size. Examine several of them, and you'll see that 9-, 10-, and 12-point fonts are generally under 3K, while the storage space needed for larger fonts, like Athens-18, Geneva-24, and New York-24 can get rather large. Add up all these fonts, and you have about 88K of font information stored in the System file. We'll discuss an efficient way to use the Font Mover later in the chapter.

■ To get back to the desktop display, click the Quit box in the Font Mover window.

The rest of the System file contains information the Mac uses to control and display the Desk Accessories, which you select from the pull-down menu under the Apple logo in the upper left corner of the Mac desktop. I'll have much to say in the next chapter about how the Desk Accessories can be used most efficiently.

◢ ◢ ◢ ◢ ◢ ◢ The Finder

The third unit of the Mac's intelligence, and the one with which you actually come into the most contact, is called the Finder. Like the System file, the Finder file is located in the System Folder, but it takes up considerably less space—46K.

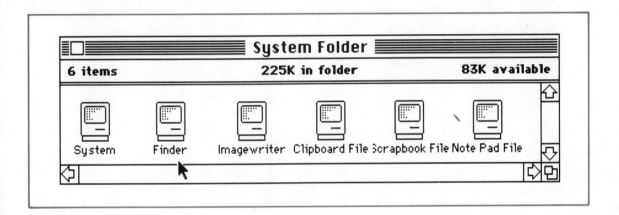

If you have ever used other personal computers, you will perceive the Finder to be in many ways analogous to what you know as the operating system.

The Finder program is responsible for quite a lot. It displays the menus across the top of the desktop, responds to your mouse-menu manipulations, displays windows and their icons on your desktop, copies documents from disk to the Mac's memory, displays disk directories, and much more. Virtually everything you do to interact with the Mac is orchestrated by the computer-coded instructions in the Finder program. A majority of the Finder program is loaded into the Mac's RAM when you insert a program disk in the disk drive. That's one reason why not all of the Mac's 128K RAM is available to your documents. However, having most of the

Finder instructions in memory helps speed things along when you select items from a menu.

One way to think of the Finder is as a helpful gnome running around inside your Mac, setting up your desktop for you, keeping track of document locations, watching out for wrong turns you might make, and advising you before a catastrophe occurs. Sometimes this gnome can be a pain in the neck, especially when it keeps asking you to swap disks. But try to remember that it is looking out for your best interests. It makes sure everything is in the right order at the end of one session so the disk can be set up quickly at the start of the next.

Does our Finder gnome have a face? Sure, it does. You see the face every time you insert a disk in response to the question mark disk icon.

It smiles for a second, then gets to work behind the scenes, hustling about at almost the speed of light.

Together, the ROM, System file, and Finder create an unusual operating environment that is far easier to conceptualize than a disk-operating system like MS-DOS (IBM PC), CP/M (Osborne, Kaypro, etc.), or ProDOS (Apple II, III). At the same time, it is forgiving if you err, and more often than not rescues you if you accidentally make a serious blunder.

Transferring Control from Disk to Disk

We now have a very important concept to discuss. It revolves around the Finder, and how it controls the Mac from the disks you put in the drive. The Finder, as we've said, has much to do with locating and transferring information onto and off the disks, while the System file holds the text fonts and the Desk Accessories. In other words, these two files contain information and programs essential to the functioning of the Mac, regardless of the application. They must be present either on the disk currently in the disk drive, or on a disk only one swap away. The Mac remembers the name of the disk with the System and Finder files on it, and will ask for that disk to be inserted when instructions from those files are needed.

The disk holding the active System Folder is called the startup disk, and it always appears in the upper right corner of the desktop. Don't be confused by the name, startup disk, however. Any disk whose icon makes it to that upper right corner position—the *pole position* I call it—is called the startup disk. And while it is true that the first disk you put into the Mac to get it "started" acts as a startup disk, other disks can take the place of the startup disk during a work session.

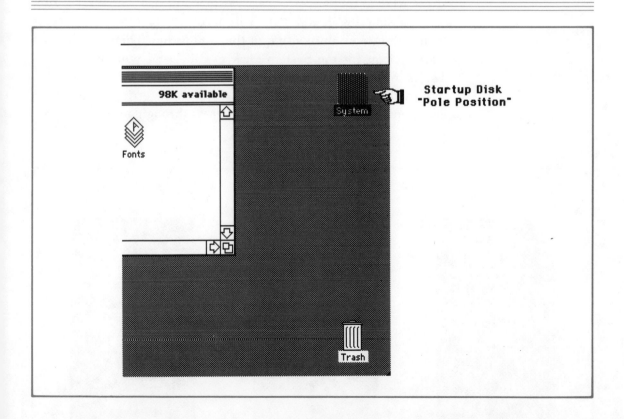

Let's say that, instead of having a copy of the System Folder on your Write/Paint disk, the System Folder was only available on the Mac System Disk. To get the Mac going in the morning, you'd insert the System Disk after you turned on the computer. At this point, the Finder from the System Disk is in charge—in control—of the Mac. If you then eject the System Disk, and insert a Write/Paint disk that does not have a System Folder on it, you will have to constantly swap disks while using MacWrite or MacPaint, because the programs frequently need resources from the Finder and System files. And in some cases, such as printing a MacWrite document, the lack of a System file on your application disk will prevent you from accomplishing the task at all.

But when you have a copy of the System Folder on the Write/Paint disk, as well as on the System Disk, an amazing thing happens (see illustration below). If you start the Mac with the System Disk (A), eject the disk, insert Write/Paint (B), and open one of the applications, the Finder on the System Disk "hands off" control of the Mac to the Finder on the Write/Paint disk—like relay runners passing the baton (C). You most likely won't notice the change, however, until you quit the application. Then you will see that the icon for the System Disk is gone, and your Write/Paint disk is in the pole position of the Mac desktop.

Why the behind-the-scenes switch? By transferring control from disk to disk, the Finder lets you progress through a series of appli-

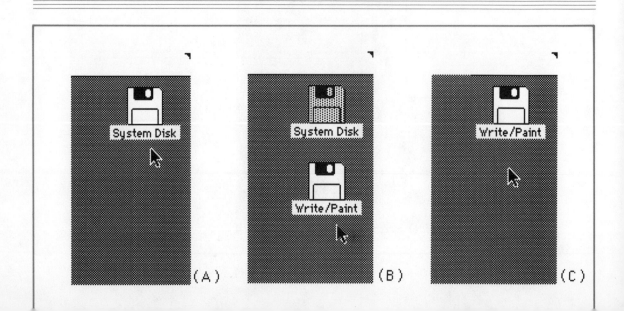

cations disks without leaving a confusing trail of disk icons behind
you, cluttering up your desktop screen.

Unfortunately, in version 1.1g of the Finder (you can see the version number by selecting "About the Finder. . ." in the Desk Accessories menu—the larger the number, the more recent the version),
the Finder on the second disk takes over only when you open an
applications program on that second disk. Future releases of the
Finder may allow you to manually change control of the Finder
through a menu selection. This fine point of the Finder can sometimes cause an extra disk swap, but, as we'll see, the extra swap
helps demonstrate what "control of the Finder" is all about.

Now that we've covered the theory, let's see how control of the
Finder and System files really works.

For our first exercise, we're going to use the Desk Accessories to
demonstrate how the System file interacts with your disks. We'll
start where we left off, with your System Disk in the drive.

- Pull down the Desk Accessories menu (the one with the Apple
  icon).

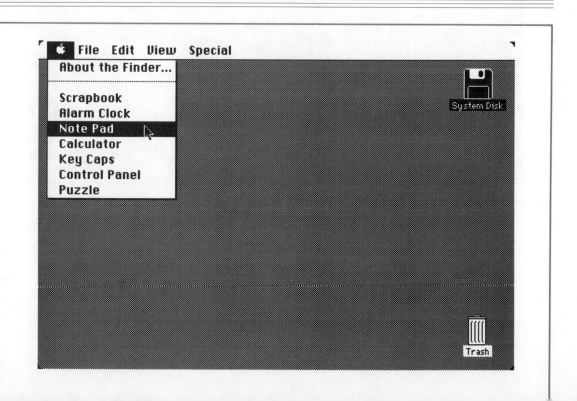

- Notice that the items in the menu are in solid type, indicating that you can select any one of them at this point. Do not, however, select anything now.
- Instead, pull down the File menu, and Eject the System Disk.
- Without turning off the Mac, insert the Write/Paint disk (or any applications disk with a System Folder on it).
- Pull down the Desk Accessories menu again, and, you'll see that this time the items in it are dimmed, which shows that you can't select any Accessory.

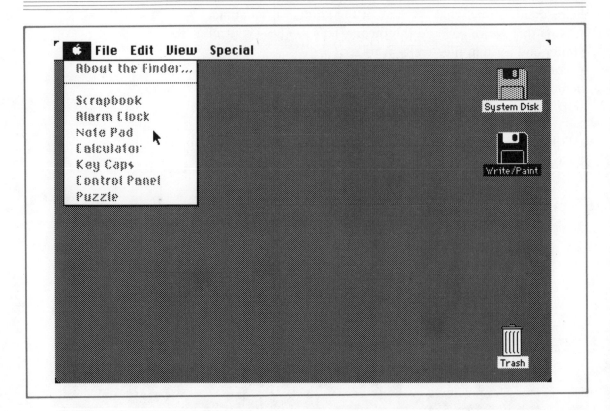

This means that Desk Accessories are available only from the disk the Mac currently recognizes as the Startup Disk—in our exercise the System Disk—which is not in the drive at the moment. In other words, control of the Finder has not yet transferred to the second disk, because we have not opened an application (which is also why the System Disk still appears in the startup disk position on the desktop).

But the plot thickens.

- With the Write/Paint (or any other applications) disk still in the disk drive, open the disk and an application.

At this point, the Mac transfers Finder control from the missing System Disk to the Write/Paint disk you're opening. In other words, it recognizes that you are no longer using the System Disk, and that you'll want to keep everything together on the applications disk you're running.

- From within your application, pull down the Desk Accessories menu to see that they are now active.
- Quit the application.

When the Mac desktop reappears, the System Disk icon is gone, leaving only your application disk icon in the startup disk position, plus the open window.

- Pull down the Desk Accessories menu.

Lo and behold, the accessories are active, this time from the applications disk.

Even if you have two disk drives, and start the Mac with the System Disk in the internal drive and the Write/Paint disk in the external drive, once you eject the System Disk from the internal drive, the Accessories will not be active until you open an application on the other disk. It is the act of opening the application that transfers control of the Mac from the System Folder on the System Disk (now ejected from the internal drive) to the System Folder on the Write/Paint disk in the external drive.

A very important point here is that failure to transfer control to the new disk results in continual disk swapping throughout your work session. Here's an experiment to show what I mean. For this experiment, you'll need your System Disk, Write/Paint disk, and one other disk, preferably one without a System Folder on it.

- Start the Mac with the System Disk.
- Eject the System Disk.

- Insert the Write/Paint disk.
- Open the disk and the System Folder so all icons of the System Folder are visible on the desktop.
- Leave the windows as they are, select the Write/Paint disk icon, and eject the Write/Paint disk.
- Insert the third disk. If it is a new disk, an alert box will ask you whether you wish to initialize the disk. Click the initialize button, and give any name you like to the disk when you're asked for one. For the sake of clarity here, call it Third disk.

Next, we're going to perform a simple copy operation on a small file (to keep the amount of swapping to a minimum). Note, however, that a copy operation is *not* an application.

- Drag the Clipboard icon from the Write/Paint System Folder window to the Third disk icon. When the Third disk icon turns dark (which it does when the pointer overlaps it), you have properly situated the Clipboard icon to accomplish the copy.

After one swap of Write/Paint and the Third disk, you are prompted for the System Disk. What happened? Why should you insert the System Disk, since it was not a part of the operation you just performed? By this point, you should be able to figure out the answer. Because you did not open an application on Write/Paint, the Finder on the System Disk remained in control (as indicated by the fact that its place on the desktop as startup disk did not change). And at the end of the copy operation, the Mac prefers to have the startup disk in the disk drive for your next operation. Thus it asked for the System Disk as the last step in the process.

■ ■ ■ ■ ■ ■
What Goes On During Disk Swapping

Disk swapping on a single-drive Mac is annoying. There's no denying it. I've discovered, however, that once I knew what was going on each time I had a disk spit out at me, I didn't mind the swapping quite as much. I resigned myself to the fact that whatever was going on inside there is in the best interest of my documents.

◢ ◢ ◢ ◢ ◢ ◢ Copying Complete Disks

The simplest way to begin to understand what's happening is to use the single-disk Disk Copy utility that comes on the System Disk.

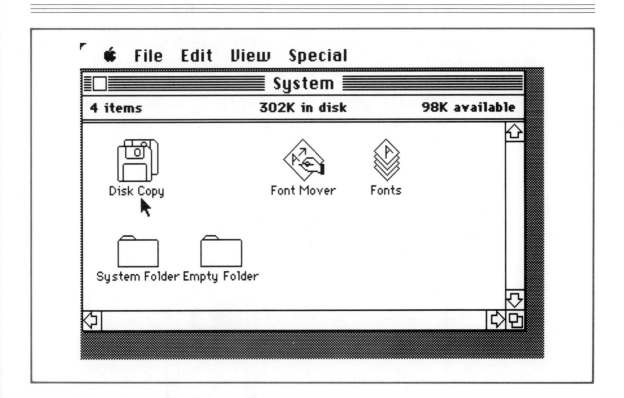

This program duplicates the contents of one disk onto a second disk. When you double-click the Disk Copy icon, you get a brief introduction, followed by a single prompt line at the bottom of the screen asking you to insert the disk you want to copy. When you place that *source* disk in the drive, the Mac makes a temporary copy in the Mac's RAM of one-quarter of the information stored on that disk.

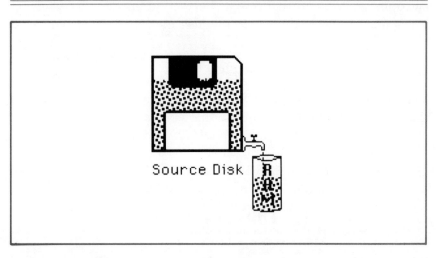

Source Disk

The Mac ejects the disk, and you're prompted to insert the disk you want the copy on. The Mac then dumps the contents of RAM onto the *target* disk.

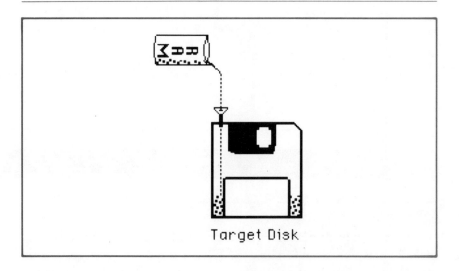

Target Disk

This process is repeated three more times until the duplicate disk is complete.

To summarize, the contents of one disk is copied, one-quarter at a time, into a holding area inside the computer, and then copied once more from the holding area to the new disk. The reason it takes four passes is that the Mac's 128K RAM can hold open only about 100K of its space at one time for this procedure. Just to achieve the clearance of 100K from the 128K of RAM, however, the Mac has to perform a few tricks, the most obvious of which is eliminating a fancy display of desktop, icons, and menus. Since the display of these things takes up memory in the Mac, such luxuries are flushed out temporarily during the Disk Copy utility process.

Copying disks with a single drive is a snap on a 512K Mac. With its expanded memory, the 512K Mac can clear enough RAM to accommodate a full disk of data. By simply dragging the source disk icon to the target disk icon, the entire contents of a 400K disk are loaded into RAM and transferred to the new disk in one swap. The four-swap Disk Copy utility program is superfluous on this model.

◢ ◢ ◢ ◢ ◢ ◢ Copying Individual Documents

Now, let's say you want to copy a folder containing six documents from one storage disk to a backup storage disk. Following the instructions from the owner's manual, you first make sure the icons for both disks are on the desktop. To do this, you insert each disk you're going to copy (from and to) into the drive, so their directories of folders and documents get stored in the Mac's memory. Even if you immediately eject the disk without opening it, you can still look at the contents of the disk by opening the dimmed disk icon of that disk on the desktop. (If, however, you open an application on one of the disks, all other disk icons and their directories are removed from the Mac desktop.)

Next, you open the storage disk containing the folder you want to copy and drag the folder icon to the backup disk icon. At that point, a small dialog box appears near the top of the screen, telling you there are six documents to be copied. Another dialog box in the center of the screen begins the prompts for inserting the appropriate disks.

```
Files remaining to copy    6
```

If you start with the storage disk in the drive, the first request for insertion of the backup disk will be to verify that: a) you have the correct disk in hand, b) there is enough room on the disk for the folder, and c) there are no other documents on the disk bearing the same name(s) as the documents in the original folder (to prevent covering up one document with a different one of the same name).

Then the Finder must start the copying process, so it asks for the source disk holding the documents. Unfortunately, there are not 100K of RAM available in the 128K Mac for this kind of copy operation, so only a small portion of the contents of the folder can be loaded into RAM on its way to the backup disk. When the first segment is copied into RAM, the original disk is ejected, and the backup requested. The RAM contents are then written to the backup disk.

If you have already performed a copy such as this, you may have noticed that the number of files appearing in the dialog box may decrease by one, more than one, or not at all during a swap. Since the Finder does not restrict the copying process to the copying of only one file at a time, if three small files can fit into available RAM space during one copy step, then they'll be transferred at once. That's why the number of files remaining to copy may decrease by two or three during a single transfer. Conversely, if a file is larger than the available RAM, the file may take two or more swaps to get its contents successfully transferred. Of course, the 512K Mac, with its ample RAM, can copy in one swap as many single files as you care to select at one time.

If you have two disk drives installed on the Mac, the amount of data transferred during each step of the copy process is no greater than with one drive. Without having to swap disks, however, you don't pay much attention to how often each disk drive motor is activated, and the entire process takes much less time since the drives keep passing the data without stopping for you to swap.

◢ ◢ ◢ ◢ ◢ ◢ Loading Documents

Let's look at another example of disk swapping to see what the Finder is doing for us. In MacPaint, you can recall a picture from the disk for editing by using the Open. . . selection from the File

Menu. When you do this, you are presented with a dialog box that features a small window onto a list of MacPaint documents on the current disk. To import a document from a different disk (storage disk), you click the Eject selection in the box, and the MacPaint disk is immediately ejected. When you insert your storage disk, the Mac reads the directory of that disk into memory and, in the same small window as before, displays the names of all MacPaint documents on the new disk. Double-click one of the document names to open it.

Immediately, the storage disk is ejected. This swap is the Finder telling you that it needs some further instructions from the Finder file on the MacPaint disk about how to load the document into memory. Once the Finder picks up the instructions, it then ejects the MacPaint disk and asks for the storage disk, so it can retrieve the data for the picture and place it into RAM.

The storage disk is once more ejected, and a dialog box asks for the MacPaint disk, in what will become a series of swaps—indeed a mystery to many Mac users. The reason for these swaps, however, is that when you are working with a MacPaint document on a 128K Mac, a duplicate of the document is also stored temporarily on the MacPaint disk (I'll explain why in a moment). When, as often happens, a MacPaint document is larger than the available RAM, you will have several swaps between the two disks as the picture is transferred, piece by piece, over to the MacPaint disk's temporary file.

Now, a word about that temporary file. With their finely detailed bits of data, MacPaint documents take up a lot of memory space. When you use the hand icon to move the picture in the window to see a different section of the picture, you've probably noticed that the Mac accesses the disk. After a few seconds' delay, the picture is restored to the screen, with the new section filled in. The Mac obtained the new picture information from the copy of the document stored temporarily on the MacPaint disk.

Good personal computing practice says that you should save your documents every 15 minutes or so, to avoid data loss in case of a power failure. When you perform a Save in the middle of your session, the disk swaps taking place copy the image from the temporary file on the MacPaint disk to the storage disk. The number of

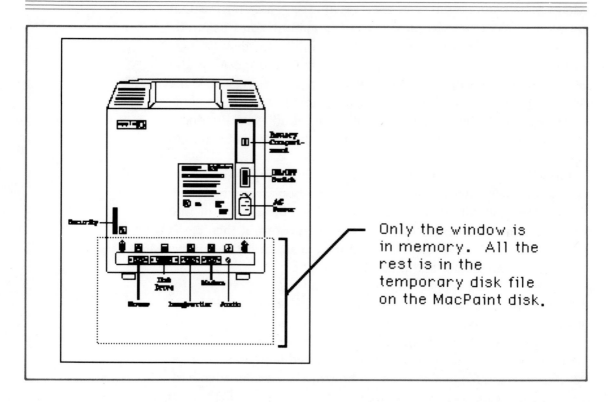

Only the window is in memory. All the rest is in the temporary disk file on the MacPaint disk.

swaps depends on the size of the document. As with the individual file copy swapping, above, the first swap is for the Finder to confirm that you have the correct disk and there is room for the document as emended. Thereafter, the swaps are purely for the exchange of file data, which may require as many as three or four swaps on a half-page picture.

Sometimes the Finder takes pity on your having to swap disks so often for a large document, especially during a Save operation to your storage disk in the middle of your session. In these instances, the Finder ends the swapping with the storage disk in the drive, rather than asking for MacPaint one last time. But the minute you attempt to use any of MacPaint's features which are not stored in RAM (going to Text, for example), you will be asked to insert the MacPaint disk again. Likewise, if you use the hand icon to move the picture, the program can retrieve its information about the rest of the picture *only* from the temporary file on the MacPaint disk.

Closing the document or performing a Save As. . . operation puts you, your document, and your disks through similar paces. Of course, if you don't make any changes after your most recent Save or Save As. . . , or if you don't want to save changes you made, there is no extra swapping, since the Finder knows that the correct copy of the document is already safe on the storage disk.

The temporary file created during MacPaint (actually, there are two files, but one is very small) may help you understand why you sometimes get the alert box about almost running out of room on the disk, and yet when you get back to the Finder on the desktop, you see you have 20 to 30K available. Since the temporary files are erased before the Finder returns you to the desktop display, you can't see that your 20K picture and its temporary copy were, in fact, getting dangerously close to filling up the disk. I'll have some specific recommendations later in this chapter on how to make your MacPaint operations smoother, with fewer swaps, and with less chance of running out of room on the disk. Also see Chapter 3 on MacPaint techniques.

In contrast to the temporary file manipulations on a 128K Mac, a 512K Mac has room enough in RAM to store a complete MacPaint picture. Consequently, there is no need for the computer to hold parts of the picture on disk. But since your latest additions and corrections are entirely in RAM, it becomes even more important to periodically save your picture on disk so that a power outage doesn't erase your most recent work.

Reducing Disk Swapping on the Desktop

During a hectic Mac work session, there may be times when you want to switch from using one application to another: MacWrite to MacTerminal, for example. The Mac is definitely capable of displaying multiple applications disks on its desktop. Four or five disks is the practical limit, although if your disks have many files and folders on them, the 128K Mac's memory can't keep track of too much directory information. A dialog box will advise you that an earlier disk icon will be removed from the desktop. But sometimes having more than one program disk icon displayed will cause the Mac to ask you to perform an unexpected disk swap, just like the one we saw a little earlier when copying a file between two storage disks. There are two possible reasons for the extra disk swaps: either the Finder has not passed control from the first program disk to the second (we went through an example of this earlier); or there is a large Clipboard File that must be copied from the first disk to the second disk. Here is an experiment to demonstrate this second point.

◢ ◢ ◢ ◢ ◢ ◢ **The Clipboard Swap**

We'll use MacWrite and MacTerminal (or any second applications disk you have handy) for this experiment. This time you'll see what happens when you have a large Clipboard File on the first program disk.

- Turn on the Mac, and insert MacWrite.
- Open MacWrite, and type two lines of text—even gibberish, if you like.
- Select the entire text and Copy it.
- Quit MacWrite. Unless you wish to save what you just typed, click "No" when you're asked whether you want to save changes.
- Eject the MacWrite disk.
- Insert the MacTerminal disk and open it so you can see the Mac-Terminal program icon.
- Open MacTerminal.

Before the program ever gets going, however, you are prompted for the MacWrite disk. What's going on behind the scenes here is that the Mac doesn't really store the Clipboard entirely in memory, but rather keeps it safe on the disk in the Clipboard File. When you change program disks and open a program that uses the Clipboard File (which is just about every major productivity program), the Mac "knows" that it must fetch the most recent Clipboard File— giving you the impression that the Clipboard is all in memory. When you opened MacTerminal, the swap with the MacWrite disk copied the Clipboard File from that disk to the MacTerminal disk, ready for you to use in MacTerminal. This will also happen even if you have two disk drives but change program disks in only one drive. And you thought the second drive would eliminate that darn swap disk dialog box!

But what if you don't want the MacWrite Clipboard—and its extraneous swap—in MacTerminal? Or how can you prevent the swap back to an unwanted startup disk as in the earlier experiment? The answer is to reset the Mac between applications.

◢ ◢ ◢ ◢ ◢ ◢ Resetting the Mac

One way to reset the Mac is to first eject the disk in the drive and turn off the computer. A few seconds later (after any residual juice in the Mac's circuits has dissipated) turn the Mac back on, wait for the question mark disk icon, and insert the new application disk. Turning a computer off and on like that, however, can cause a power surge inside the machine, which puts a strain on the components inside, especially the video display tube. It also strains the power switch, a mechanical device that deteriorates with excessive use. Instead, I recommend you install and use the Programmer's Switch, which came packaged with your Mac (instructions for installation are found in the owner's manual). This switch is intended primarily for program developers who often find themselves in need of getting out of a programming jam caused by some unforeseen bug. Of the two buttons, labeled Interrupt and Reset, you'll use only the Reset button, which is located closest to the front of the Mac.

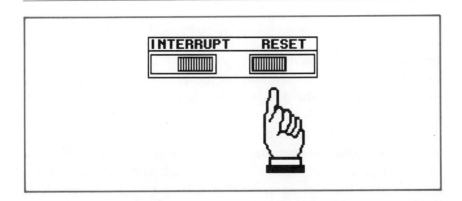

To reset the Mac with the Reset button, first eject any disks in your drives. Then press and release the Reset button. A second later, the screen goes blank, the Mac beeps, the screen flashes on and off once more, and the familiar question mark disk icon appears on the screen, ready for you to insert a startup disk of your choice.

It is important to remember, however, that the Reset button operation momentarily cuts off power to the memory, thereby erasing its contents. Of course, when you are shifting between two programs for two completely separate tasks, this is fine, because the second program doesn't need any Clipboard or other assistance from the first disk. But if you are counting on the Clipboard to transfer text or a picture from one program to another, you should not reset the Mac between programs. If you do, the Clipboard (or the trail leading back to the Clipboard file) is erased right along with the rest of the memory.

Two cautions are in order, however. First, when you have the Programmer's Switch installed, don't place anything, such a book or a lamp, near the switch that might bump the buttons while you're using the Mac. If someone should walk by your desk and accidentally bump that book, which, in turn, hits one of the buttons, your current document could go blooey. Second, use the Reset button *only after you have ejected all disks.* Beyond those two warnings, the Reset button is not only safe, its use could prolong the life of your Mac's key components.

The rule of thumb to follow, therefore, is to reset the Mac and start fresh every time you start a new application.

◢ ◢ ◢ ◢ ◢ ◢ Eliminate Swapping a Phantom Disk

By now, you've probably noticed that when you eject a disk from the Mac, the disk icon remains on the desktop, but in a dimmed form. Even though the disk is no longer in the drive, the Mac still has a record of the disk's contents in memory (open the dimmed disk icon, you'll see a window of other dimmed icons). I call this ejected-disk icon a *phantom* disk—a shadow of its former self. And, like many phantoms, this one can come back to haunt you—with a request from the Mac to insert that disk, even though you don't need it anymore.

What is the reason for this swap request? If you open the phantom disk icon, adjust its window, or move an icon in its window, the Finder will insist on recording those changes on the disk. It will ask for the actual disk in order to effect those changes, however, only when you do something that removes the icon from the desktop—if you open an application or eject another disk. The Finder does this so that any changes you make to the desktop will be duly recorded and reproduced when you insert the disk during another work session.

To avoid being prompted for the phantom disk, don't open a phantom disk icon or, if it is already open, don't move any of the icons in the window or select the Close All option from the File menu. If you think you might want to look at the document icons of a particular disk after it is ejected, leave the window open when you eject it, and then don't close it. The Finder will have recorded the open window on the disk as it was ejected. Unless you have a fetish for closing all your windows (or inserting a disk that has all windows closed), don't bother changing or moving the windows. The phantom disk will disappear from the desktop as soon as you open an applications program from an active disk. Just bear in mind that the Finder won't quietly remove a phantom disk from the desktop if you mess with it.

Alternatively, if you close all the windows on the phantom disk, you can drag the dimmed disk icon to the Trash. As long as the icon is not a startup disk, the Mac won't blink an eye, as you clear off your desktop.

Working Disk Strategies

In this section, I will give you guidelines to follow in making backup copies of your program disks. Backup copies of program disks should be the ones you use in your everyday Mac work. I get queasy about using the original disks, since something can go wrong—and the more expensive the program, the more bizarre and damaging the "wrong" thing will be. Such is Murphy's Law, as updated to reflect the personal computer age. Strategies for making working copies of MacWrite and MacPaint apply to many other programs, so don't think this discussion is limited to those two programs only. Copy-protected software, like Multiplan, present particular problems, and I'll discuss them as well.

This entire discussion, of course, is based on the assumption that you will be using separate disks for your programs and storage—a practice I will emphasize in the next chapter. A program disk has too much space taken up by necessary files—the program and System Folder—to offer enough free space for storing anything but the documents you are working on at any given moment. Long-term storage should always be on separate storage disks. I know, you're going to tell me what a nuisance it is to have to swap disks all the time by keeping documents on storage disks (I'll show you some ways to minimize the problem later in the chapter). But when you are left with less than one-quarter of a disk for document storage, it doesn't make economic sense to make copy after copy of your favorite applications just to store a dozen documents. Sony, Apple, BASF, and Memorex will be happy, but your budget won't be.

◢ ◢ ◢ ◢ ◢ ◢ System Disk and Font Mover

Were it not for the very important Font Mover program, the System Disk would be practically superfluous. That one program, however, and its associated Fonts file combine forces to give you tremendous flexibility in the text fonts you can use in many programs.

But just because you won't be using the System Disk except to alter the text fonts for an applications disk doesn't mean you shouldn't keep a backup copy of it. A general rule to follow in all personal computer work—whether dealing with 3½-inch microdisks like on the Mac, 5¼-inch disks like on the IBM PC, or 8-inch disks on sophisticated CP/M systems—is *Never use the original disk for your work.* The reason for this is that you never want to expose your original disk to the risk of being damaged either while in use or simply in transit. Additionally, there may be a time when you will want the original disk in its virgin state—perhaps just to see how differently your current working disk has evolved from the original. If you keep your original disks in a safe place and do not alter them in any way, you always have a master reference to turn to in time of need. Then, if your working disks should become damaged or lost, you can always make a fresh copy of the original disks, just as if you had bought a new set.

Another reason I recommend making a backup copy of your System Disk is that I am now going to suggest a method of maintaining your fonts and using the Font Mover program different from what Apple prescribes in its manuals. You'll be trashing everything on your working System Disk except what you'll need for creating font libraries for your program disks. In addition to freeing up more disk space, this should help simplify the moving of fonts, especially the importation of new fonts, like the Seattle font, which you can extract from a Multiplan program disk (for details, see the end of this section). It will also allow you to more quickly change the selection of fonts in the System file in case you find it necessary to add a new font to programs like MacPaint, MacDraw, MacWrite, or Microsoft Word.

Our main goal here will be to compile a complete catalog of fonts in the Fonts file of your working System Disk. From there you will be able to use the Font Mover to assemble a smaller, more selective array of fonts for individual applications programs. At the same time, we'll be clearing enough space on the working System Disk for you to create a System file that contains the entire Fonts file—a task not possible without lots of disk space. This will be the fastest way for you to load variable-font programs, like MacWrite, Mac-Paint, and MacDraw, with every available font, in those situations that demand it.

- First, copy the entire System Disk onto a new disk (use the single-drive Disk Copy program on the original System Disk if you have only one disk drive and 128K).
- If the new disk needs to be initialized, initialize it when prompted.
- Name the new disk "System Disk," just like the original.
- When the copy procedure is completed, eject the original disk, and put it away.
- Reset the Mac.
- At the question mark disk icon, insert your newly made disk.
- If your Mac is equipped with a second drive or 512K RAM, you can trash the Disk Copy program now. Having two drives or all

that memory obviates the need for this utility (and you'll always have the program on your original System Disk if you ever need it).

- Open the System Folder.
- Select the Scrapbook File, Note Pad File, Clipboard File, and Imagewriter, either by using the pointer to draw a marquee around them all or by selecting one, pressing the Shift key, and then selecting the others one by one.
- Drag them all to the Trash. You won't be needing these files at all on the System Disk, so confirm in the dialog boxes which will appear that you wish to erase these files. You should have only your System and Finder icons showing in the System Folder window.
- Click the Font Mover or Fonts icon (either one) to bring up the Font Mover program.

The next step involves copying every font from the System file to the Fonts file, thus creating a catalog of every font available to you.

- The most effortless way to do this is to click the topmost font in the System file window, and drag the pointer beyond the bottom of the window.

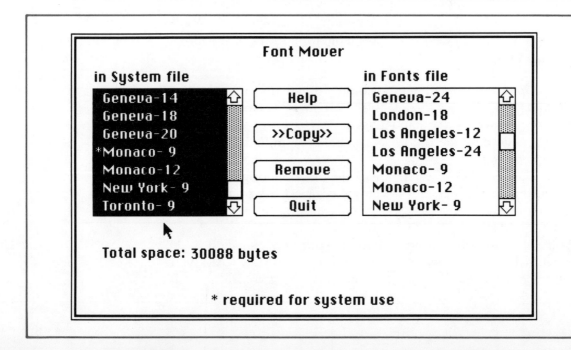

Holding the mouse button down with the pointer below the window causes the window to scroll vertically, selecting all fonts to the bottom of the list.

- Click the >>Copy>> command to copy all selected fonts to the Fonts file. (The arrows point in the direction—left or right—in which the copy operation will work.)
- After a short while, you may see one or more dialog boxes, like the one that follows, advising you that some fonts are already in the Fonts file. Click OK to acknowledge these messages.

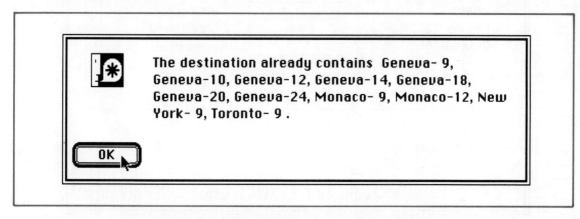

- When the copy procedure is finished, and with all fonts still selected in the System file listing, click the Remove command in the window.
- A dialog box tells you that some fonts cannot be removed. Click OK.

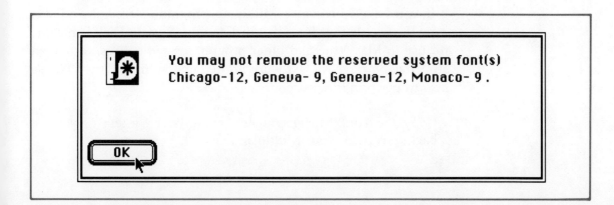

What you now have is a System file with only four fonts listed (these fonts, marked with asterisks, are the ones the Finder uses for window and desktop displays) and a Fonts file with a complete list of every font available on the Mac.

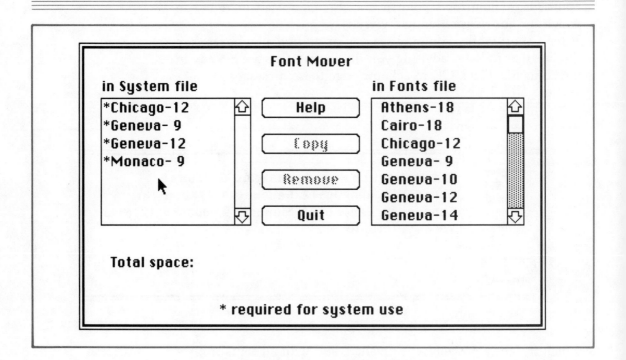

This completes the making of your working System Disk. The Fonts file on your System Disk is now essentially your master fonts library. Only Copy from it, and never Remove fonts from the Fonts file. We'll use the Font Mover and this master Fonts file to create font libraries for MacWrite and MacPaint in the next sections.

If you have Microsoft's Multiplan program, I recommend you copy the Seattle font from that disk to your System Disk Fonts file, for use in MacWrite and other programs. Seattle-10 is, to me, an attractive typeface for text work printed on the Imagewriter. Here's how to perform the procedure.

■ Copy the Font Mover program from your System Disk to a backup copy of your Multiplan disk.

- Double-click the Font Mover icon that is in the Multiplan disk window.
- The Seattle-10 and -20 fonts are listed in the System file window below the asterisked system fonts. Select both Seattle fonts and >>Copy>> them to the Fonts file.
- Quit the program. In the Multiplan disk window is a fonts icon labeled Fonts. Click the icon and type "Seattle" to rename the icon.
- Copy the Seattle font icon to the System Disk.
- Double-click the Seattle icon—not the Font Mover icon—on the System Disk to start the Font Mover program.
- Select both Seattle fonts listed in the Seattle file, and <<Copy<< them to the System file.
- Quit the program.
- Double-click the Fonts icon on the System Disk to restart the Font Mover program. This time, all the fonts in the Fonts file will be listed on the right.
- Select both Seattle fonts from the System file list and >>Copy>> them to the Fonts file. They are now a part of your master library.
- Quit the Font Mover program and trash the Seattle icon from the System Disk window. You should also trash the Seattle and Font Mover icons from your Multiplan disk to open up spreadsheet storage space on that disk.

◢ ◢ ◢ ◢ ◢ ◢ **MacWrite**

Making an effective MacWrite working disk takes a little more care initially than what you did for your System Disk, but the effort will be well worth it when you start using the program on a day-to-day basis.

Since the program arrives on a separate MacWrite disk, the fastest way to start the process is to make a complete copy of the MacWrite disk. The following instructions are for a single-drive 128K Mac.

- Turn on (or reset) the Mac and insert the original MacWrite disk.
- Double-click the disk icon to open the window.
- Double-click the Disk Copy program icon.
- In a moment, a description of the program appears on the screen, with a box for you to click to continue. Click the box now.

- The Mac ejects the disk and prompts you to insert the disk to copy from. Simply reinsert the MacWrite disk.
- When the program asks you to insert the disk to copy to, insert a blank disk. Initialize the disk when asked to do so.
- When prompted for the new disk's name, type "Write".
- After four swaps, you have a complete duplicate.
- Eject the original disk and press the Reset button.
- Insert your new Write disk.

For a single-drive 512K Mac, the procedure is simpler.

- Turn on (or reset) the Mac and insert the original MacWrite disk.
- Eject the disk, and insert a blank disk. Initialize the disk when asked to do so, and, when prompted, type the new disk's name, "Write".
- Drag the dimmed original MacWrite disk icon to the new Write disk icon.
- You'll be asked to confirm whether you want to copy the contents of MacWrite onto Write. Click OK.
- After only a couple of swaps, the complete copy will be made.
- Eject the original disk and press the Reset button.
- Insert your new MacWrite disk.

If you have two disk drives (with either Mac), the procedure is simplest of all, since there is no swapping required.

- Turn on (or reset) the Mac and insert the original MacWrite disk in the internal drive.
- Insert a blank disk in the external drive. Initialize the disk when asked to do so, and, when prompted, type the new disk's name, "Write".
- Drag the original MacWrite disk icon to the new Write disk icon.
- You'll be asked to confirm whether you want to copy the contents of MacWrite onto Write. Click OK.
- After considerable disk drive activity, the complete copy will be made.
- Eject both disks and press the Reset button.
- Insert your new MacWrite disk in the internal drive.

Next, you want to get rid of excess baggage which is taking up space on your disk by dragging a few icons to the Trash. You don't have to Empty Trash every time you bring a document there unless you want to see immediate results in the amount of space available on the disk.

Once you've gone through the MacWrite manual and the exercises with the Sample Memo, you can delete that document, freeing up 3K of disk space. Whether you want to delete the single-drive Disk Copy program from your MacWrite working disk depends on your system configuration and the way you will be managing your storage disks. If you have a second disk drive or 512K RAM, there is no practical use for this program. On a 128K single-drive system, however, you may wish to use Disk Copy later to make backup copies of your storage disks.

Since it has an effect on our creation of a work disk, let's look more closely for a moment at the problem of backups. There are two ways to back up your work. One way is to keep a duplicate set of all your storage disks—one each for MacWrite, MacPaint, Multiplan, etc. In this case, the Disk Copy program (for a 128K Mac) will be useful in making a duplicate of your storage disk whenever you're finished with an application session. This method is expensive, however, since you will have at least three active disks for each application (the working program disk, one storage disk, and one backup storage disk). A second, more economical way is to have a single disk for all backup storage. To this disk you transfer individual files as they are updated from a diversity of applications or applications storage disks. In this case, you won't be using the Disk Copy utility to back up files, and it can thus be left off your MacWrite working disk, freeing 6K. It is safely on your System Disk if you ever need it.

Next, we can eliminate two files from the System Folder that we don't need at the moment.

- Open the System Folder.
- From the row of six icons, delete the two that won't affect your MacWrite abilities in any way: the Note Pad File and Scrapbook File, freeing up a total of 12K.

As we'll see in detail in the next chapter, when it comes time for you to use these applications, the Mac automatically creates the appropriate files for you.

You can free up more space on the disk by selectively removing fonts you aren't likely to use. Most guides to the Macintosh I've read suggest that you copy the Font Mover and Fonts file from the System Disk to your working application disk in order to select fonts. I don't like this method, however, because it entails far more copying and file manipulation than is really necessary. Instead, use the System Disk you prepared earlier to assemble a new System file for your MacWrite disk.

- Eject the MacWrite working disk and insert the System Disk (your working one).
- Open the disk and the Font Mover program.
- Using techniques outlined earlier in this chapter, select fonts from the Fonts file that you'll be using in MacWrite and copy them to the System file.

Your choices here are limited only by the kind of work you'll be doing with MacWrite, and how varied and/or fancy you anticipate on getting with your documents. Seattle-10 is a nice sans-serif font for text (if you transferred it from a Multiplan disk), while pictographs from Cairo-18 may come in handy for highlighting within some documents. Remember that your MacWrite documents probably won't be as elaborate as will be the text you add to MacPaint documents. Chances are that most word-processing applications won't need a type size any larger than 14-point for headlines.

If you're not sure which fonts to use at first, I can recommend the following for most straight text work:

- Geneva-9
- Geneva-10
- Geneva-12
- Geneva-18
- Geneva-20
- Geneva-24
- New York-10
- New York-12
- New York-20
- New York-24

If you can obtain the Seattle font, then add Seattle-10 and -20 to the list.

I've included some large fonts in this list because if you intend to print documents in the highest quality on the Imagewriter, you should have in the System file the size that is *double* the size you'll be using. For example, if you use New York-12 as your regular text font, it is recommended that you have New York-24 in the System file as well. See Chapter 4 for more details on fonts and printing text.

- When you're finished selecting and copying your MacWrite fonts, quit the Font Mover program.
- Open the System Folder of the System Disk to display the icons of the System Folder programs.
- Eject the System Disk with the windows still open.
- Insert your MacWrite working disk (no need to open it).
- Select the System icon from the System Folder window and drag it to the MacWrite disk icon.
- A dialog box asks if you want to replace the System file on the MacWrite disk with a file of the same name from the System Disk. Click OK.

The copying (and swapping) you'll be doing here will be to transfer a copy of the newly formed System file with your selected fonts onto your MacWrite working disk.

When the copying is complete, you will probably end up with between 150K and 190K available on the Write disk, depending on how many fonts you put in your new System file. Later in this chapter, I will show you what you will be doing with all that space.

▲ ▲ ▲ ▲ ▲ ▲ **MacPaint**

Creating a working MacPaint disk is just as easy as making the MacWrite disk was, because Apple supplies a separate MacPaint master disk in the software package. On a 128K Mac, use the Disk Copy utility on the System Disk to make a duplicate of the Apple MacPaint disk onto a fresh blank disk, which you can name "Paint." On a 512K Mac, drag the MacPaint icon to the fresh blank disk icon. Drag to the Trash any files you don't need, like the Note Pad and Scrapbook, from the System Folder.

Because MacPaint is sure to bring out the creative genius locked inside you, I recommend you create a MacPaint disk System file with as many fonts as possible. That way, there won't be a font you'll be lacking. San Francisco is, perhaps, one font you won't need, unless your MacPaint document is intended to resemble a ransom note. (I have to admit to once using the font for just such a document—disguising an invitation to a baby shower as a ransom note.) If you don't want to include every font, you should at least be sure to include the Cairo font in your selection for your MacPaint disk. See Chapter 3 for a complete list of the predesigned pictographs available to you with this font.

To make your MacPaint font collection, go back to the System Disk and invoke the Font Mover program. When you do, the System file lists the fonts you installed on your MacWrite disk. You can either remove them all (the asterisked ones will remain) in order to start fresh or you can just build onto the list from the catalog in the Master Fonts file, using the <<Copy<< command. If you've trashed all the extraneous files from your System Disk as recommended earlier, you'll be able to create a System file duplicating the complete Fonts file. Replace the original MacPaint disk System file with the new one, just as you did with MacWrite.

◢ ◢ ◢ ◢ ◢ ◢ **MacWrite/MacPaint Working Disk**

Believe it or not, after all this talk about making separate MacWrite and MacPaint working disks, it may sound odd that I'm going to recommend that you make a working disk that combines the two programs. But there's a good reason for it, if you qualify under the following two situations: 1) you have a single-drive Mac, and 2) you will be importing MacPaint pictures into MacWrite documents.

If both of these circumstances ring a bell with you, then you'll save yourself some time in the future by making a combination working disk. With both programs on one disk, the Clipboard File is readily accessible to both programs, so there is no disk swapping between applications.

This combo disk will be actually little more than a duplicate copy of the Write/Paint disk you received with these programs. Use the Disk Copy utility from the System Disk to make the working copy on a 128K Mac. On a 512K Mac, drag the Write/Paint disk icon to the blank disk icon.

Note that with these two programs on one disk, you don't have much room left for working with a document. Avoid storing documents of any sort on this disk. Also, be careful of the number of fonts you import into the System file. The tendency will be to want every font you have on the MacPaint disk. Unfortunately, that is not possible. Look for ways to open at least 35K of available disk space, including trashing the Scrapbook and Note Pad files if you don't use them. Every kilobyte counts on this combination disk. I suggest you use this disk *only* when creating a MacPaint picture for quick transfer to a MacWrite document. Otherwise, use your specialized Write and Paint disks, since they have room for all the fonts plus an acceptable workspace.

▲ ▲ ▲ ▲ ▲ ▲ Copy-Protected Working Disks

With the exceptions of Microsoft BASIC and a few other programs, most *third-party applications* for the Macintosh (i.e., software published by companies other than Apple) are copy-protected to some degree. How, then, can you make a working disk from a program that supposedly won't let you copy it? The answer is that some copy-protected disks do let you make a *pseudo-copy*.

There is a way to make a working copy of a disk that adheres to Microsoft's copy protection scheme to help reduce the risk of damaging your original disks. Unfortunately, the copy you make is not exactly a complete copy. It requires the momentary insertion of the original disk to reassure the program that you in fact have possession of the original disk. You only have to do this swap once per session, as long as you keep the Mac turned on and don't reset it.

When you start the program from the copy, it looks to a particular memory location for the presence of a Master disk code. If the code is present, the copy is satisfied that you have possession of the original disk. If the code is not there, the copied program ejects the disk and requests insertion of the original—so much for storing the original disk in a safe place off-site.

The question will come, then, whether it's worth the trouble to make such a pseudo-copy of a protected program disk. My answer is most definitely in the affirmative, even though on both a single- and dual-drive system it means an extra swap when you first use the program in each session. Let's just say that using the copy as the work horse during the computing session is cheap insurance to protect your investment in the original disk. If you or the Mac somehow damage the original disk while it's in the disk drive, which is much more likely if you use it full-time, you'll be out of the game until you can get a replacement from the software supplier—a process that can take a week or two. Don't let that happen to you.

◢ ◢ ◢ ◢ ◢ ◢ If You Run Out of Disk Space

Almost nothing is worse than getting the warning box that alerts you to the fact that your disk is almost full, and that you have to delete or move some documents from the disk to continue. Before you can expect to go on with your program by deleting a file or two, it will help if you understand something about the Trash.

Just because you place a file in the Trash doesn't mean that you're going to have extra space on your disk instantly. Here is an exercise to show what I mean.

- Place your MacPaint working disk in the Mac.
- Open the disk window so you see the amount of disk space available. Note how much space is available.

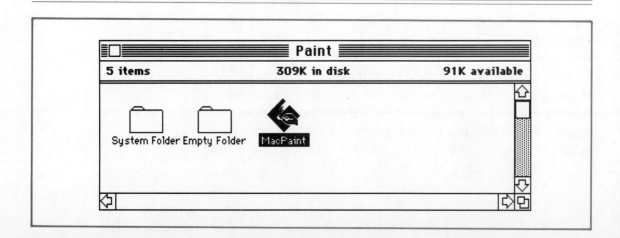

- Select the MacPaint program icon with a single click.
- Pull down the File menu and select Duplicate. A Copy of Mac-Paint icon appears on the desktop. Notice that the available space has been immediately affected by making a copy of a file.

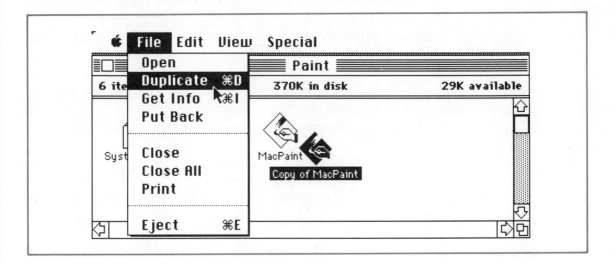

- Drag the Copy of MacPaint icon to the Trash.

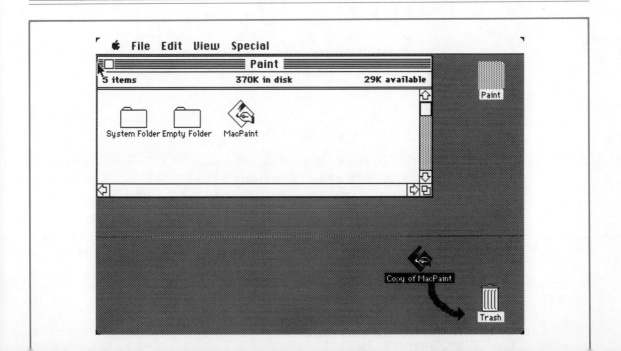

■ Reply OK to the box that wants verification of deletion of an application program.

Now, note that a) the disk drive was not activated (so nothing happened to data stored on the disk), and b) the amount of available space remains unchanged. If you make a mistake in dragging the wrong icon to the trash, you can recover it immediately by opening the Trash, fishing out the icon, and dragging it back to its original window. But if you're intent on eliminating a file, you have three ways to remove it to free up space on the disk: 1) perform an Empty Trash command from the Special menu, 2) open an application, or 3) eject the disk.

Therefore, follow these guidelines if you run out of space:

1. If you forgot to remove a temporary copy of a document (which you've stored on a separate storage disk), or if you keep frequently-used documents on the program disk, look into your program disk window for nonessential files you can put in the Trash.
2. If you have used the Scrapbook or Note Pad for any reason since you made the working disk, there will be icons for those applications in the window. Provided you don't need the information stored in either file, drag them to the Trash.
3. Now Empty Trash. A few kilobytes of space will open up on the disk.

More often than not, it is merely for the want of a couple of kilobytes that a program runs out of room on the disk.

◢ ◢ ◢ ◢ ◢ ◢ **Storage Disks**

Creating an empty storage disk is about the easiest disk maneuver you can do with a Mac. There's no disk swapping involved, even on a single-drive Mac. There's no icon dragging or file copying, either.

A Mac document storage disk need start out as nothing more than a completely empty disk, after it is initialized. *Initializing* a disk—Macintosh terminology for the more computerese term, formatting—is a procedure that goes on behind the scenes in your

Mac. As your disk spins during initialization, the Mac is in a sense painting parking lot lines on the disk. The disk surface is being subdivided into numbered sectors where your documents will be parked when you save them to disk. Since most computers using the 3½-inch microfloppy disks format them differently, it's much cheaper for you to buy unformatted disks and then initialize them as they're needed.

- With the Mac turned on, and the Finder already loaded into the machine by way of an application or System Disk, simply insert a new disk.
- A dialog box alerts you to the fact that the disk is unreadable and needs to be initialized. Click OK.
- After the disk is initialized, and you have named it ("Storage" in our example), open it.

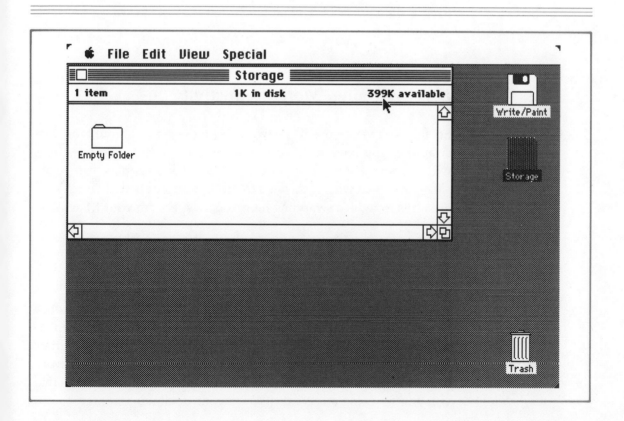

You see a virgin disk, with only one empty folder (from which you can make more), and the fact that 399 kilobytes are available to store your documents. The Finder uses one kilobyte as overhead to keep track of where things are (or will eventually be) on the disk. As the number of documents stored on the disk grows, the overhead also grows—to about 5K. The rest is for your storage.

It is important to realize that copying the System Folder or even just the Finder from the System Disk (or other applications disk) to your storage disk will *not* help you eliminate swapping when accessing documents on the storage disk. Recall what we learned earlier about the Finder. As long as a program disk starts the Mac going, the Finder on that disk will prevail *until another applications program is started.*

Therefore, start your storage disk's life with the full 399K. If you're prolific or prone to experiment (how can anyone resist Mac-Paint?), you'll start filling up storage disks soon enough without having the clutter of a gigantic System Folder crowding you out.

Less Swapping, More Productivity

So far, you've seen several ways to reduce the amount of disk swapping you have to do at the desktop level. But there are times while working within applications that disk swapping can really slow you down when you need to be at your productive best. There are ways to reduce swapping here, too, to speed up your Mac work.

◢ ◢ ◢ ◢ ◢ ◢ Saving Without Swapping

If you wondered earlier why I made a big point of clearing off a large amount of space on application program work disks, the reason is that I'm going to show you how to use that space to eliminate disk swaps on a single-drive system while still saving your work every fifteen minutes or so, as recommended. This assumes that you will be using a second disk for your document storage.

Normally, when you start an application and load in a document from a storage disk, the Finder remembers which disk you used to retrieve the document. Therefore, when you go to perform an intermediate save of your latest emendations or additions, the Finder automatically signals you to swap disks so it can save the latest edition on the storage disk. With even a small file, this will take no fewer than two complete swaps. In all likelihood, however, it will be three or four swaps with a typical document. With this kind of extra handling in store for you, you're not as likely to perform as many intermediate saves as you should—perhaps causing severe heartbreak if something goes wrong with the power or the Mac.

There is a better way, however.

- Open a document from within an application. After a couple of swaps, the program disk will be in the disk drive.
- The first time you're ready to store an intermediate version of your document, invoke the Save As. . . command instead of the Save command.

In most programs (like MacWrite and MacPaint) you get a dialog box guiding you through the procedure of doing a Save As. . . operation. The name of the current file is highlighted, and the name of the program disk is in the right half of the box.

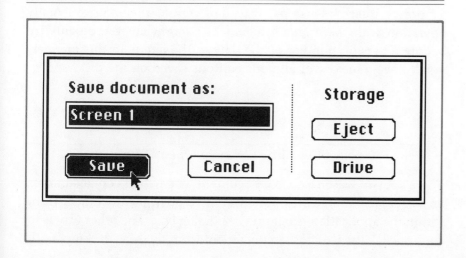

- Click Save without touching any keys on the keyboard (if you touch a letter or number key, the current name of the document will be removed from the box, and you'll have to retype it).

What's happening here is that your original document on the storage disk remains intact, while you save a copy of it temporarily on the application disk. Then, every time you issue a Save command, the Finder thinks you want it to update the document on the application program disk—which, in fact, you do. This way, you won't have to swap any disks while you merrily save your changes as often as possible.

When you're finished editing the document, you can then issue the Save As. . . command once more, eject the program disk, insert the storage disk, and click Save in the dialog box. This procedure copies the document back onto the storage disk, automatically replacing the old version with the new. You'll have to perform a couple of swaps to get the document back on your storage disk, but you've saved yourself a lot of swaps during previous intermediate saves.

When you return to the Mac desktop, be sure to Trash the temporary copy of the document from your Write disk. You don't want this needless file to rob your Write disk of valuable storage space.

Incidentally, this method provides you with the luxury of keeping early versions of your document intact on the storage disk—just in case you find your corrections are worse than the original. To preserve earlier versions, instead of making the final Save As. . . operation with the original document name, change the name by adding a version number or the date to the name. In this manner, you'll have a history of all your editions saved on the disk.

◢ ◢ ◢ ◢ ◢ ◢ **A Streamlined Way to Open Documents**

There are two ways to open a document when you keep documents on a separate storage disk. One way is to open the document from within the application program via a dialog box. The other way is to double-click the icon for the document from the Mac desktop. Both methods entail some disk swapping on a single-drive Mac, but oddly enough, I find that the method that involves one more swap is actually less tedious and much faster than the other way.

Let's compare the steps involved in opening the same sized Mac-Paint document two different ways. Method No. 1 is the way of opening from the dialog box within an application, while Method No. 2 is the icon approach.

DIALOG BOX METHOD	ICON METHOD
1. Insert MacPaint disk.	1. Insert MacPaint disk.
2. Open MacPaint disk.	
3. Open MacPaint program.	
4. Close "untitled" window.	
5. Select "Open" from File menu.	
6. Eject MacPaint disk.	2. Eject MacPaint disk.
7. Insert Storage disk.	3. Insert Storage disk.
	4. Open Storage disk.
8. Select and Open document.	5. Select and Open document.
9. Insert MacPaint disk.	6. Insert MacPaint disk.
10. Insert Storage disk.	7. Insert Storage disk.
11. Insert MacPaint disk.	8. Insert MacPaint disk.
	9. Insert Storage disk.
	10. Insert MacPaint disk.

If you look at these two procedures carefully, and envision the mechanics of each, you'll notice that the dialog box method starts with a lot of mouse and desktop manipulation before getting to the swaps. The icon method, on the other hand, is almost all disk handling.

Which of these two methods is better? I suppose it depends on the humor of the user, but I prefer to let the Finder do most of the desktop and window work for me behind the scenes. The less I have to precisely maneuver the mouse, the better. I just hunker down and accept the swapping as a matter of course.

▲ ▲ ▲ ▲ ▲ ▲ **Swapping with Finesse**

Also on the subject of swapping disks, I've found that the procedure can be made less tedious if I prepare myself physically for the swaps. Trying to do a swap with one hand is very tiring. From an ergonomic point of view, the one-handed method takes too much energy to be a pleasant experience.

I recommend using the two-handed method.

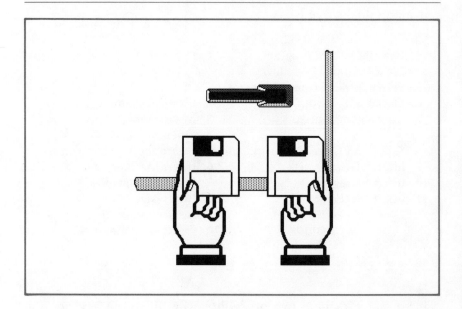

Hold the disk you're going to have to insert in one hand. When the disk from the machine is ejected, grab it with the other hand. Keep shuffling the disks, but let one hand be in charge of your program disk, the other in charge of the storage disk. The individual "reads" and "writes" of each disk don't take long, so you won't be left holding a disk too long. In fact, if you are poised, ready to grab one disk and insert the other, you will get through the swap session much faster than by fumbling around with one hand.

■ ■ ■ ■ ■ ■

Two-Drive Tips

Just adding a second disk drive to your Mac doesn't automatically mean you're the slickest Mac user on the block. You still have a few techniques to learn that can make your job a lot easier and faster.

◢ ◢ ◢ ◢ ◢ ◢ **Changing Drives**

For many dual-drive Mac users, there seems to be a bit of confusion surrounding how to know which drive is the "active" drive, and how to switch the active drive from internal to external, or vice versa. If you've worked with other dual-drive computers before, the active drive concept is the same as that of the *default* drive—the drive that is summoned for a read or write on the next command.

To solve the mystery, let's work with MacWrite in the internal drive and a storage disk in the external.

- From the desktop, open a document in the storage disk window by double-clicking the document icon in that window.
- After several seconds, MacWrite will load, and then the document will be in the display.
- Select Save As. . . from the File menu.

You'll notice that on the right side of the dialog box, the name of the MacWrite disk is shown. That means that the internal drive— with the MacWrite disk—is the active drive. This might seem counterintuitive to you, because you opened the document from the external drive. I agree.

- To change the active drive to the external drive, click the Drive button (below the Eject button). The storage disk name now appears in the dialog box.

■ Click the Cancel button. This action merely closes the dialog box. The external drive is still the active drive.

Therefore, any time you want to change the active drive, summon the Save As. . . dialog box, and click the Drive and Cancel buttons.

There should be little need, however, to change active drives except when you're opening a document from a different drive, or when you want to save your current document on a disk other than its original. When you load a document into an application, the Mac remembers both the name of the disk and which drive it came from. When you invoke the Save command, the revised document automaticallly seeks its original disk and drive, no matter which drive is the active drive. Similarly, certain behind-the-scenes procedures (things we'll be discussing later, like the temporary picture files MacPaint creates and the Command-Shift-3 snapshot command) write files only to the disk with the application program and/or the System Folder, no matter which drive is the active drive. In general, then, you can pretty much leave the work up to the Mac until you need to deliberately read or write to a different disk drive.

◢ ◢ ◢ ◢ ◢ ◢ **Opening Documents**

When it comes to opening a document, with a program disk in the internal drive and a storage disk in the external drive, you will be better off in the long run if you open a document by double-clicking the document icon from the storage disk. Here's why.

In order to open a document from inside a program like MacWrite or MacPaint, you must first close the "untitled" screen, and then select the Open command. From there you must go through quite a bit more mouse manipulation to select the external drive, and find the document in the small document window in the dialog box. Save yourself all the hassle by opening the document from the storage disk document.

Another fact worth remembering is that even if you view the contents of your storage disk document folders by name, size, date, or kind, you can still open the document by double-clicking it in its nonicon listing. Just place the pointer anywhere along the text area of the line associated with the desired document. Then double-click. It's just like double-clicking an icon.

▲ ▲ ▲ ▲ ▲ ▲ **Ejecting Two Disks**

With the addition of a second disk drive comes the extra hassle of having to eject a second disk. If you've upgraded to a second drive after using only the internal drive, your inclination will be to eject each disk individually, selecting each disk icon with the pointer beforehand. Frankly, I'm lazier than that, so I let the Mac do the dirty work for me.

The crux of the issue is the method of selecting both disk icons in one fell swoop, and then issuing one Eject command that covers everything selected. The Mac gives you no fewer than four ways to select both disks. Some methods are more sensible than others, as you'll see.

One way to select both disks is to use the Select All command from the Edit Menu. When you invoke this command *with all windows closed*, all disk icons and the Trash are selected. Selecting the Eject command makes the Mac wrap up things in each disk and eject them in turn. Don't worry. The Mac won't eject the Trash in your lap. It essentially ignores the command to eject the Trash or any icon outside a window that is situated on the desktop (you'll see why you'd have icons outside the window in later chapters).

This method, however, isn't going to work for you if you keep any window(s) open. The problem is that when you issue the Select All command, the Finder selects all the icons in the active window only. What you want is to be more specific in the selection of icons—the disks.

If the disk icons for the two disks currently in the system's drives are adjacent to each other on the desktop, then you can use the marquee to draw a box around the two disks while holding down the mouse button. When you release the button, both disk icons are selected. Then you can invoke the Eject command, which works on each disk in turn.

But if your desktop has more than two disk icons and they are not adjacent to each other—say they're the first and third icons in a column—you'll have to select the icons differently. Point to one icon and select it. Press the Shift key on the keyboard and select the other icon. Now you can invoke the Eject command.

One thing you don't want to do is to select a disk that you have already closed and ejected—a phantom disk. If you do, nothing bad happens to the computer or the disks, but you are prompted to insert that phantom disk because the Finder, in reply to your Eject command, wants to double-check that it has properly closed the disk. What a waste of time. So be sure that your Eject command applies only to those disks currently in the drives.

Finally, here is the fastest, most effortless way to eject disks. It involves using the keyboard equivalent commands for the Select All and Eject mouse commands. With all desktop windows closed (a procedure which can be sped up by selecting the Close All command from the File menu), type Command-A, followed immediately by Command-E.

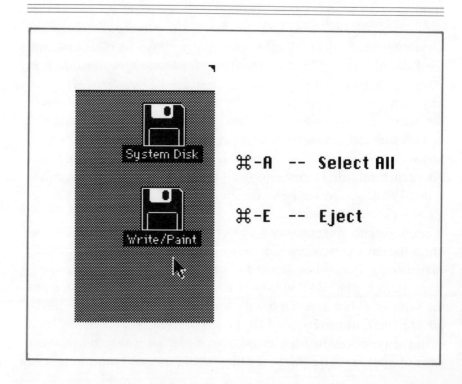

This sequence performs the same functions as pulling down the Edit menu for the Select All command, and then pulling down the File menu for the Eject command. The best part about this keyboard equivalent method is that you can type in these commands in rapid succession, and then start straightening your physical desk while the Mac does its work of selecting, updating, and ejecting the disks one by one. This is the method I use most frequently.

Managing Disks with a 512K Mac

Throughout this chapter I've hinted about the improvement in disk management possible with a 512K Macintosh. The most noticeable improvement is in the significant reduction in disk swapping when copying disks and files. You need at most one complete swap to copy an entire disk onto a blank. My guess is that anyone who invests in a 512K Mac will probably also have a second disk drive anyway, so the disk swapping improvements will go largely unnoticed.

◢ ◢ ◢ ◢ ◢ ◢ RAM Disks

But there is an optional software program available that turns part of your 512K of RAM into an electronic equivalent of a disk drive. This type of program goes by different names, but most people call it a RAM disk. On your desktop, a RAM disk looks just like another disk icon. You can copy files to it and from it. You can transfer applications programs and the System Folder to it. You can also use it for temporary document storage, provided you copy the document back to a real disk before turning off the machine.

If you had unlimited memory for your RAM disk, you would get the most impressive performance from your applications by transferring the System Folder and all applications to the RAM disk when you turn on the Mac in the morning. It takes literally two seconds to open or close programs like MacWrite or MacPaint from a

RAM disk, because, instead of retrieving the programs from the disk, the Mac fetches them from memory—the fastest storage facility on the Mac. With all your programs on the RAM disk, you could leave the Mac turned on all day, with information from a variety of programs—spreadsheet, database, telephone dialer, whatever—available in a couple of seconds. But back to reality.

Because the Mac needs at least 128K of its 512K to operate like a Mac, the largest a RAM disk can ever be is 384K. In practice, RAM disks are a bit less. Now, that means that you have less room than a standard disk—which has often proven to be too small for your work. Therefore, you have to consider a couple of options.

The biggest gobblers of RAM disk space, unfortunately, are the System file and the Finder. It is these files that give you incredible speed into and out of programs when they're in the RAM disk. But if you copy these two files to the RAM disk, you are severely limited in the number of applications you can have ready at your fingertips. Therefore, if a program's speed is of utmost importance to you, then you should copy the System file and the Finder to the RAM disk, but you will have to be satisfied with working with only one or two programs on the RAM disk at one time.

If you can sacrifice a little performance, however, you can keep the System Folder stuff on a disk in one of the Mac physical drives, and copy many more applications programs to the RAM disk.

Of course, there are going to be problems with copy-protected programs. The Microsoft program series isn't too difficult to work into RAM disk, since you can copy the programs daily to the RAM disk from the Master disks—which takes care of Microsoft's copy protection scheme. But many other programs, like pfs:File and pfs: Report won't let you copy them to RAM disk at all.

The other drawback to RAM disk is that the minute you take away from the 512K Mac's total memory, the machine acts like a 128K Mac to most of the software that you run on it. Therefore, if a program offers enhancements when running on a 512K Mac—like larger documents in MacWrite—you won't get the full benefit of your loaded Mac unless all the memory is free for the program.

Another factor worth remembering is that most 128K programs operate more efficiently on a 512K Mac, often just as if working from a RAM disk. The reason is that instead of reaching out to a program disk for supplemental instructions (called program segments) as on a 128K Mac, a program running on the 512K Mac has ample room in memory to retain those instructions after they're used once. In MacWrite, for example, the first time you select Insert Ruler from the Format menu, the program fetches the program segment with instructions on inserting rulers. On a 128K Mac, the ruler segment may later be overwritten (*purged* in Mac programmer talk) by another segment, like the one that displays the header screen. But on a 512K Mac, the ruler instructions stay in the vast memory, and are recallable in an instant.

What this discussion boils down to is that if you use one program predominantly throughout the day—and that program doesn't require more than 128K to work productively—then you may be ahead in performance if you load that program and System Folder into a RAM disk. But if you switch around from program to program, you should probably skip the RAM disk and let the 512K Mac load in all the pieces of each program as you use them. By mid-1985, there will be software that will let you load more than one program into the 512K memory, and you'll be able to switch programs without going to the desktop. That, in my estimation, will be the most efficient use of the 512K Mac's memory.

Among all the Macintosh models, the Macintosh XL, when expanded to its full 1 megabyte RAM capacity, has an ideal memory setup. RAM disk software usually grants you as much memory for the RAM disk as the program can find in the machine. Typically, a 1 megabyte Mac XL offers more than 700 kilobytes of RAM disk, which is plenty for the System Folder and several applications. Or, you can select about 500 kilobytes for the RAM disk, and still keep enough RAM available for 512K applications like Jazz and Think Tank 512.

Hard Disk Pros and Cons

I've used three of the first hard disks available for the Mac for a couple of months. The models were the Tecmar MacDrive 5 megabyte cartridge hard disk, and the Davong Mac Disk and Corvus 10 megabyte fixed disk system. The details of my experience can be found in a review of these products in *Macworld* magazine (vol. 1, no. 6, December 1984). Rather than get into the specifics of these three products, I will limit my discussion here to the advantages and disadvantages of linking a Mac to a hard disk.

First of all, and by way of explanation, a *hard disk* is a very precise device that crams more data per square centimeter on a hard metallic platter than can now be imagined for a floppy disk like the microfloppies the Mac uses. We're talking many millions of bytes on a hard disk, not just the puny 400,000 of the Mac floppy disks.

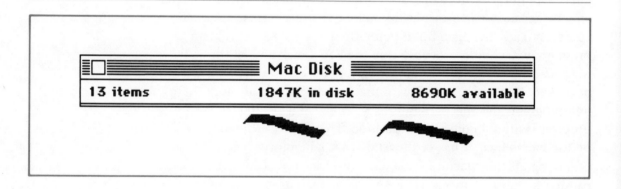

As a result of the increased data densities, much faster disk rotation (3600 r.p.m. vs. 360 to 602 r.p.m on the Mac floppies), and other circuit details, a hard disk can transfer information onto and off the disk surface at a fantastic speed compared to what happens on the Mac floppies.

The entry fee, however, is not cheap. Hard disks start at about $2000, and work their way up as the storage capacity increases. Some of the hard disks currently available can be used as shared hard disks, that is, more than one Mac in an office environment can link up to a single hard disk to share files and applications. (Apple will also offer such a device in the second half of 1985.) This use of a hard disk makes economic sense, since the high cost of the hard disk can thus be spread among several workstations.

▲ ▲ ▲ ▲ ▲ ▲ Advantages

The most significant advantage of a hard disk to a Mac user is increased speed for those operations that involve writing or reading information on a program or storage disk. Noticeable improvements in the time it takes to load a program, write a printed copy of a MacWrite document to the disk before printing, shifting around a MacPaint document with the hand icon, and quitting programs are attractive incentives for going with a hard disk.

Having all that disk space, of course, is also attractive. By storing all your programs (at least those that let you do so—see below) and documents on one huge disk, you don't have to deal out microfloppies anymore to load a document.

▲ ▲ ▲ ▲ ▲ ▲ Disadvantages

Accompanying all that disk space, however, is the opportunity for your desktop and file organization to get out of hand. Storing information on a hard disk takes discipline to organize your files so you can find them easily later on. A hundred files can get pretty mind-boggling if you can't find the one you need in a reasonable amount of time.

The Finder (version 1.1g) also presents a problem for some of the hard disks because it is incapable of keeping track of a large number of files. Under ideal conditions, the Finder can manage at most 240 separate files. But when you start organizing files into folders—which is essential for you to find your way through a hard disk directory—the total number of files the Finder can manage drops dramatically to less than 100. The Corvus disk addresses this problem to a degree by letting you subdivide the vast disk space into smaller volumes, each of which behaves like a separate disk (unfortunately, you can't have more than two such volumes on the desktop at once). Moreover, as the number of files exceeds about 50, the time it takes to return to the desktop from an application increases noticeably. Some of these problems will likely be cured by software improvements and in later versions of the Finder, so you should consult the hard disk manufacturers about their current progress in this area.

Another disadvantage crops up because some software is not copyable to the hard disk, while other software, with less stringent copy protection schemes, makes it cumbersome to do so. The pfs: File and pfs:Report series from Software Publishing Corporation, for example, cannot be copied to a hard disk. But if you copy Microsoft's Multiplan or Chart to a hard disk, the copy works in the same way as a floppy disk backup copy, as noted earlier in this chapter. In other words, the first time you try to use the program after you turn on the computer, you are prompted to insert the original disk. So, if you think you'll be saying "goodbye" to your floppies by getting a hard disk, think again.

Also annoying (to me, at least) is that with the way the early hard disk drives are being designed (to connect to the Mac via the modem or printer port), you can't use the hard disk as a startup disk. On its own, the Mac doesn't know to configure the serial port to accept high speed data as if from a disk drive. You must start up the Mac with a special floppy disk supplied by the hard disk manufacturer. This floppy configures the Mac so that it recognizes that data coming in the serial port is coming from a disk drive. It also means that there is one more floppy you need close by.

In early 1985, a new company, General Computer Company (215 First Street, Cambridge, MA 02142) introduced an internal hard disk for the Mac, called HyperDrive. It is a 10-megabyte disk that is dealer-installed inside the Mac cabinet, and includes a fan that also mounts internally to help push out the extra heat generated by the drive. An intriguing feature of the HyperDrive is that you can start up the hard disk without having a floppy disk in the internal disk drive. While this system looks inviting (its file management software is about the best I've seen for a Mac hard disk), you should also realize that buying such a device from a new company has its risks. If, two years from now, the extra HyperDrive circuit board that goes inside your Mac, or the disk drive itself, should develop trouble, there's no assurance that the company will still be in business to service this very specialized peripheral.

One more hard disk solution is the 10 megabyte disk that is built into the Macintosh XL. Even though the disk is integrated into the system, the problems of the Finder, noted above, still hold true. Moreover, if you prefer the 128K and 512K Macs because of their diminutive appearance on your desk, then you'll realize that the XL means more than just extra-large memory and disk space.

◢ ◢ ◢ ◢ ◢ ◢ Recommendations

Although the speed enhancement is nice, I've found that a Mac with two floppy drives—one internal, one external—is more than acceptable for most situations. For increased speed while running an application, upgrade your Mac to a 512K machine. When double-sided floppy disks are available, an 800K external disk drive should solve any problems you might have with too small a disk capacity.

If, on the other hand, you intend to add more Macs to your hard disk for a shared system, then a high capacity (20 megabytes or more) hard disk may be a wise choice. Moreover, depending on the demands of the software you use, you might be able to get by with 128K Macs sharing the hard disk, keeping your workstation investment relatively low.

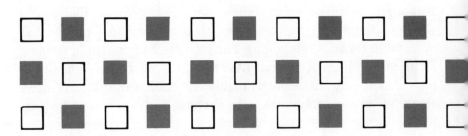

ONE OF THE elements of the Macintosh that makes it a "super" computer is the way the screen works: how choices are presented in menus, how icons represent documents, and how icon manipulation resembles tasks we're familiar with. The tips in this chapter will help you move around and organize your Mac screen like a real pro. You'll also learn about ways to organize your documents so you can find them again with the least fuss. All it takes is a little insight into how the key elements work.

Desktop Fundamentals

So far, we've been using the term, *desktop*, rather freely. I suspect that for some users, the notion of the Macintosh display screen representing a desktop might be a little difficult to grasp. After all, we're accustomed to a desktop being horizontal, resting under our elbows, and with plenty of surface area on which we can dump anything we don't want to carry. In contrast, the Mac desktop is

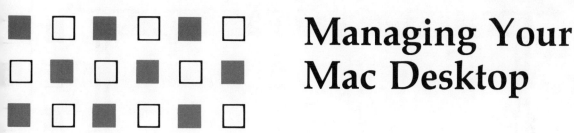

Managing Your Mac Desktop

vertical and two-dimensional. With a traditional desktop, you can usually see the lumps where things are stacked on top of each other. But on the Mac desktop, you can have several things on top of one another, yet the 9-inch screen is no fatter there than anywhere else on it.

▲ ▲ ▲ ▲ ▲ ▲ **Conceptualizing the Electronic Desktop**

To help you visualize the Macintosh desktop concept, in the illustration on page 76 I've taken the basic Mac desktop and given it a more traditional appearance, adding three-dimensionality to a number of elements.

The grey area (corresponding to the large grey area on the Mac screen) is your desktop working area. This is where you can spread your stuff out so you can see as much or as little as you want at one time.

Readily available on your desktop are your disk(s) and trash can. Every time you open a disk (double-clicking on the desired disk is

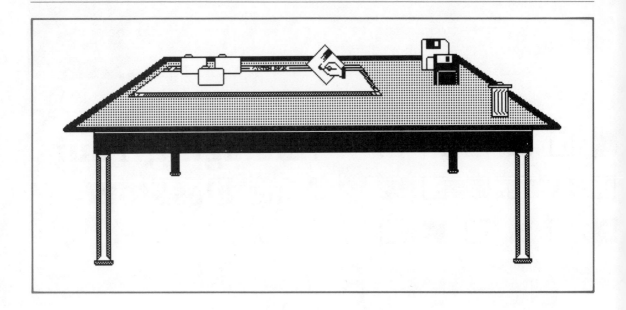

the fastest way), it's like opening up a portfolio on which you can spread out or organize related documents. Maybe you'd rather think of the open portfolio as a desk blotter designated for a particular task. Although Apple likes to call this white area the *active window*, it might be easier to think of it as the current work area, where your attention is focused for the next operation. In this work area are icons for the programs contained on the disk—like MacWrite and MacPaint—and for documents you have created using those programs. There are also at least two file folders. We learned about one, called the System Folder, in the last chapter. The other, labeled Empty Folder, is actually an almost inexhaustible stack of empty file folders. I'll have more to say about folders later in this chapter.

Just like a physical desktop, the Mac desktop can be arranged to suit your tastes. You can, for example, have more than one window visible on the desktop at one time. But as with physical desks, a Mac desktop can get messy. In fact, if you let your Mac desktop get carelessly messy, you can momentarily lose track of things. Fortunately, nothing is lost on the disks when this happens. It's just that somewhere, underneath several layers of windows, can hide a window or document you need, but one you can't get to without closing or moving the others sitting on top of it.

▲ ▲ ▲ ▲ ▲ ▲ Basic Organizational Skills

Before we get too deeply involved with how you should organize your Mac desktop, let's investigate a few basics. The three points we'll consider are: 1) how changes to your desktop affect what's stored on your disk; 2) the significance of the View menu selections; and 3) the right and wrong way to set up windows on the desktop.

Here's an exercise that will demonstrate in experience and pictures how well the Mac keeps track of the desktop for you:

- Turn on your Mac (or reset it if it is already on and the disk drive(s) empty).
- Insert the System Disk (your working copy, of course).
- Open the System Disk.
- Open the System Folder.
- Pull down the View menu and select "by Size." The System Folder icons are converted into text descriptions.

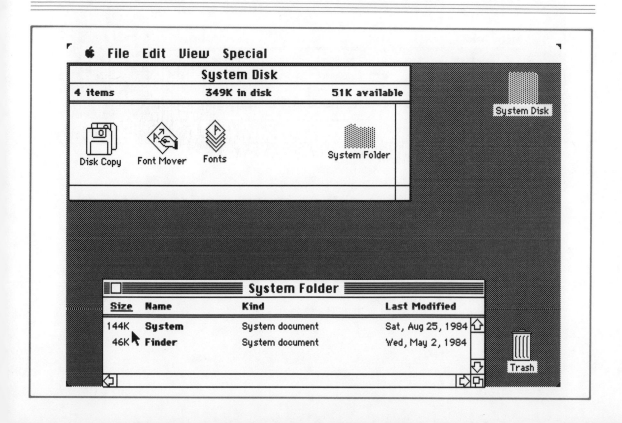

■ Placing the pointer in the size box at the lower right corner of the System Disk window, drag the size box as close to the upper left corner of the window as possible.

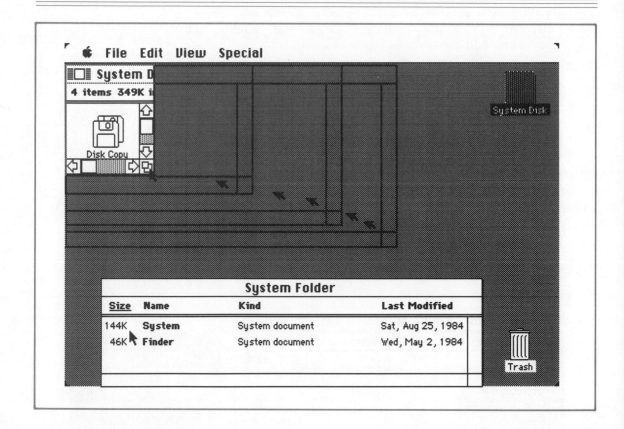

- With the pointer on the title bar of the same window, drag the entire window to the very center of the screen.

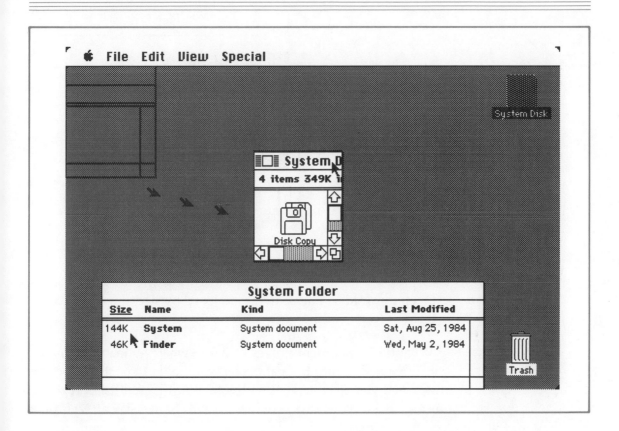

- Pull down the File menu and select Close All. Both windows close into the disk icon.
- Eject the disk.
- Now reset the computer (which wipes clean the Mac's memory), insert the same disk and open it. Notice that the window is in the same shape and form as you left it.

■ Use the scroll bars if necessary to bring the System Folder icon into view.

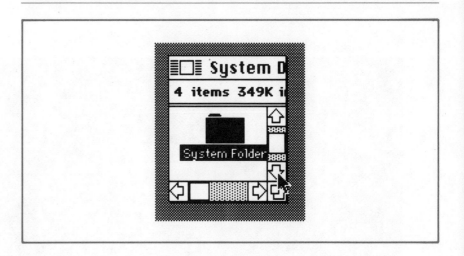

■ Open this folder. The contents are listed by size, the way you left them.

What this experiment proves is that in whatever manner you organize your desktop, the parameters and layout are stored on the disk when you eject it. That means that if you establish a regimen for organizing your disk windows, it will be consistent each time you open a disk.

■ Now that I've made my point, restore your desktop to its original layout (as in the illustration on page 76).

◢ ◢ ◢ ◢ ◢ ◢ The View Menu

While seeing programs and documents in their icon form is one of the most appealing features of the Mac desktop, you may find yourself wishing to see more revealing directories of files. That's what the other choices in the View menu are for. As you may have noticed in our last exercise, the View menu applies only to the active window, and it affects only one window at a time. Therefore, if you have five windows on your desktop at one time, you could conceivably have each directory listed in a different manner—icon, size, name, date, and kind.

All four text-oriented directory listings display the name of the file, its size (in kilobytes), what kind of file it is (e.g., document, application, folder, etc.), and the date on which it was most recently modified.* The manner in which the text directory is organized can be seen by looking for the underlined column heading (note that "Size" was underlined in the System Folder menu line when selected). The decision to choose one of the text listings instead of the icon listing depends on the kinds of documents you work with, how many will be in a folder, and which listing makes it easiest for you to find a particular document.

The alphabetical listing (by name) is the most practical if your directory will be holding many small files of the same kind—a couple dozen letters created by MacWrite or Microsoft Word, for example. But if you have a storage disk directory that contains documents from many different programs, grouping the files by kind will bring together those that apply to your current program.

Fortunately, no matter how you set up your directory window, you can always change it by selecting a different option from the View menu. But you should establish a convention for yourself and adhere to it as much as you can.

Text directories, by the way, work like the icon directory in two important respects. First, the same level of organization established for the icon directory applies to the text directories. Therefore, a folder is listed as a folder; to see a listing of its contents, you must open that folder. Second, you can open a document, folder, or program from the text listing by double-clicking the listing, just as you double-click an icon. For copying (dragging) documents onto another disk or into a folder, however, you must be in the icon directory.

*Incidentally, the "kind of document" column reveals the exact kind of document—"MacDraw document," for example—only if the applicable program(s) is (are) on the desktop. Otherwise, the listing simply says, "document."

◢ ◢ ◢ ◢ ◢ ◢ Window Edges

When you start manipulating your windows around the desktop, take a lesson from the smarts built into the Mac. Watch how the Mac handles it.

- Start the Mac with the System Disk (if you still have the System Disk in the Mac from our last exercise, that's fine).
- Open the disk so the System Disk window is on the desktop.
- Drag the Empty Folder out of the window to the right edge of the desktop, somewhere below the disk icon.
- With the Empty Folder icon selected, pull down the File menu and select Duplicate. An icon named Copy of Empty Folder appears next to the original.

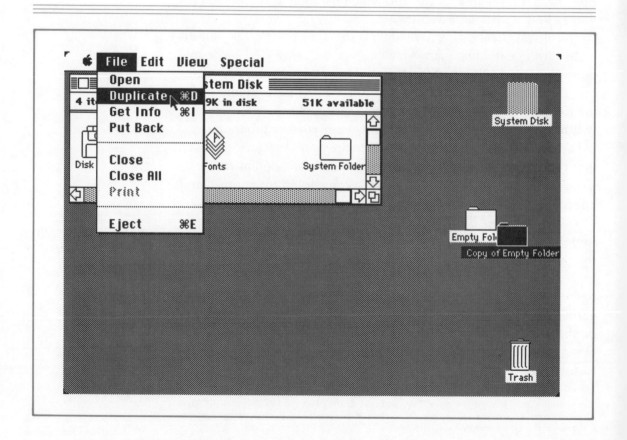

■ Double-click the original Empty Folder icon. Notice where the
Mac places the Empty Folder window in relation to the System
Disk window.

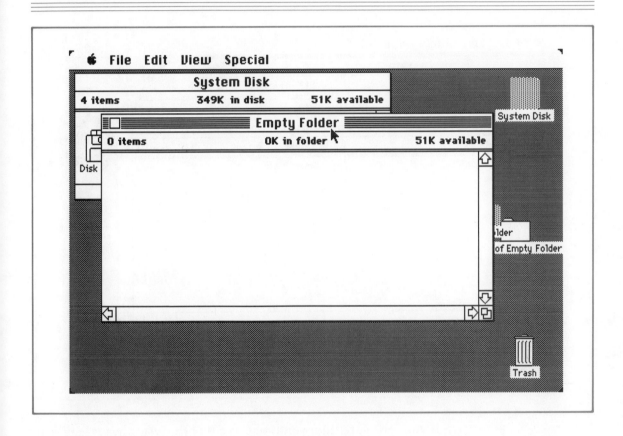

■ Double-click the Copy of Empty Folder icon. Notice where the Mac places its window in relation to the Empty Folder window.

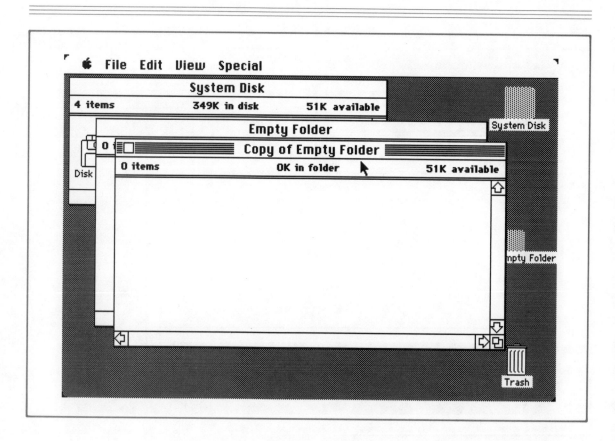

If you look carefully, you'll observe that the Mac always leaves at least some small part of earlier windows showing on the screen. That, of course, allows you to move the pointer to that sliver of window, click the mouse, and bring the old window back to the foreground. There is no little wisdom in this arrangement, for it is easy to accidentally cover up one window with another. Here's an example of how easily you can bury a window:

■ Continuing where you left off, place the pointer in the size box at the lower right corner of the Copy of Empty Folder window.

■ Drag the box to the upper left, until the window is about half its
original size.

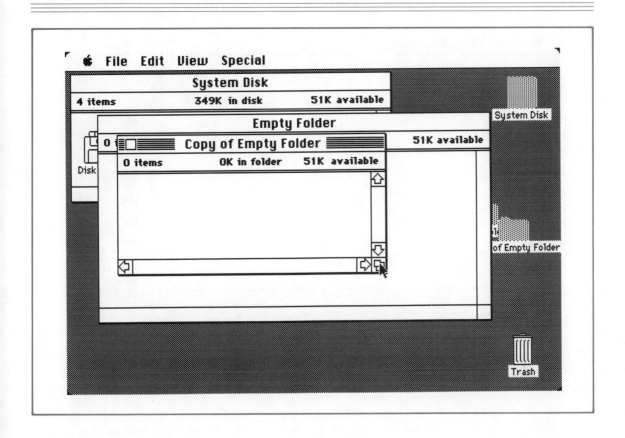

■ Click anywhere in the Empty Folder window.

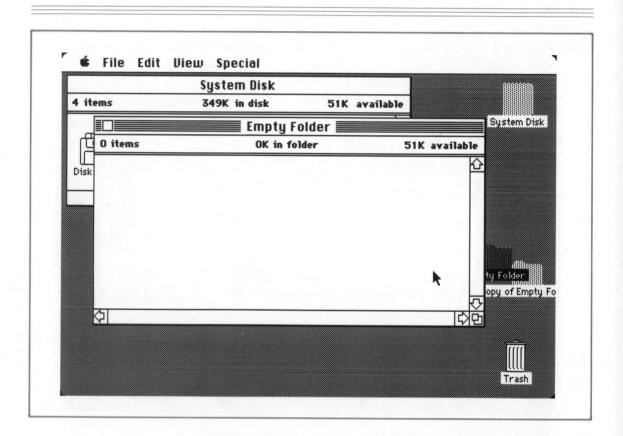

When the Empty Folder becomes the active window, it covers up the smaller window. If you want access to the buried window, you'll have to move the top window, close the top window, or double-click the Copy of Empty Folder icon—all solutions that place an extra step between you and the next task you want to perform in that window.

To avoid this potential problem, and still have the flexibility of arranging your desktop to suit your whim, you should follow the guideline implied by the Mac's own desktop arrangement scheme. Never knowingly position two windows from the same disk—or disks you use together, such as a MacPaint disk and its storage disk—in exactly the same spot.

Ideally, you should endeavor to make your adjacent windows approximately the same size. Otherwise you are more likely to run into the covered window problem demonstrated above.

Before we leave this discussion, let's restore our desktop to its original order.

- Close the top, Empty Folder, window to prove that the little one is still there.

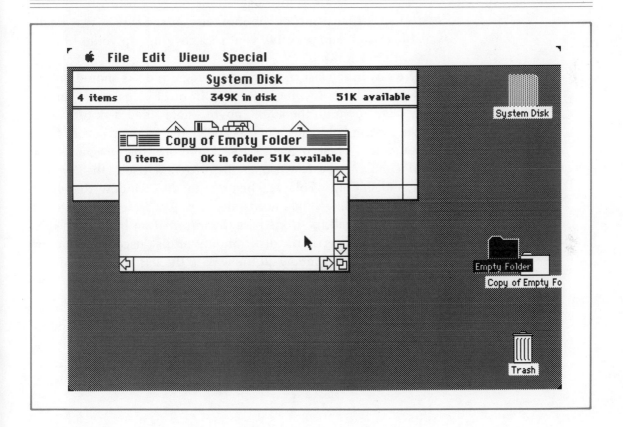

- Close the smaller window.
- Drag the Copy of Empty Folder to the Trash.
- Drag the Empty Folder icon back to the window.
- Select Clean Up from the Special menu to align the icons.

◢ ◢ ◢ ◢ ◢ ◢ Organizing Your Desktop: A Plan

As with a physical desktop, the Mac desktop can be neat or messy, fancy or plain. With the exception of the placement of disk icons, which the Mac dictates along the right margin, you are free to place windows and icons wherever you like. With all this flexibility, however, sometimes it's good to have a solid foundation to start with—a workable plan that adheres to good Mac practice, but adaptable enough to suit your work habits.

Therefore, here are some suggestions on how to organize your desktop such that it makes the most use of the screen real estate available to you, and prevents you from covering up your old windows with new ones.

As we saw in the last chapter, your program disks should not be used for long-term document storage. In most cases, there simply isn't enough room on the 400 kilobyte single-sided disk to handle the Mac System Folder (as much as 263K), the program (easily 40 to 80K), and lots of storage besides. Therefore, the program disk should contain very few icons: the program itself, the System Folder, and an Empty Folder. The program disk window, therefore, can be very small, a single horizontal strip just wide enough to let the Mac display all the icons plus the information bar, which lists the number of items on the disk, amount of disk used, and amount available. Push the window all the way to the left and top margins of the screen. As we'll see in the next section, however, you may never need to look at this window, so its exact position is not critical.

■ Arrange your MacWrite disk window, so your desktop looks like
the illustrated screen. The order of icons in the window is not
important.

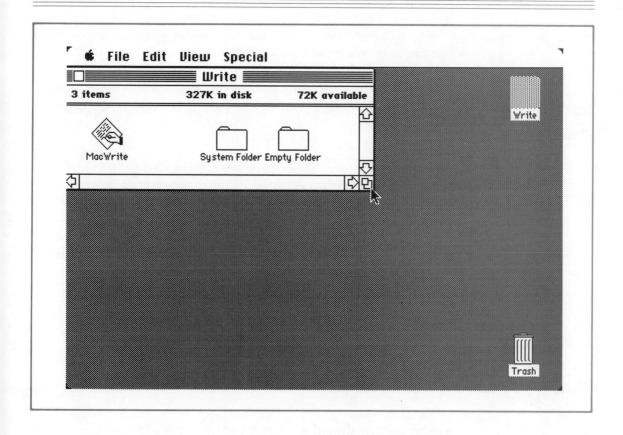

- With the MacWrite disk window still open, eject the disk.
- Insert the storage disk you'll be using with the program.
- Open the disk.
- Using the size box, adjust the size of the new window until it is as wide as possible, still leaving room for two columns of disk icons along the right edge of the screen.
- Arrange your documents (preferably grouped in file folders) in one horizontal row across the top of the window. If you have more than five files, start a second row.
- Drag the window size box to adjust the bottom of the window up as close to the top row of icons as the Mac will let you, thus making a horizontal strip similar to the one you made for the program disk.

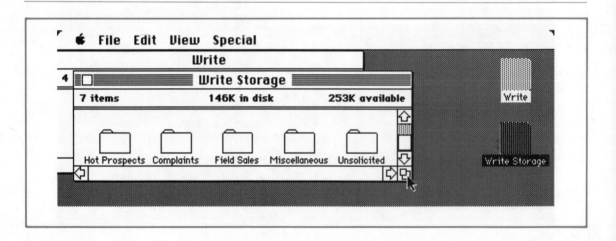

- If necessary, drag the entire window down and to the right just enough so you can see the name of the Write disk at the top of the desktop and a one-eighth to one-quarter inch sliver of the program window at the left margin.

Next we have to arrange the windows from the folders.

■ Open one folder, and position its window just below the storage
disk window you just made.

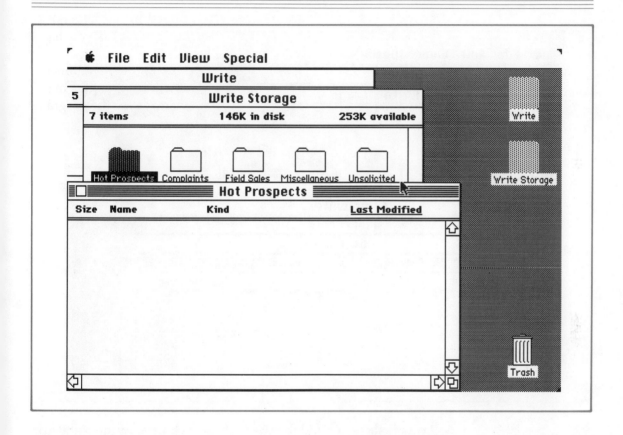

- Open each of the other folders one at a time, positioning each window just below and slightly to the right of the one before it, until you have what looks like a staggered stack of windows. Be particularly careful to make the right edges look like steps on a staircase.

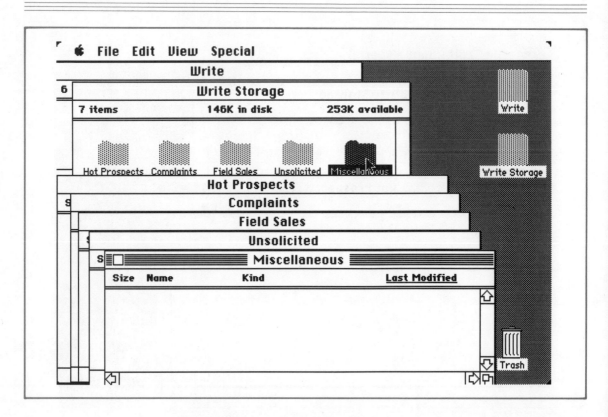

- Arrange the icons and the size box for each window such that you can see as many documents as possible inside the window without scrolling.

Folders with the most documents should be planted first, since they will need the most space to display all icons at once. Remember, too, that you can change the display of any window to be organized by date, time, size, or kind.

With this folder window arrangement, no matter how many or how few folders you open, you will not accidentally cover up an entire folder on the desktop. You will also be able to make any one of them an active window by clicking the part of the window showing from behind the others. Of course, if you make one of the windows closest to the top of the screen the active window, you will cover the contents of some other windows.

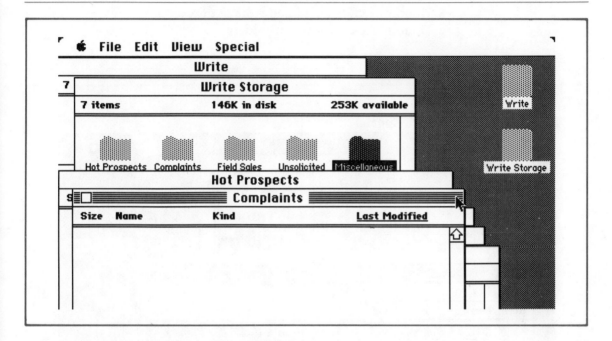

To return the display to the point where you can read all window titles, simply click the top right corners of the covered windows (starting with the window nearest the top of the screen), stepping down the "staircase" formed by the upper right corner of each folder window.

Now, watch the Mac speed through an otherwise time-consuming task.

- From the pull-down File menu, select Close All. One-by-one, the windows fold, until all windows are stowed safely in the disk icon.
- When you eject the storage disk, all the window location information will be written to the disk in the process.

One helpful thing to know about the Mac's windows is that as long as the disk icon is still on the desktop, every window from that disk is stored in the Mac's memory for your perusal, even without the disk in the drive.

- Eject the storage disk (if you are asked to insert the Write disk, do so).
- Double-click the dimmed storage disk icon.
- Double-click a couple of folders.

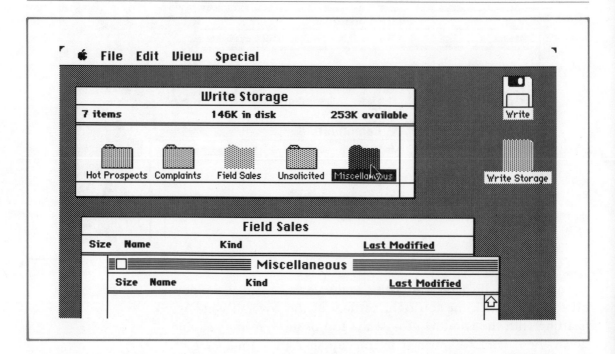

- Pull down the File menu and select Get Info.

All the information about the disk's directory is stored in memory, as long as the disk's icon still appears on the desktop.

◢ ◢ ◢ ◢ ◢ ◢ **Superfast Program Desktop**

Up to now, we've been discussing the Mac desktop only in terms of using the windows that are created whenever you open a program or storage disk. But for those who are impatient, and who don't like to keep clicking the mouse to get to a frequently used program or document, you should use a feature of the Mac desktop that short-cuts around the mouse.

The secret of this technique is that you don't need a disk window open to initiate an action on the Mac. For example, if you were to drag the MacPaint icon from your program disk to any grey area on the desktop, you could close the disk window, leaving only the trash, disk, and program icons on the screen. To start the program, simply double-click the MacPaint icon, just as you would do if it were inside the window.

Moreover, if you quit the program and eject the disk, the Mac-Paint icon stays in its spot on the desktop, even though the program is safely stored on the disk. The next time you start up the Mac with the MacPaint disk, the MacPaint icon will appear on the grey desktop precisely where you left it. You won't have to open the disk window to gain access to the program.

This feature works not only for programs, but for documents as well. So if you have a storage disk that you use for correspondence to be printed on a MacPaint-designed letterhead, then you can leave the blank letterhead document on the desktop, and select it as soon as the disk and document icons appear on the desktop screen. The Mac will then automatically look for MacWrite—whose icon is in the unopened window—or any other word processing program you use, and load it automatically. Some disk swapping may be necessary on a single-drive system, but no more than if you had opened the document from a more traditional disk window.

As an alternative, you may be tempted to use the Set Startup command of the Special menu. This command instructs your disk to automatically open a program or document as soon as you insert the disk as a startup disk. In other words, it bypasses the desktop and goes straight into an application. I personally don't like this option. The little time it might save when I need that application at start up is overshadowed by the time wasted when I *don't* want the program to start right away. For example, if I want to check the available disk space before embarking on a project, I have to wait for the program to load, quit the program, and wait for the display to return to the desktop—essentially backtracking through the System Startup procedure. No, I'll stay with my handy program icon next to the disk, and control my own destiny.

Document Fundamentals

Now that you understand what the Mac desktop environment is, it's time to get closer to the documents you work with daily. We'll start by understanding things about file names that the Mac manual doesn't tell you.

◢ ◢ ◢ ◢ ◢ ◢ How to Name Documents

The Macintosh is one of the most forgiving personal computers when it comes to naming documents. Most other computers place severe limitations on the way you can give names to files you store on disk. The result is usually an unintelligible list of files that even the one who named them can barely decipher. To see what the file contains usually means opening it from the appropriate application—a time-consuming task.

Naming and renaming files on the Mac are simple procedures, but sometimes the flexibility built into the system can hinder, rather than help, productivity. Therefore, it will help to follow a few simple guidelines and be consistent.

The Mac allows you to assign a document name up to sixty-three characters long (usually during a Save As. . . operation). That's plenty of space to identify even the most bizarre file you could ever concoct. But in practice, you should endeavor to keep your file names as short as possible. Moreover, if you have several documents that are related to one another, like segments of a MacWrite document, you should pay attention to how you differentiate the names of those pieces.

Here are some examples of what I mean.

If you look at the way the Mac places icons in a window, you'll notice that although the pictures are separated by more than enough space, the document names can easily run into one another if they are too long. If one document name is longer than the space available for it, then it may cover part of another name or be, itself, partially covered by another name.

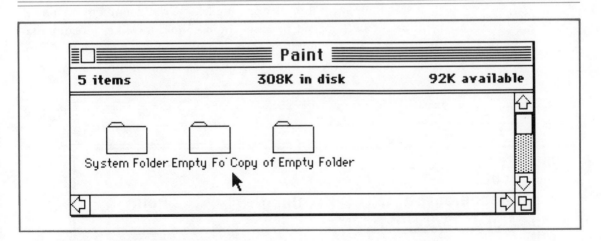

The factor that governs which name covers which is simply the document that has been most recently selected. Any time you click a document, its full name appears, at the expense of the display of longer names from adjoining documents.

You can, of course, reorganize your desktop so that documents with extra long names are located on separate lines or in different sides of the window. By dragging an icon to the far right side of the window, for example, it will stay in its own little area even when you issue the Clean Up command.

Since the font used for document names is a proportionally spaced one, it is difficult to lay down a hard and fast rule about the number of characters you can cram into a document name before the name starts to impinge on another name's territory. You can put about eighteen lower case *i* letters in the same space that you can put only about seven lower case *m* letters, so the exact number of letters you use will depend on the overall makeup of the name. But if your names stay within ten to twelve letters, you should be safe in most circumstances.

There is another document name issue that you must be aware of, however. In many Macintosh programs, when you attempt to open a new document, the computer presents a dialog box with a list of files on the disk. This list is housed in a small window within the dialog box. When it comes to holding long document names, this window is less forgiving than the icon label arrangement, because the document name must either fit within the confines of the window or be *truncated*—cut short—to fit.

If you have several parts of a long MacWrite document on a disk, you might be tempted to label them something like, Documentation Part 1, Documentation Part 2, and so on. But look what happens when you try to open one of these from within MacWrite.

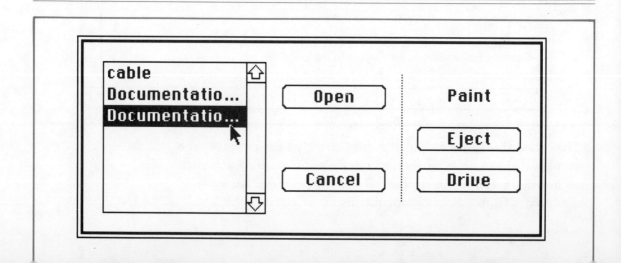

The window lists the files as, "Documentatio...." You don't know which part is which. Therefore, you should put the differentiating element of the document name at the beginning. Alternatively, you can keep the common name to about eight to ten characters, while appending a number to signify which part is which (such as Doc1, Doc2, etc.). Again, the font used for this window is proportionally spaced, so the exact number of characters that can fit will vary with your document name.

Don't forget, however, that although you should keep the document names as short as possible, you still have a place with plenty of room to describe each document, and thus, help you identify its place in the cosmos long after you've forgotten the meaning of the abbreviated name. Each document has a Get Info box that contains three lines of about eighty characters each (a total of more than 240 characters) in which you can type a complete description of what the document is, what other pieces belong in it, and so on. Use this box for specific identifying information.

◢ ◢ ◢ ◢ ◢ ◢ Changing Document Names

Quite often, as a project progresses, you discover that the file names you used for some early pieces of the project don't really convey the meaning you think they should. Or the project may take a different direction than originally intended, making the first document or folder names illogical. That's the time to change the names.

There are several ways of changing document and folder names on the Mac, depending on how much of a change you need to make. Names can be changed only on a disk currently in a disk drive.

Here are examples of three ways of changing document names, depending on the extent of the change. The first two make use of the fact that if you need to change only part of the name, you can edit it very much like you do with MacWrite, including double-clicking one word to select it. You can do this by moving the screen pointer over any document name, so that the arrow changes to a text pointer, the same kind you have in MacWrite and MacPaint to indicate where you want the next piece of typed text to appear.

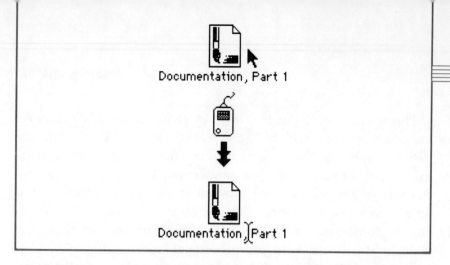

For the first method, if you have a typographical error, the fastest way to correct it is to place the text insertion pointer after the erroneous letter(s) and backspace over the error(s). Type the correct letter(s) as needed.

Second, to change or delete a complete word, place the text pointer over the word and double-click. (Be sure the pointer has changed to the text pointer before you double-click. If it is still the arrow, you will accidentally open the document.) When you double-click the text, both the icon and the word are selected. To get rid of the selected word you can use the Cut option from the Edit menu if you like, or simply press the backspace key. Press the backspace key once more to move the text insertion pointer flush against the word to the left to remove the extra space that was originally between the two words.

Third, the fastest way to give a document a completely new name is to simply select the icon and start typing the new name. The old name instantly disappears, as newly typed letters begin filling up the space below the icon. The Mac is smart enough to know that you want the name centered underneath the icon, so it takes care of that for you.

▲ ▲ ▲ ▲ ▲ ▲ **Organizing Your Documents**

One thing that will most certainly slow down your search for a specific document is a storage disk with a dozen or more documents in the window. Instead, exploit the Mac's abilities to give names to disks, folders, and documents to organize your work and simplify your desktop. As with all organizational tasks, it's a case of giving it a little forethought to save yourself lots of time later on, when you are in the biggest hurry.

To organize your Mac work most effectively, you should examine the ways you use the computer. It may take some time for identifiable patterns to develop adequately for you to see how to best use the disk-folder-document strategy. The first tendency for new Mac owners is to store a conglomeration of documents— MacWrite documents, MacPaint pictures, Multiplan spreadsheets—on a single storage disk. There is a feeling that each disk should be used to its fullest extent, and that empty space on a disk is wasteful. Unfortunately, this breeds organizational problems.

It is best to maintain separate storage disks for each applications program you use. That means one for MacWrite, one for MacDraw, one for Microsoft Word, etc. If you perform work that exchanges information between programs—like moving data from Multiplan to Microsoft Chart, or from MacPaint to MacWrite— then maintain a joint storage disk for those documents that are used on more than one applications program. When it comes time to exchange or merge the documents, there will be less disk searching and swapping.

Chances are that you will have one primary application, perhaps word processing if you're a writer, graphics if you're an artist, or financial modeling if you're a manager. With this primary application, you will be generating a disproportionately high number of documents compared with other applications. If this is the case, you should analyze the categories of documents you create regularly, and maintain separate disks for each category. For example, if word processing is the chief application at your Mac workstation, then you will probably want to keep your correspondence, weekly reports, Psychology class papers, English book reports, etc., on separate storage disks. Label the disks accordingly (e.g., Letters, Weeklies, Psychology, English).

Then, within every disk, group your documents into logical folders. For speed in locating a particular document, it is important to keep your desktop windows as clutter-free as possible. Folders help you do this, by keeping from sight everything that might throw you off the track.

A sales executive, for example, with lots of correspondence, and a specialized disk for it all, might find that the letters regularly fall into a few categories: replies to unsolicited sales inquiries, letters to potential customers, memos to field salespeople, and letters to current customers with problems or complaints.

To keep his correspondence in order, he could set up a storage disk with file folders for each category. First he would line up his folders as a separate row in the main window and then shrink the window with the size box so that only one row of icons shows in a horizontal strip across the top (as shown in the illustration on page 90). If needed later, other documents and folders can be accessed by selecting the window and scrolling to them.

Next, he would set up folder windows as shown in the illustration on page 92, as previously discussed. As he opens each folder for the first time, he could use the View menu to select the option that makes it easiest for him to locate a particular letter.

If you have a storage disk organization like this, open only as many folder(s) as you need in order to find the document(s) you wish to review or revise. To view the contents of a folder that is already open but covered by another window, it's perhaps faster to double-click the folder icon in the topmost window rather than trying to figure out which sliver of the bottom window layers belongs to the window you want.

It is important to remember, however, that when you create a new document, and perform a Save As. . . operation, the document is not automatically placed into a folder. It appears, instead, on the disk window (the Write Storage window in the illustration on page 92). To move the document to the proper folder most easily, first select the folder window in which it belongs (if it is not already the active window) to bring it into view. Next, select the MacWrite Storage window and use the vertical scroll bar to bring the new document icon into view. Finally, drag the icon to the folder window. Even though the folder window may be viewed in a text format, and your dragged document is in icon form, the document is moved into the folder and its directory format changed accordingly.

Those involved in college coursework can utilize the same principles of organization to keep notes, papers, and other material in order. If you transcribe lecture notes over to the Mac (or perhaps take notes during class on a portable computer and transfer them to the Mac back home—see Chapter 6 for details on how to do this), you would group your notes in a folder called Class Notes or something similar. You can use the same storage disk for your term papers, but since such assignments usually come very infrequently, you can probably get by without setting up a folder for them. On the other hand, if you use the Mac to collect research materials for a paper, you should group the research results and the term paper into one convenient folder. That way, when you open the folder, all relevant documents are readily visible in the window.

Using the Mac's Desk Accessories

A physical desktop frequently has a number of accessories, such as a calculator, a clock, a note pad, maybe even a small electronic game tucked away in a drawer for when you're thoroughly bored with what you're doing. The Mac desk has these, too. They're standard features of your Mac desk, and are always available to you, even while running most programs. To help you visualize how the Mac's desk accessories figure in the Mac desktop scheme of things, I've added them to our earlier Mac desktop conception.

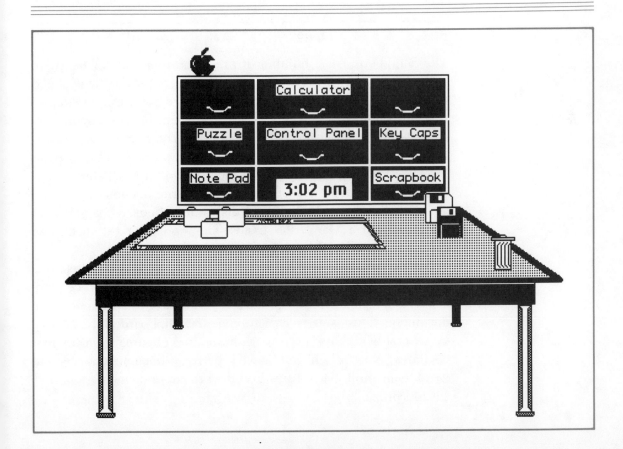

To work with these items, you need to pull down the menu from the Apple logo. Here, then, are the desk accessories you have at your fingertips and some ideas on how to use them to your best advantage.

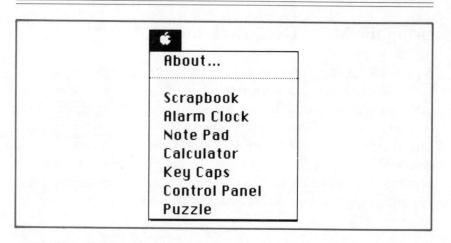

◢ ◢ ◢ ◢ ◢ ◢ **Scrapbook**

The Scrapbook has a number of practical applications when used with virtually any program. The Scrapbook consists of blank sheets of paper which let you store commonly used pictures, paragraphs, charts—whatever—so you'll always have them at your disposal, regardless of the application you're running. You might have a favorite drawing that you like to include at the top of a MacWrite page. Instead of having to retrieve the picture from a MacPaint storage disk, and then copy it over to your MacWrite document, you can simply call up your Write/Paint disk's Scrapbook while you're in the middle of a MacWrite session, summon the right sheet, and copy it in the MacWrite document where you need it.

The Scrapbook is also helpful if you need to copy more than one picture or block of text from one document to another. Since there is only one "page" to the Clipboard, you'd have to switch between documents to transfer each picture via the Clipboard. But by filling up several Scrapbook pages with individual pictures from the first document, you only have to switch between documents once, and paste those multiple pictures into the second document.

Another practical example of using the Scrapbook is to save typing in word processing. Let's say you have written a superb way to close off a letter to sales prospects. To make sure your purple prose is not lost, you can copy that section over to a Scrapbook page. It will always be on that program disk for later use, or until you decide you'd rather store something else on that Scrapbook page.

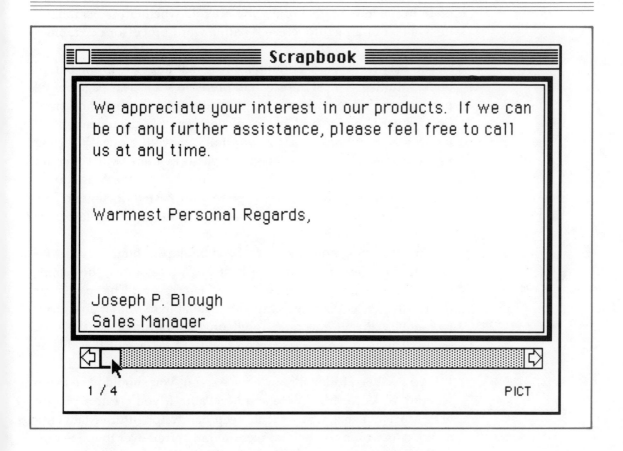

To flip through your Scrapbook, you use your mouse pointer and the scroll bar at the bottom of the Scrapbook window. The fastest way to scroll over to a Scrapbook page you want to use is to click the scroll bar arrows or the grey area on the bar on either side of the white square (the square indicates the relative position of the pages within the Scrapbook). Each time you click the mouse button, the white box moves down the scroll bar toward the pointer, and the next Scrapbook page comes into view. The relative distance the white box moves along the scroll bar with a single click depends upon the number of items stored in the Scrapbook.

Note, too, that the page numbers in the lower left corner of the Scrapbook window indicate how many total Scrapbook pages are stored as well as the number of the one currently displayed (e.g., 1 of 4). In the lower right corner you are told whether the Scrapbook item is text or a picture (created with a word processor or graphics program).

You may feel unsure about putting something new in the Scrapbook. Intuitively, most of us would prefer to see a clear page before pasting a picture or document into the Scrapbook—but the Scrapbook never opens to a blank page. With another document showing in the Scrapbook window, you might have the queasy feeling that the document you're about to paste in there will cover up something already in the Scrapbook. Fortunately, the Mac knows enough to assign a brand new page to your pasted document. The most recent additions are at the lowest page numbers of the Scrapbook.

One interesting note about the Scrapbook. Although this feature is grouped together with a bunch of desk accessories, the Scrapbook might actually be called a "Disk" Accessory. The reason for the distinction is that the Scrapbook available to you at any given moment is always the one stored on the startup disk (the disk whose icon is in the *pole position* on the desktop) even if that disk is not currently in the drive. An example should help explain this.

If you've been following my advice so far, you should have made working disks for MacWrite and MacPaint. If you create a picture with MacPaint that you want to keep handy for future MacWrite documents, you must get that picture transferred over to the Scrapbook on the MacWrite disk. Calling up the Scrapbook while in MacPaint and pasting the picture to it records the picture only on the MacPaint disk's Scrapbook. Later, when you go to retrieve the picture from your MacWrite disk, you won't find your picture, because while you are in MacWrite, only the MacWrite disk Scrapbook is accessed.

To resolve this dilemma, you must:

- Copy the picture while in MacPaint (it goes into the Clipboard temporarily).
- Quit MacPaint.
- Eject MacPaint.
- Insert MacWrite *without* first resetting the Mac.
- Open MacWrite (to transfer control of the Finder).
- Open the Scrapbook.
- Then Paste the picture into the MacWrite Scrapbook.

As a space-saving measure, you should know that the Scrapbook is an expendable file on your desktop. When you make the working copies of MacWrite and MacPaint, you also copy the original disk's Scrapbook. That means that the renowned fish, fancy borders, and all the other pages of the Scrapbook were deposited on your new disk. Altogether, the original Scrapbook takes up 10K of disk space, and can grow to fill up nearly all available space on the disk if you keep adding things to it.

If you don't need the pictures from the original disk's Scrapbook—they're stored on the original disks, so they won't be lost—you're better off trashing the Scrapbook icon located inside the System Folder. Fortunately, this act does not actually eliminate the Scrapbook accessory from your desktop or disk—just its current contents. Even though the Scrapbook file is not on the disk, once you summon it from the Apple menu, the Mac knows to create a Scrapbook file for you. When you close the application, you'll see the Scrapbook icon sitting in the disk window again. For the sake of good organization, drag the icon over to the System Folder.

Because an empty Scrapbook takes up only 2K of disk space, it may not seem important to free up only 2K on a 400K disk. But once you see the "almost out of memory" dialog box a few times, you'll be eager to locate an extra 2K, which may save you such hassles.

◢ ◢ ◢ ◢ ◢ ◢ **Alarm Clock**

The Macintosh has a built-in clock, which is powered by a replaceable battery. The clock keeps track of the date and time even when the machine is turned off. The importance of this feature should not be overlooked. By having the computer keep track of date and time, your documents and disks are automatically date-stamped each time you save a document or initialize a disk. As we've already seen, the date stamping of documents can help you organize your files when viewing documents in chronological order. Moreover, you can use the dates to help you reconstruct your progress through a project, if necessary.

To make the time appear on the screen, pull down the Apple menu and select "Alarm Clock." The clock appears in its own window near the upper right corner of the screen.

To set the clock (for daylight savings time, for example) or alarm, you need to go further into the clock window. Move the pointer over to the flag icon at the right of the clock window, and click the mouse. The flag goes down, and the window enlarges to reveal another numeric display and three icons.

The second numeric display line is where any setting you wish to change—time, date, alarm time—appear. To change the time, click the clock icon.

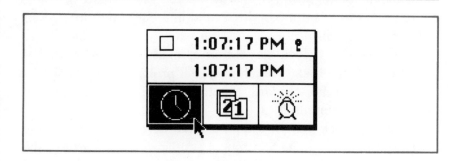

Its square is highlighted, and the current time appears digitally in the window, counting up the seconds in step with the original clock display. If you move the pointer over the numbers in the second line, the pointer arrow changes into a cross. This is to help you carefully position the pointer over the hours, minutes, or seconds—whichever needs adjustment.

Let's change from daylight saving time to standard time by shifting the hour back one. Position the pointer anywhere over the hours digits and click. The hours digits are highlighted, and two small arrows (up and down) appear at the right end of the line.

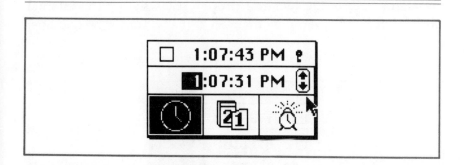

These arrows are like the up/down buttons you might find on a digital clock's setting controls. Each time you click the up button with the hours digits highlighted, the hours increment by one. Clicking and holding the up button causes the digits to race ahead. All you need to do is move your hours digits back by one, so click the down-arrow button once. When you're done, click in the window anywhere outside of the second line, and the time takes effect immediately. Note, however, that when you begin to set the time, the seconds stop counting in the second line. Since the clock resets to the time shown in the second line when you click that you're through, the Mac's clock may be off as many seconds as it takes you to change the hour. Therefore, you'll probably want to set the clock against a time standard, like the one offered over the telephone in some communities.

To set the clock against a time standard, you need to set the hours and minutes digits to a time a couple minutes ahead of the current time. Set the seconds digits to zero (if your time standard issues a signal on the minute). Then get ready to click the mouse outside of the second line (but within the clock window) as soon as you hear the time signal (actually, you need to anticipate the "gong" by about one-half second). That will start the clock silently ticking away in step with the "real" time.

The central icon represents a calendar. Click the calendar icon. It is highlighted, and the date, as kept by the Mac's internal clock, is displayed in the second line. Adjustment of the calendar digits requires the same up/down arrow procedure as setting the clock.

Next click the alarm clock icon. The icon is highlighted, and the second line displays the time to which the alarm is set. Changing the alarm time is the identical procedure as setting the internal clock. Notice, however, the little icon at the left of the second line.

This is a picture of the lever on a traditional alarm clock that turns the alarm on or off. When the lever is in the up position, the alarm is set to "ring." The alarm clock icon confirms this by showing the bell atop the clock ringing. Clicking the lever down disengages the alarm, and the alarm clock icon returns to its quiet mode.

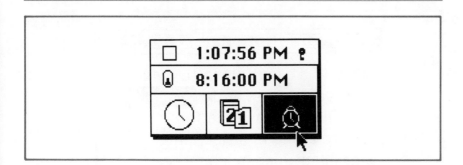

The Macintosh must be turned on for the alarm to sound at the appointed time, although you can be doing any application you please. The alarm doesn't stop the program or do anything else except that, when the time comes for the alarm to go off, you hear a single beep from the Mac's internal speaker, and the Apple logo in the top menu bar flashes on and off (alternating between highlighting and normal). If the alarm is set to ring, and the alarm time occurs while the Mac is turned off, the Apple logo will flash immediately when you put in your first startup disk. The flashing Apple is signaling you to check the time. Retrieving the Alarm Clock from the Desk Accessories pull-down menu turns off the flashing Apple—but the alarm stays set, ready to ring the next day, if you don't change it. It's a great way to signal the lunch hour, by the way.

◢ ◢ ◢ ◢ ◢ ◢ **Note Pad**

There isn't an executive desk in the world that doesn't have some kind of note pad either right by the telephone or handy in the top drawer. In the Macintosh desk, it's handy in the top drawer. The Note Pad acts in some ways like the Scrapbook, but is intended for text only. The pages are smaller, and when you bring out the Note Pad from the Apple menu, you are automatically in a text entry mode (with the pointer converted to the kind used in the MacWrite word processing program).

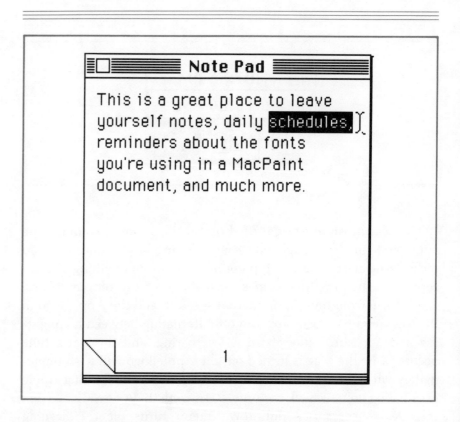

Unlike the paper note pad you may have on your desk, Mac's Note Pad has eight active pages which stay on the pad at all times. You can flip through the numbered pages, as you would a paper pad. To flip from page 1 to page 3, you move the pointer to the dog-ear on the lower left corner of the pad and click. Before your eyes, page 1 literally peels back to reveal page 2. Repeat the procedure once more to get to page 3. To go in the reverse direction, click the mouse with the pointer over the extreme lower left corner of the pad.

Pages on the Note Pad are big enough for about fifty words, so you can see they are intended only for brief notes to yourself. The Note Pad is a good spot to place notes about some important document or picture you're working on. For example, if you are using a particular font and font size for various parts of a chart, you should leave yourself a note about what size is used in which part. Then, when you come back to complete or edit your illustration the next day, you will be able to recreate the fonts without trial and error, or relying on your memory.

As you've seen earlier, the Note Pad is an expendable file from the System Folder if you need to squeeze every byte of space from a Mac disk. The Note Pad file gets no larger than its minimum 2K, but even that small amount often makes a big difference.

◢ ◢ ◢ ◢ ◢ ◢ Calculator

Every executive desk these days also has an electronic calculator nearby. The Mac holds one as part of its Desk Accessories. It never fails that when you're involved in some kind of work—even writing a memo—you need to do some figuring. Mac provides an unusual on-screen calculator.

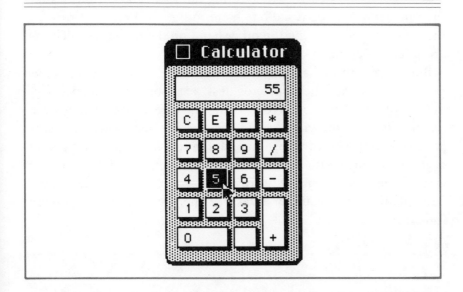

It looks like a pocket calculator you might carry along in your briefcase. But instead of having buttons you press with your finger, you use the mouse to point to the numeric buttons and press the mouse button. As you click a number, its key turns black. The number appears in the digital display when you release the button.

This calculator uses algebraic logic, like most consumer calculators. That means to add 2 plus 3, you enter the first digit (2), the operation (+), the second digit (3), and then press the equals key (=) to see the answer in the 13-digit display. Although the Mac calculator doesn't have any special functions other than the basic four arithmetic functions, you can enter very large or very small numbers in exponential notation. Here's how.

The exponential notation for one million—a one with six zeros after it—is 1E6 on this calculator (you may be more familiar with the form 1×10^6). To enter the figure, click the E key and the exponent, 6, on the calculator. The display shows 1E6. If you then click an operation, like multiplication, the number appears in its ordinal form, 1,000,000. If a number has too many digits for the calculator's display, then the number will automatically be displayed in exponential notation. The Desk Accessory calculator can accommodate numbers within a range of 1E4932 to 1E−4920, numbers surely large and small enough for anyone using a four-function calculator.

A fast, two-handed way of entering numbers and operations for the calculator is to dedicate one hand to the top keyboard row for the numbers, while using the other hand on the mouse to click the arithmetic operations.

But a funny thing happens when you use the Mac's optional numeric keypad with the calculator desk accessory. The keypad layout of arithmetic functions follows not the legends on its own keys, but the keys on the video calculator. I'm not sure whether this is good or bad. If you're accustomed to the real keys after doing a lot of numeric entry with software like Multiplan, then the calculator arrangement will seem awkward. But if you use the numeric keypad only with the calculator accessory, then you may not notice the legend discrepancies.

▲ ▲ ▲ ▲ ▲ ▲ Key Caps

Before we discuss exactly what the Key Caps accessory is, and how you'd use it, we need to talk about a term that is often used without a lot of explanation: *character set.*

A character set is the list of letters, numbers, punctuation marks, and other symbols that a computer is capable of producing without any special programming. Usually, this means all the characters that can be produced by typing keys on the keyboard either singly or in combination (as with the Shift key). Some computers are rather limited in the variety of characters accessible from the keyboard, but the Mac is relatively prolific in this regard, providing many useful symbols for currency, math, and copyright notations, plus many foreign language letters and accents. All characters can be typed directly from the keyboard (in most fonts), with the special symbols usually requiring keyboard combinations with the Option or the Shift plus Option keys. The problem, however, is knowing where these extra symbols are located on the keyboard. That's where the Key Caps accessory comes in.

You can use the Key Caps as a built-in reference guide to the special symbols, and as a convenient way of creating a math formula, short foreign phrase, or other piece of text using special symbols. When you first call up the Key Caps accessory, you see the keyboard replica as shown in the following figure.

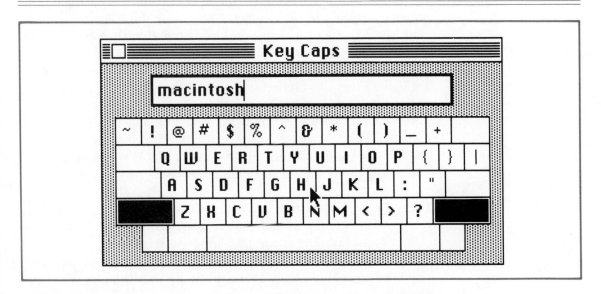

To place a character in the Key Caps display, you can either type on the keyboard or click individual keys with the mouse. For capital letters, press a Shift key on the keyboard (the mouse only works on the character keys, space bar, and backspace key), and either type the key or click the key with the mouse. Press an Option key on the keyboard to see the special symbols in the Mac's character set, and as before, place them in the display by typing on the keyboard or clicking the mouse.

To use the Key Caps effectively, create your phrase or formula in the display at the top of the keyboard depicted in the Key Caps window. Then you select the text, copy it, and later paste it into your document. Here's an example of building a French phrase for inclusion into a MacWrite document.

For this exercise, we will create a copyright line, attributing the copyright to a French school called, aptly enough, *L'école Française.*

- Open the Key Caps accessory if you haven't done so.
- Press the Option key to find the copyright symbol key (©).
- Click the key with the mouse pointer.
- Type L' on the keyboard (or click the mouse on the appropriate keys—pressing the Shift key for the capital *L*). Use the standard apostrophe key.
- Creating the accent mark over the *e* takes two keystrokes. With the Option key pressed, type the acute accent (´) on the *e* key. Nothing appears in the display. Then press the *e* key by itself— both the letter and its superimposed accent mark appear in the display.
- Continue typing (or clicking) the letter until you reach the ç in *Française.* Press the Option key to find the ç key (the *c* key, as it turns out), and type the letter.
- Finish typing the rest of the word.

Next, we want to transfer this text into a MacWrite document (it could also go into a MacPaint picture as well).

- Place the pointer just to the left of the copyright symbol in the display. Press the mouse button and drag the pointer across the one-line display. The entire text line is selected.
- Select Copy from the Edit menu. Since nothing was typed beyond the last *e*, the empty space to the right of the text won't be copied.
- The text is now in the Clipboard. You can open MacWrite or MacPaint (if not already open) and paste the text into any document.

If you plan to paste into a MacPaint picture, I recommend you select the font, font size, and font style *before* performing the Paste operation, because you will have difficulty changing these attributes later. For MacWrite, you must first paste the text, *then* change its attributes if necessary. And, unless you cut or copy something else to the Clipboard, the text stays there, ready to be pasted each time you need that special text in your document.

Of course, you don't need to have Key Caps present on the screen to take advantage of special characters, since you can type the two-key or three-key combinations directly from the keyboard. But having Key Caps on screen allows you to proceed with the alternate character set without having to refer to the manual to see which key is which.

In fact, if the document you're working on happens to include many foreign phrases or math formulas, you can use a dual window trick. By moving the Key Caps window to the very bottom of the screen (so the space bar row of keys is off the bottom edge), and shortening the depth of the MacWrite window with its size box, you can have a ready reference of the special characters on screen at all times.

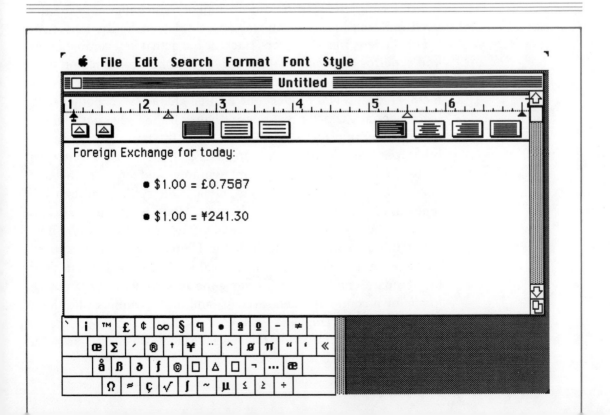

Simply press the Option or Shift-Option combination to see the characters in the Key Caps window, and type them from the keyboard. As long as the MacWrite window is the active one, the characters will appear in the document, and not in the Key Caps display. This operation seems to violate the belief that you can have only one working window operating on the Mac at once, but it definitely works in your favor. Since the keys on the Key Caps window are highlighted every time a real key is pressed, the display can be rather distracting while typing. If so, you may want to cover the Key Caps window with the MacWrite window until you come to a point where you need Key Caps assistance.

There's a catch, however, to all the character set flexibility which Key Caps offers. Not all fonts contain every character of the extensive Mac character set. Chicago (the Key Caps font), Geneva, and Monaco have the most extensive character sets. When a character is not available in a font, it appears on the screen instead as a small square. If you're unsure a particular character is available in the font you're using, go ahead and create the text with Key Caps (or straight from the keyboard if you know the character key combinations). Pasting the text to your document and changing to the desired font will reveal which characters didn't make the transition.

Fortunately, the Mac keeps track of the actual key combinations you type for a special character. Even if a key combination produces an empty square in one font, that key combination is remembered, and will produce the desired character in another font. If the special character text doesn't have all the right characters in the font you're using in MacWrite, select the text and choose another font from the font menu. In MacPaint, first select a font, then paste the text into the MacPaint window, and undo if the text doesn't look right. For both programs keep cycling through the fonts until you find one that has the characters you need and matches the style of your document's font as closely as possible.

If you buy your Macintosh in the United States, the standard character set (the characters on the real keyboard) is different than the standard character set for someone in Europe. Each language has its own common letters, accents, and other symbols, and these are parts of that language's standard character set. Therefore, it wouldn't be practical to use the special Macintosh characters (with the Option key) for extensive work in a foreign language when a foreign language keyboard is available. But if on occasion you need to reproduce a phrase from German or a mathematical formula that uses Greek symbols, then you will find Key Caps a convenient way to gain access to the special characters of Mac's character set without looking up the key combinations in a manual.

◢ ◢ ◢ ◢ ◢ ◢ **Control Panel**

The Macintosh Control Panel is the most interesting-looking display of all the desk accessories. In this window there are adjustments for a number of things that affect how you and the Mac communicate with each other. It gives you considerable influence over the keyboard and display. We'll examine each control, starting at the top center, and working our way clockwise around the panel.

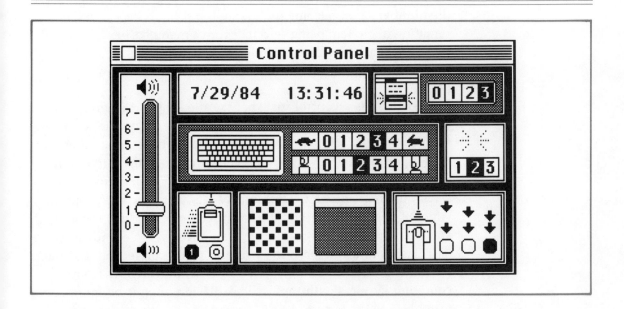

At the top is another display of the time and date, as maintained by the computer's internal battery-operated clock. You can use the control panel to adjust the clock and calendar, in precisely the same up-down button method as we saw on the alarm clock.

In the upper right corner you can control the number of flashes an item makes when you select it from your desktop or from a menu. Your choices are: no flashing (0), 1, 2, or 3 rapid flashes. The reason you might like to have the icon flash is that it offers instantaneous feedback of the Mac acknowledging your choice and doing something about it. Without any flash, especially if you work quickly on the Mac, you sometimes have the feeling that perhaps the computer is doing something else with its disk drive instead of fetching the program or performing the task you really want— pull-down menus can disappear before you're sure you made the right selection. With the flash, your selected icon stays on the screen for a second, confirming your choice. Moreover, if you select the wrong choice, at least the flashing gives you a chance to see what you did wrong, thus making it easier for you to recover your original status.

To choose the number of flashes you want, place the pointer over the appropriate number and click. When you do this, not only does the number's box become highlighted, but the little graphic representation of an item being selected from a menu flashes accordingly to give you an onscreen example of your selection. I leave it set to three, since I appreciate as much feedback to my actions as possible.

Next there is a control for what is called the *text insertion pointer*. Anytime you are about to type text—into a page on the Note Pad, for example—Macintosh produces a cursor at the point where the next typed character will appear. The cursor is nothing more than a thin vertical line, which would be very difficult to find on a crowded screen unless it flashed. This control lets you specify the speed at which it flashes. At speed 1, it flashes about every two seconds; at speed 2, it flashes slightly slower than once every second; at speed 3, it flashes at a rate between two and three per second. For most people the middle setting will be fine, while converts from other computer systems with rapid cursor flashing might be more comfortable with the fastest setting. As you change the setting, a sample text insertion line flashes at the set speed, giving you the chance to see it before leaving the Control Panel.

At the lower right corner of the Control Panel is the control for the mouse that determines how quickly after an initial click you need to press the mouse button a second time so the Mac interprets it as a double-click. If you specify a fast double-click (the control panel selection with the arrows closest together), and double-click at a slower rate, then the Mac interprets the clicks as two separate single clicks. I recommend setting this control as shown in the previous illustration—at the fastest setting. It forces you to be more deliberate in your double-clicking, but more importantly, it prevents you from accidentally double-clicking an icon, when you actually mean to click it once to select it, and then maybe a second time to drag it.

At the bottom middle of the Control Panel is a most interesting control. It lets you redecorate your desktop as often as you like.

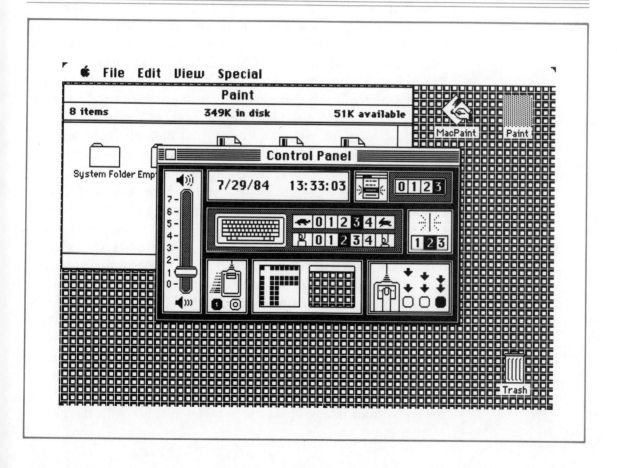

When you turn on the Mac for the first time, the desktop looks grey. Actually, the grey is composed of alternating black and white dots. To see the pattern of light and dark that makes up the desk, look at the bit pattern in the left-hand box in this section of the Control Panel. The right-hand box is a miniaturized representation of an entire desktop screen, complete with menu bar along the top. If you don't like the grey, place the pointer over the miniaturized white menu bar and start clicking through the library of patterns. You'll be an interior designer in no time. The patterns are the same ones available in MacPaint. To see what the pattern actually looks like on the desktop, click the pointer anywhere on the pattern in the miniature desktop on the Control Panel.

Some of the patterns are mighty bizarre when used as a background to your desktop (see the illustration on page 121), but for a change of pace, they may be just the ticket to brighten up your day. Some users may also find that under different lighting conditions, either a darker or lighter background is easier on the eyes. You might want to change the setting for daytime and nighttime use. You can even adapt (edit) any pattern you like by using the pointer to fill in or remove bits by clicking at any point in the left box. There are only sixteen million patterns you can create.

Desktop patterns really affect only the desktop when you are working with your disks and file icons. While it does change the background of the MacWrite screen environment, you don't see enough of it for a change to make any difference. And in MacPaint, the background is unaffected by a change in this Control Panel setting.

The next control to the left lets you select between two different methods of mouse tracking. This factor lets you determine how the pointer on the screen reacts to the way you move the mouse on the tabletop. The normal setting for mouse tracking—and the one I recommend—operates in such a way that as you move the mouse faster in any direction, the pointer on the screen accelerates even more in that same direction. The other setting is *linear*, meaning that the pointer moves in direct proportion to the speed of the mouse on the table top. The normal setting lets you cover more ground on the screen without taking up as much tabletop space with the movement of your mouse. But when you move the mouse slowly for precision work, the pointer-mouse speed relationship is identical to that of the linear selection. The only difference between the two occurs when moving the mouse at high speed.

If the long control along the left side of the Control Panel resembles a volume slide control on a radio, that's because this control adjusts the volume of the beep used to signal startup, warning boxes, and the alarm. The volume you choose should depend on where the Mac is going to be set up. In a noisy office environment, a high setting (6 to 7) may be necessary to make sure you hear things such as the alarm. But in a one person office, a low setting (1 to 2) is enough for most people to hear the beeps when needed, without the sound being intrusive. Since the beeps are also there as a warning, it's not a good idea to turn the volume all the way down to zero.

Finally, we come to some keyboard adjustments, located in the center of the Control Panel. The top control is for the rate at which keys are repeated. When you press and hold down a key, the Mac repeats the key for you automatically. You can adjust the speed at which the characters repeat on the screen whenever a key is held down. Notice that the range of numbers on the screen indicates which end is faster (the hare) and which end slower (the tortoise).

The bottom keyboard control may be a difficult concept for some users to comprehend because the manual calls it Keyboard Touch. When you hear this term, you immediately think it has something to do with the pressure needed to make contact with the key. Of course, in a computer keyboard like the Mac's, that factor is designed into the keyboard, and is not under control of the computer. Instead, Keyboard Touch here refers to the length of time required to hold down a key before it starts to repeat. A good typist's fingers will skip from key to key so fast that no finger will linger long enough for it to start repeating on a normal keystroke. That same speedster will want repeating keys to start repeating quickly so as not to ruin the established typing rhythm. A slower typist, on the other hand, will often let the fingers rest on the keys a bit longer. If the Keyboard Touch is set too quickly, then you'll get what appears to be a lot of double keys appearing on the screen, and your first thought will be that there's something wrong with the keyboard.

And if you're so slow that you're uncomfortable with the idea of repeating keys, you can set the bottom control to zero, turning off the feature.

◢ ◢ ◢ ◢ ◢ ◢ Puzzle

The last desk accessory is a puzzle. It's no hot-shot video game, but rather an electronic adaptation of a novelty puzzle we all worked on as kids.

It has fifteen numbered, sliding tiles in a grid of sixteen squares. Your job is to move the tiles around until they line up in numerical order starting at the upper left corner and working across each row. To move the tiles in the Mac version, you position the pointer over a tile near the blank square and click. If the tile you're pointing to can move, it zips over to fill in the blank spot. You can also move whole rows of tiles by placing the pointer at one end of a row and clicking.

Every time you call up the puzzle from the Desk Accessories menu the tiles are scrambled into a different order. Who knows? Maybe one day you'll call it from the menu and it will be perfect from the start.

This completes our desktop discussions. By now, you should be an expert on all features of the Mac operating environment that are common to all programs. Next, we will look at ways to speed up some popular applications.

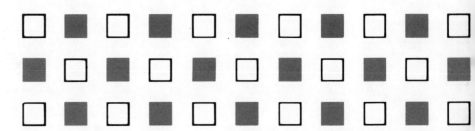

IF YOU'RE LIKE me, you have probably spent more time on your Macintosh playing with MacPaint than with any other single program. There's something about this program—its ease of use, its library of built-in commands—that encourages you to experiment. Eventually, you look for excuses to use MacPaint in your work, perhaps to add some ornament to an otherwise formal presentation, or to design a clever letterhead for your children to use. But if you use MacPaint seriously for your work—illustrating articles, preparing advertising layouts for clients, or creating finished art for a class assignment—you will be particularly interested in some of the program's less obvious features and how to exploit them.

Here, then, are a number of techniques I've discovered over many months of using MacPaint for work and play. I am no artist, to be sure, so anything I've done here can be easily mastered by anyone.

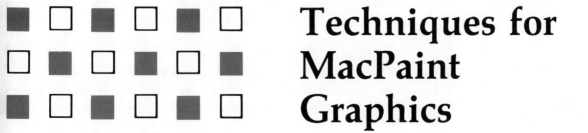

Techniques for MacPaint Graphics

MacPaint Rulers

Quite often, you find yourself wanting to recreate on the Mac a picture or other graphic image that already exists in print. Since there is no easy way to trace a printed image without a special jig for the mouse or a copy of the image on a clear acetate sheet taped to the screen, you might want to draw on the MacPaint screen according to precise ruler measurement. But MacPaint does not have a way built into it for you to accurately measure an image on the screen as you're drawing it.

To solve this problem, I've created horizontal and vertical rulers that fit along two adjacent edges of the MacPaint window. They measure five inches across by three inches down, and are marked off every one-eighth inch. I keep the rulers in the Scrapbook on the

MacPaint disk so I can copy and paste them to my work area whenever I need them.

In designing the rulers, actual measurements were calibrated on a printout from the Imagewriter. This was essential, because an Imagewriter printout doesn't hold entirely true to the proportions shown on the screen.

Making the rulers for yourself is a little tedious, but the powers of MacPaint make it considerably easier than you might imagine. Let's make the horizontal measure first.

- Open MacPaint and immediately summon FatBits.
- Use the pencil icon to lay one vertical marker of eight bits. The fastest way to do this is to hold down the Shift key (to keep the line straight) and mouse button while you drag the pencil pointer.

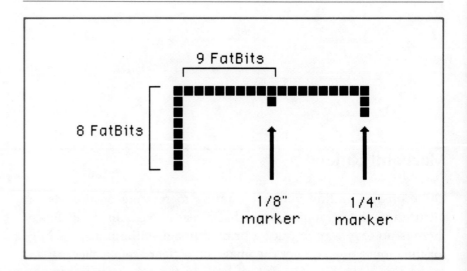

- Then, beginning next to the topmost bit of the vertical marker, lay nine horizontal bits, using the same straight line technique (the Shift key) as before.
- Below the ninth bit, place a single bit marker. This is a one-eighth-inch marker.

- Lay nine more bits to the right, and mark the end with two vertical bits as the one-quarter-inch marker.
- While still in FatBits, use the marquee to select the line you've made thus far in such a way that the left side of the marquee overlaps the long initial marker at the left and the bottom line of the marquee is on the same line as the bottom bit of the one-quarter-inch marker.

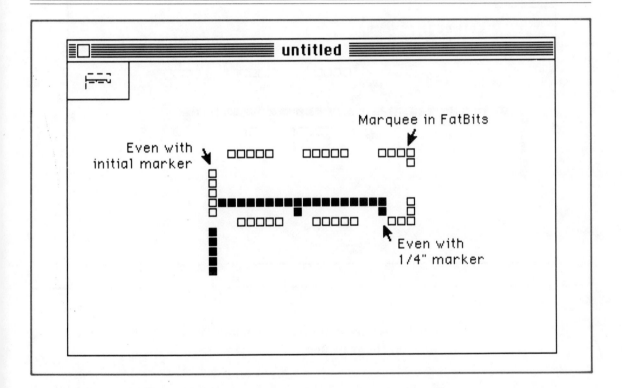

- Now drag the line to the right while holding down the Option and Shift keys. Pressing those two keyboard keys retains the original image in its location, while assuring that the drag you're about to do stays on the same horizontal line as the original image.

- When the left edge of the Select rectangle covers the one-quarter-inch marker, release all the keys and mouse button.

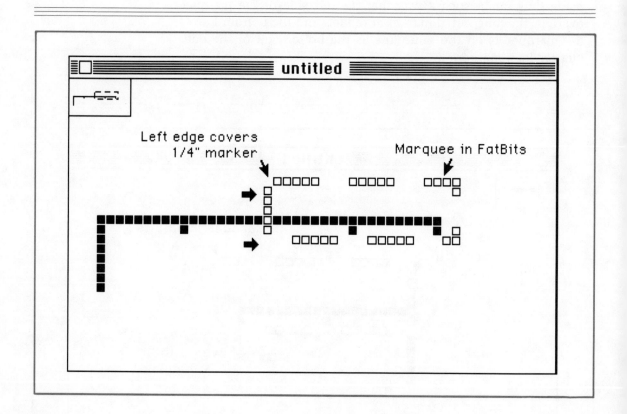

- Click the mouse button once in an empty portion of the screen to turn off the marquee.

You're now up to a one-half inch ruler.

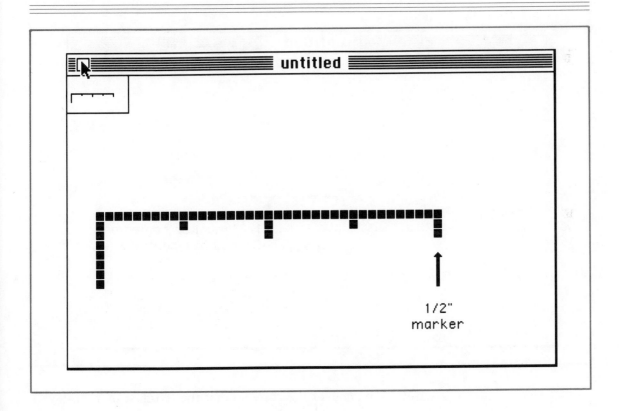

- Exit FatBits.
- Use the marquee to encompass the entire image you have so far.
- While holding down the Option key, drag a copy of the half-inch line a couple inches away from the original.
- With the marquee still around the image, select the Flip Horizontal command from the Edit menu.
- Next, use the lasso to draw a rough circle around the image you just flipped.

- When the image starts sizzling, drag it up to the right edge of the original image.

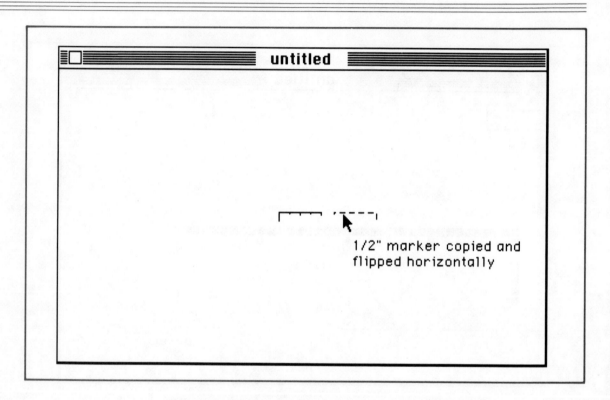

- Carefully maneuver the copy so that the leftmost marker covers the rightmost marker of the original line—you want them to overlap. Also make sure the horizontal lines are perfectly even.
- When you're satisfied that all is in order, click the mouse button with the pointer away from the image.
- If the maneuver didn't work out just right, select Undo from the Edit menu, and start the last procedure over.

You now have a one-inch line.

The next steps are larger repetitions of the previous ones. Use the lasso and Option key to make a copy of the one-inch line; then, pressing both Option and Shift, drag the copy to the right, making sure the end markers from each image precisely overlap. Now you have a two-inch line. Repeat this procedure with the two-inch line to bring the ruler out to four inches.

To get the last, odd inch, the easiest way is to lasso the entire four-inch line and, again using both the Shift and Option keys, drag the copy over to the right only one inch. Make sure the markers line up precisely all along the ruler.

Numbering the ruler is a simple task at this point.

- Plant the text insertion pointer in a blank area of the screen, and type the numbers one through five with a couple of spaces between each number. For my ruler, I used the Monaco-9 font.
- Then use the lasso to select and drag each number to its respective marker on the ruler, placing the number above, and as close as possible to, the horizontal line (with a little care, you should be able to get the numbers within one FatBit of the line).

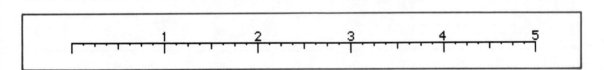

When you're done with the horizontal ruler, use the hand icon to move the page so that the ruler is along the very top of the window. You'll be using the area beneath it for the creation of the vertical ruler.

Since you're already an expert at making a horizontal ruler, you'll find it's easier to create the vertical ruler initially as a horizontal one, which you will later rotate into vertical position. The only difference between the horizontal and vertical rulers is that the vertical ruler needs the insertion of one extra bit for every one-half inch (the Imagewriter prints seventy-four dots per inch vertically and seventy-two dots per inch horizontally). That means that somewhere along the first one-half-inch section of the ruler you make, there must be an extra FatBit thrown in.

Therefore, to make the vertical ruler, you should start the same way you did for the horizontal one, except that in one (and only one) of the first one-eighth-inch markers, you have to add a tenth bit. Be careful, however. When you double the images of the first one-quarter inch, there will be an extraneous FatBit in the second one-eighth inch rule. You'll have to use FatBits to find and remove the extra bit. Once you have the first half-inch completed, however, you can flip it and duplicate it with the lasso and Option key, just as you did before, to make a ruler that extends this time only three inches. The MacPaint window won't accommodate a vertical ruler any longer than that.

The final step involves moving the vertical ruler into position.

- Use the marquee to select the ruler, and then select the Rotate command from the Edit menu to make the ruler vertical. The Mac flips the ruler somewhere near the center of the screen.
- While the marquee is still around the ruler, drag it to the left margin of the screen, so it doesn't touch the top ruler.
- Then lasso the vertical ruler and carefully position it so that the markers in the upper lefthand corner meet at a right angle such that the corner pixel appears to be missing, as shown in the following figure.

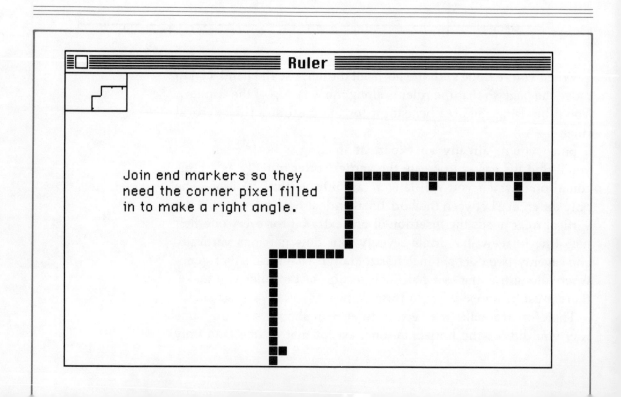

- Go into FatBits to fill in the single, corner pixel.
- Finally, use the same technique you used for numbering the horizontal ruler to place numbers on the vertical ruler, but this time, add the zero to the upper left corner so it applies to both the horizontal and vertical rulers.

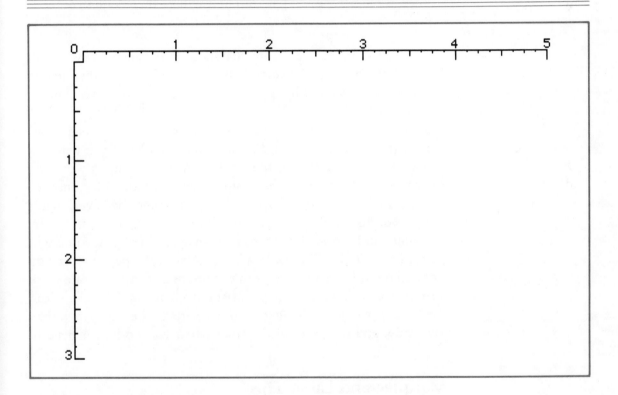

At this point, you should use the lasso to select the entire ruler. It's a lot easier than it looks.

- Place the lasso icon in the upper right corner of the screen and press the mouse button.
- Drag the lasso to the left, along the very top of the screen, by keeping the lasso *outside and above* the window as you move to the left (as long as you hold down the mouse button—and press it initially *inside* the window—the lasso will not change to an arrow). The line you leave behind is perfectly straight, against the top margin of the window.

- Keep the lasso outside the window, and continue to drag it down the left margin, and about halfway across the bottom margin.
- Release the mouse button, and the entire ruler should sizzle.
- Select the Copy command from the Edit menu.
- Summon the Scrapbook from the Desk Accessories menu and paste it in there. Even though you won't be able to see all of the ruler in the Scrapbook page, all of it will be there when you need it.

I also recommend you immediately save the picture as a Mac-Paint document, called "Ruler," on an archival storage disk just in case something should happen to your MacPaint work disk and its Scrapbook file.

To use the ruler, simply open the Scrapbook to the page containing the ruler, copy it, and paste it into your MacPaint window. It may not be accurately centered when you paste it, so while the ruler is still sizzling after the Paste command, move it against the top and left margins of the window. Bear in mind, however, that if the area in the window where the ruler is to go contains an image, the ruler will be pasted right over the image. Therefore, you might prefer to move the window to a blank area of the page before you bring in the ruler. There, you can use your ruler in a separate work area to create your precisely measured elements. Then you can copy and paste those elements to other parts of the page when they are ready, and erase or cut the ruler when you no longer need it.

Marquee and Lasso Tips

You saw in the last section that you can use the marquee in Fat-Bits—something you may not have realized before (the lasso also works in FatBits). What you should know about these two tools are: how to use the marquee to size images to a desired proportion; a shortcut for using the lasso; and deciding which tool to use for different situations.

◢ ◢ ◢ ◢ ◢ ◢ **Precise Image Stretching and Shrinking**

One of the features of the marquee is that, with the Command key, you can stretch or shrink an image contained in the rectangle by pulling on the corners. Even though, with the help of the Shift key, you can stretch it horizontally or vertically you may still find the operation very haphazard when it comes to precisely sizing an image. Moreover, since you usually perform the stretching in a blank work area and then move the image to where it's desired, all too often the image isn't stretched to the exact dimensions required of the space. And if you try to stretch the already stretched image, you will notice that the bit pattern of the image is slightly different from the original (some lines are distorted). Each time you stretch the same image, it distorts even more. Unless you keep a copy of the original image, the original bit pattern is lost. There is, however, a good way around this problem.

- Create your original image wherever it is convenient.
- When it's completed, lasso the image.

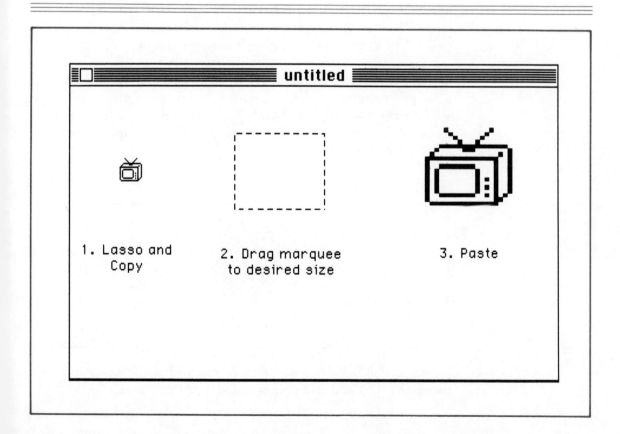

- Issue the Copy command (from the Edit menu or Command-C).
- Select the marquee and map out on your picture exactly where you want the image to fit. Let the edges of the marquee's rectangle delineate the proportion and size you want the image to fill.
- Then issue the Paste command.

After a bit of disk work (no swapping), the image will be sized to the exact proportions of the rectangle you have specified. The image will still be sizzling from the original image's lasso, so you can use the pointer to move the copy around in case you need to slightly readjust its location.

◢ ◢ ◢ ◢ ◢ ◢ **Lasso Shortcut**

Using the select lasso in a finely detailed drawing is not the easiest thing to do on MacPaint, since you are essentially asked to use the mouse to draw a freehand circle around an object you wanted moved or deleted. And for nonartists, a freehand drawing with the mouse is difficult. There is a shortcut, however.

To appreciate the shortcut, let's use an example.

- Draw a fairly large, filled circle in a MacPaint window. Use a snappy pattern.
- Then select the lasso and draw half-way around the lower part of the circle. Do not complete the loop at the top. Now release the mouse button.

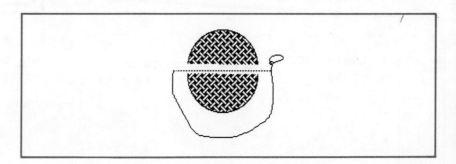

Notice that MacPaint automatically completed the lasso line between the start and end points and selected that area.

■ Now, drag the lasso from the same start point, but go to about one o'clock and release the button. This will give you a feeling for how MacPaint automatically closes the lasso in a straight line between the start and end points.

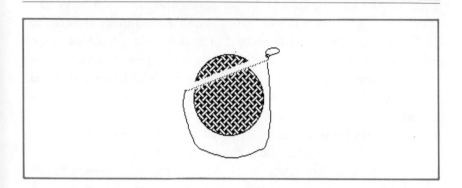

■ Experiment more with the lasso and the circle.

The shortcut, then, allows you to select a shape by drawing only as much lasso line as is needed for MacPaint to close the line with a straight one, and encompass the entire shape.

■ Using the same circle, draw around it, but this time starting above and to the left of the circle.
■ Stop dragging the lasso in a corresponding location at the right. You don't have to worry about bringing the lasso line all the way around to the starting point to select the shape.

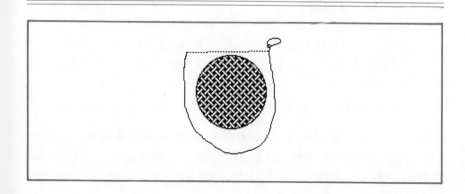

Since the circle is inside the area prescribed by the semicircle formed by the lasso, the entire circle is selected.

◢ ◢ ◢ ◢ ◢ ◢ Marquee or Lasso?

If you've played around with the marquee and lasso, you may have noticed that they treat the objects they surround quite differently. Understanding these differences can make your job of editing a picture much easier, and will give you more professional results.

Perhaps the best way to get a feeling for the difference between the two is to try both methods in the following example. Using first the marquee, then the lasso, try to move a circle on the screen in such a way that it is tangent to a diagonal line. If you use the marquee rectangle, no matter how closely you move the rectangle to the rim of the circle, the final result will always show gaps in the diagonal. That's because when you use the marquee, absolutely every pixel within that rectangle moves around with the primary object. Even though the area around the image (but inside the rectangle) looks blank, the operation actually drags all the blank pixels with the image.

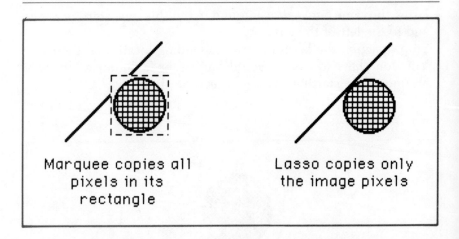

Marquee copies all pixels in its rectangle

Lasso copies only the image pixels

But if you use the lasso, no matter how bizarrely you trace a line around the primary image, only the primary image is selected. An outline of the selected image sizzles on the screen, so you can see what you've affected. You can then drag the circle over and carefully place it right against the line.

If you take the power of the lasso one step further, you will perhaps recognize that since the lasso activates only the precise image you're working with, you can more easily overlay images atop one another without leaving the unwanted white space made by the white pixels of a marquee rectangle.

For example, let's say you're making a map, and you want to depict the intersection of two roads as the location of a particular town. The town marking is a circle with a dot in the middle. If you make the town marker in open space and then drag it to the intersection, you can try to use the marquee, making the rectangle as small as possible, while keeping it just outside the boundaries of the marker. But when you drag the rectangle, its outer boundary and all white pixels therein are also dragged, leaving gaps in the road at the intersection.

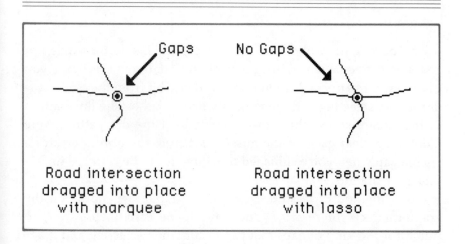

But if you use the lasso, you don't have to be careful about where you make the lasso, and still when you drag the marker to the intersection, there are no gaps at all. It's as if only the marker's image were pasted directly on top of the road markings. The differences between the two methods is most evident under the scrutiny of FatBits.

The lasso presents interesting properties when you use it to select shapes having solid borders. As long as the border is solid, the interior space prevails over any other image it may overlap. But if you remove even one bit from the border, the interior space becomes, in a manner, transparent. See example (B) in the following illustration, where I've selected and dragged the circle onto the square with the lasso.

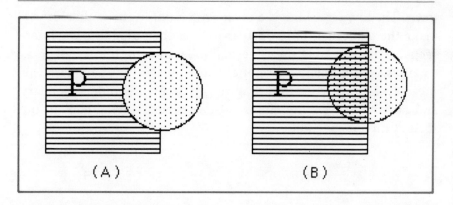

(A)   (B)

The border was solid, and the dot pattern inside the circle appears painted on a white, opaque background. But in this figure you can see what happened when I removed one bit from the circle border before selecting and dragging it with the lasso. The line pattern of the square shows through the circle as if the dot pattern were painted on clear glass. If the missing bit from the border creates a visible gap when you're finished dragging, it can be restored in Fat-Bits after the move.

Either method of lasso dragging is desirable, depending on the graphic effect you're after. You have to be careful, however, to watch for the kind of gaps that can occur when selecting and dragging text characters onto a filled space with the lasso. The previous example (A) shows how the interior space of a dragged letter covers up the line pattern, while prior pixel removal in (B) (and subsequent pixel restoration) allows the line pattern to show through. Of course, the marquee method does not offer any transparency whatsoever.

In general, then, you should use the lasso whenever you want to drag an object such that its destination will be directly atop or tangent to an image already planted on the screen, or when a marquee rectangle would otherwise cover up an existing image. Use the marquee whenever the area surrounding the destination of the image to be dragged contains no images that would be covered by the marquee rectangle. And use the lasso, less one border pixel, to select and drag an image to overlay another like a transparency.

Designer Aids

Now we come to some practical and fun MacPaint work. You'll practice design techniques the pros use, like getting quickly in and out of FatBits, making soft corners, combining multiple shapes into one larger one, moving your entire drawing around the page, and keeping your picture pieces in line with each other. You'll also finally get the low-down on the mysterious Grid feature.

◢ ◢ ◢ ◢ ◢ ◢ Speeding In and Out of FatBits

It's no secret that a shortcut into FatBits is to double-click the pencil icon, and I hope you used it when working on the rulers. But it is less well known that getting FatBits to immediately display the area of the screen you want (instead of "feeling" your way around with the hand icon) and exiting FatBits can also be sped up by a couple of tricks.

Before going into FatBits, there are two quick ways to instruct MacPaint what you want FatBits to be focused on when it throws on the microscope, depending on which icon you have selected when you need FatBits. With the marquee, lasso, or hand icon selected, simply click (without actually lassoing or putting a marquee around anything) those pointers where you want to work with Fat-Bits. Then double-click the pencil icon. You'll be right on target. This technique also works if you click any of the other icons in the precise spot. The problem with doing this with the other icons, however, is that they all leave some kind of mark on the page where you click the icon. With some marks, like from the line and shape icons, it's not too serious because only one extra bit has been drawn on the screen, and that bit can be removed very quickly the minute you're in FatBits by moving the pencil to the offending bit and clicking it to white. The paint bucket and spraypaint can, however, can cause considerable damage to your picture, so don't use these icons as FatBit locators.

The most efficient method for getting into FatBits is available only if you're using the pencil icon. All you have to do is place the pencil point at the spot in the picture you want to see in FatBits, press the Command key, and then click the mouse button. In a flash, you're in FatBits at the precise location—all in one step.

Exiting FatBits can be simpler than even double-clicking the pencil icon. In fact, there are two "secret" ways.

One method is the reverse of the one-step Command key-pencil icon combination, above. With the pencil icon selected, press the Command key, and click the mouse anywhere in the window—in either the FatBit or regular size window. The pencil will not leave any marks on the picture. (This Command key sequence to exit FatBits does not work when other icons are selected.)

In the second method, all you have to do is move whatever pointer you're using in FatBits to the "regular size" window in the upper left corner of the MacPaint window and click the mouse. Instantly, you're back to the original screen.

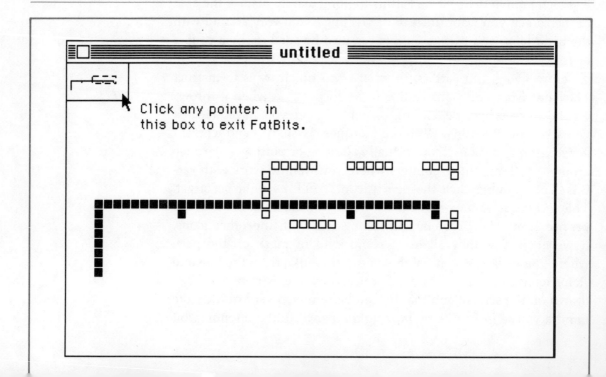

Also, while you're in FatBits, save yourself a lot of pointer manipulating and mouse clicking by using the built-in shortcut that
turns the pencil pointer into the hand icon at the press of the Option key. As long as you hold down the Option key, you can move
the page around (within the limits of the regular size window) and
make FatBit changes much faster this way.

In fact, with the Option and Shift key shortcuts imbedded into
several MacPaint icon features, I find myself keeping one hand
hovering near the keyboard just about all the time. Not only am I,
thus, more prone to use the shortcuts when I need them, but my
productivity improves markedly.

⫝̸ ⫝̸ ⫝̸ ⫝̸ ⫝̸ ⫝̸ **Softening Corners of Squares**

You may have already seen and admired some carefully crafted
pictures created on MacPaint, or even the simple icons that the
Macintosh uses for directory displays and the like. Yet, when you
try to replicate them, they just don't seem right. One of the techniques that icon designers use is to round off square corners in
simple line art. Rounding corners is different from using the
rounded-corner square icon of MacPaint, since in some sizes and
proportions, this function tends to create corners that are too
rounded, making some rectangles look almost ovoid.

In small images, especially those of the icon size, you may have
to look very closely to notice that what the artist has done to round
that corner was to use FatBits and simply remove the corner pixel.
Look at the difference the removal of ten pixels (one from each corner of the Mac cabinet and video screen) makes when I draw the
Macintosh icon.

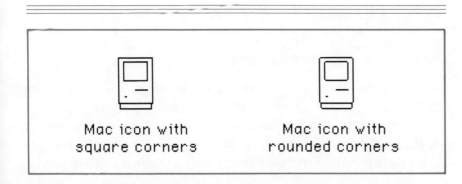

Mac icon with   Mac icon with
square corners   rounded corners

If the original rectangular image is much larger, then you need to use a variation on this theme to bring the "roundedness" of the corners into correct proportion. Instead of just removing a single bit, form a short diagonal at each corner.

The next figure illustrates four types of FatBit corners (three of them rounded) on a right angle drawn with a one-pixel-wide line.

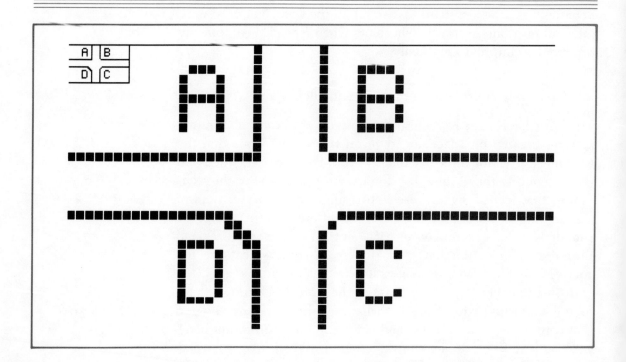

Corner A is the standard right angle, while corner B is the kind I used on the Mac icon. Look at the normal size results for all four corners in the upper left corner of this figure.

◢ ◢ ◢ ◢ ◢ ◢ Combining Linear Shapes

Although the library of built-in shapes (rectangle, circle, polygon, etc.) on MacPaint is diverse enough for most pictures, there are times when you want to draw a shape not available on the palette. At the same time, you may feel you don't have the artistic abilities to create the desired shape by using the mouse in a freehand style.

Don't feel bad—it's a very common feeling with those of us who aren't graduates of a fine arts academy.

It is possible, however, to utilize many of MacPaint's powers in such a way that you actually use two or more built-in shapes to create custom shapes that fit your picture idea. Essentially, the procedure involves overlapping standard shapes and then erasing the bits that don't belong there—and it's quite a bit easier than the sculptor's job of cutting away everything that isn't the statue. Let's look at a couple examples of techniques you may want to use in some of your own pictures.

I'll illustrate the first few techniques by showing you how to make an organizational chart a little more interesting than simple boxes and straight lines. We'll do that by making the lines look more like pipelines, complete with smoothed corners and shading.

First I lay out the boxes representing the individuals to be represented on the chart.

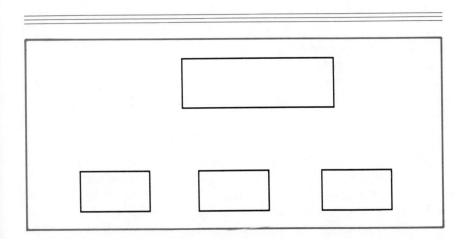

Next, I connect the boxes with pipelines, which are made, like the boxes above, using the rectangle. It's important, however, to make sure that the rectangles making up the pipelines are of equal width. To do that, I use the cross-hair pointer, which MacPaint provides whenever I click the rectangle icon. This is a valuable measuring tool, and is something you should experiment with to fully understand its properties.

One important characteristic of the cross-hair pointer, like most pointers on the Macintosh screen, is that whenever any pixel of the pointer is over a black pixel already in the window, the pointer's pixel turns white—in other words, the pointer is always the opposite of the pixels beneath it. This allows the pointer to stand out, no matter what the screen image is. Leaving our incomplete organizational chart for a moment, try the following exercise which illustrates the use of the cross-hair pointer as a measuring device.

- Click the rectangle icon, drag a rectangle of any size, and release the mouse button.
- Now carefully move the pointer to one of the rectangle's corners. Practice moving the pointer slowly in one-pixel increments, if possible, in the vertical and horizontal direction, while watching the characteristics of the pointer and the pixels of the rectangle beneath it. Notice how the rectangle lines become white whenever the pointer's lines cross it.

```
Cursor lines
reverse when
directly over
rectangle
corner
```

- Try to move the pointer to the precise corner of the rectangle such that the center of the pointer is exactly on the corner point of the rectangle. The corner should be obscured by the pointer.
- Draw another rectangle, and this time, without releasing the mouse button, use the pointer to measure the width of one side. Notice how easy it is to match the width of the pointer with the length of the side.

I use this pointer measure to make skinny rectangles for all kinds of things, but especially when I want to make a number of them, all of equal width (and where simply copying one standard rectangle won't work). Until you train your eye to recognize the properties of the cross-hair pointer, your rectangles might be off by a pixel; even so, in most cases there won't be a noticeable difference. Such is the luxury of high resolution graphics.

Now, back to our organizational chart, I've connected the boxes of the organizational chart with these skinny rectangles.

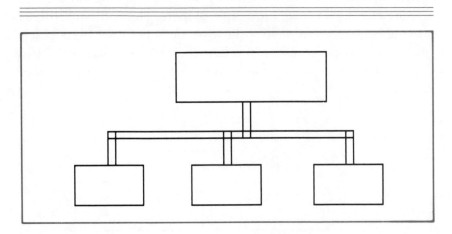

At this point, we have a bunch of rectangles with all kinds of extra, overlapping lines where they meet. Using FatBits and the pencil icon, I attend to each intersection of rectangles and remove all extraneous black pixels. Now the individual rectangles have been converted into one, multiple-armed pathway from box to box.

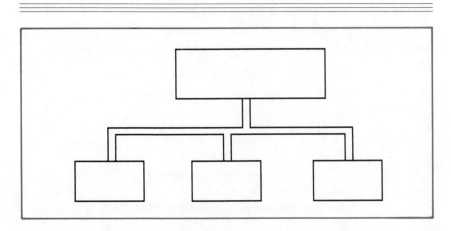

The next task is to round off all the corners of our pathways. Since the rectangles here are more like tubes, you must smooth the corners on both the inside and outside of each corner. For this kind of rounding on the outside corners, I prefer the more diagonal type of rounded corners (example C in the figure on page 146) instead of the missing pixel type. To my eye, it presents a less severe, more artistic appearance. But since the inside corner is a tighter curve, I use the missing bit corner (example B) there. Thus, still in FatBits, I use the pencil icon to remove the three outside corner black pixels and replace them with one pixel on the diagonal joining the two arms. For inside corners, I simply remove the one bit at the point of the corner.

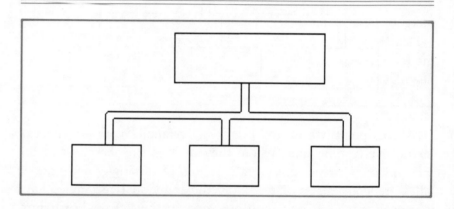

At a "T" intersection, I round the two corners as inside corners, by removing single bits at the corner points.

I exit FatBits and select a pattern from the palette. Then I select the paint bucket icon from the left and fill the tubes with the pattern.

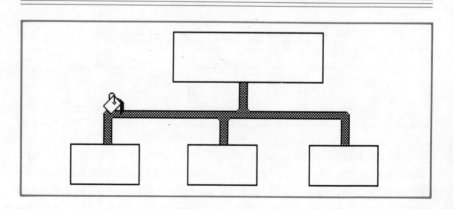

If I don't like the pattern I've chosen, I can erase it immediately by selecting Undo from the Edit menu, and try a different pattern.

▲ ▲ ▲ ▲ ▲ ▲ **Combining Curved Shapes**

Now let's see how to combine two curved shapes to fashion an irregular shape. I once designed a map that was going to some friends. It included an area of the Pacific coast that was well known for whale watching. Therefore, it was only fitting that the ocean off the coast on my map include the picture of a few whales half submerged in the water. Here's how I went about it.

I started with two ovals. The first was a very long one, to capture the form of the whale's back. My vision of a stylized whale had a head more severely sloped than the rear portion, so I drew a second, almost circular oval. Then I selected the second oval with the lasso, and dragged it to the large oval, placing it such that the two were tangent to each other as shown in the following figure.

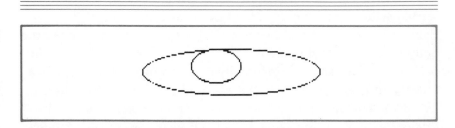

Next, I drew a horizontal straight line near the middle of the two ovals, indicating where the waterline would be.

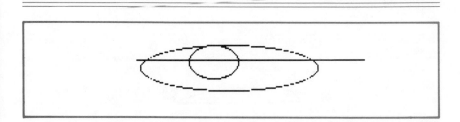

With the eraser, I removed all of the ovals' lines below the waterline. Then I turned to FatBits to help me clean up the details, removing all extraneous oval outlines above the waterline except for the hump that becomes the whale's body.

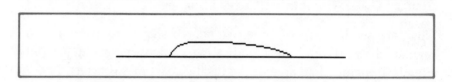

Near the head, I added an eyeball by planting a couple of pixels, and then added a jet of spray from the whale's blow hole.

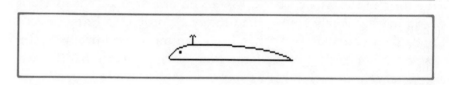

To create a small tail in a separate work space on the screen, I started with a small circle, erasing all but a tiny arc in the lower right quadrant—this will become the part of the tail that links the body to the pair of flippers at the very end of the tail. For the flippers, I drew two small, horizontally oriented ovals adjacent to each other, and dragged them to the exposed tip of the arc. I then selected the tail assembly with the lasso and dragged it to the right side of the body at water line. It took a little more work in FatBits to beef up the arc to make the tail look in proper proportion with the rest of the body. Then I added ripples to the water line in random locations by replacing a few pixels of the line with pixels in the shapes of inverted V's.

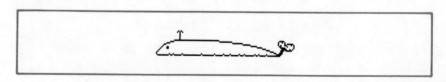

The result was anything but a true representation of a whale—nor was it intended to be. The purpose of this demonstration, however, is to show you how to think of complex forms in terms of combinations of simple forms. If you had even a smidgen of art in grade school, you may remember how you learned to draw a horse's body by first sketching a few contiguous ovals, then joining them across the top and bottom to form the torso. After that, you erased the parts of the ovals you didn't need anymore. The principle holds true for MacPaint . . . but without the erasure marks of your deletions showing on the screen.

◢ ◢ ◢ ◢ ◢ ◢ **Repositioning Large MacPaintings**

When you start creating a picture, it is very easy for it to grow larger in one direction, such that when you perform a Show Page, the picture is off center on the page. And, of course, as it appears on Show Page, so will it appear on your printed page. One feature of Show Page often overlooked by MacPainters is that you can correct this problem by moving your entire image around on the page to center it properly.

An important note about Show Page belongs here. When you invoke Show Page, you must realize that in order for the program to reduce your picture to fit within the MacPaint window, the Mac is only approximating your painting. There aren't enough pixels on the screen to portray every pixel from the original. Therefore, you may notice from time to time that a line or two is missing from the picture shown in the reduction. Due to the nature of the way the picture is reduced for Show Page, it is the horizontal lines that are occasionally left out by this miniaturization process. But don't worry, they're still in the Mac's memory or on disk. And despite this minor drawback you can still see an image's main elements and outline to get the idea of where your picture is placed on the page. In addition, this approximation of the picture should be enough for you to estimate how the overall picture is turning out, since you can't see it all from the MacPaint window.

While in the Show Page mode, you have only two ways of influencing your document. One is to move the MacPaint window to another portion of the page; the second to move the entire picture on the page.

To reposition the MacPaint window, move the pointer to anywhere within the dotted-line rectangle, which represents the viewing window, and drag it to the target area you want to work on next.

If it is important for you to work on a precise segment of a picture, the Show Page method of moving the window is faster than using the hand icon in regular size to push and tug at the paper under the MacPaint window. With a 128K Mac, the hand icon doesn't let you see exactly how much of the picture outside of the original window you've brought into view—until the program can fetch the new part of the picture from the disk. Each time you move the paper with the hand icon, even if only one pixel in any direction, it entails a relatively lengthy disk access. Moving the window with Show Page gets you to the desired location in only one motion and two disk accesses. (On a 512K Mac, dragging the picture with the hand icon brings the rest of the picture into view instantaneously without disk access—by far the most efficient way to zip around your picture.)

The second power within Show Page is the ability to move the entire picture around the page. To accomplish this, position the pointer anywhere within the boundaries of the picture—but not within the dotted-line box representing your viewing window.

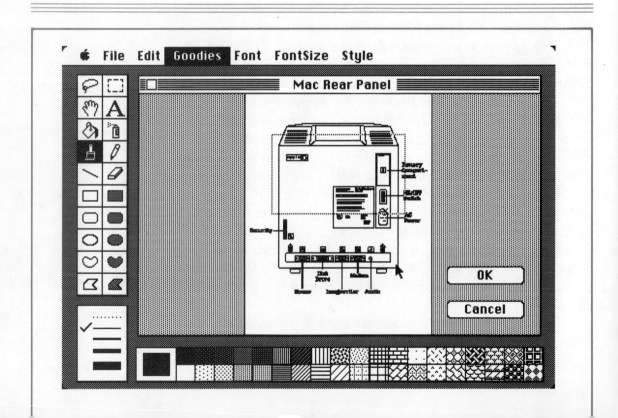

You can then drag the drawing all over the page, placing it wherever you need it. If the entire picture fits within the viewing window, you'll have to first move the window's dotted rectangle out of the way so you can drag the picture. With this power at your fingertips, it's not necessary to guess where on the page you should start your picture. Adjust it later if you need to.

Be careful, however, to keep the Show Page miniature drawing on the page. If part of the picture runs off the page, whatever doesn't show will be erased forever when you click the OK button. Even Undo can't resurrect the missing art.

A limitation of this convenient picture moving feature, however, is that you can move only the entire picture—not just one part of it, as you can within MacPaint by selecting a segment with the select rectangle or lasso. But you can combine the powers of several features to accomplish the same thing. Here's an example.

If you have two main elements of a picture and need to move them closer together, you might think you're in big trouble because both images take up practically an entire MacPaint window. If you select nearly the entire window with the marquee or lasso, you won't be able to drag the image very far, because you will erase any part of the image that slips outside of the window. Thus it would seem that if you have just a little room in the window to move the image, you would have to creep your way around the picture, alternating between selecting the image, dragging it a few millimeters, selecting the hand icon, moving the paper an equal distance, and repeating this procedure forever until you have moved to where you wish the picture segment to be. If that were the only way to do it, I'd sooner print it out the way I had created it, and perform an old fashioned cut-and-paste procedure with scissors and rubber cement.

Fortunately, there's a better way.

- The first thing you must do is get one of the segments into full view in the MacPaint window.
- Then select the entire segment by using either the marquee or lasso (the marquee is faster, but the lasso will be better if you need to carefully adjoin or overlap this picture with the other segment). Make sure that you leave a space of at least one bit be-

tween your picture and the window borders so there is room for the marquee or lasso dotted lines.

- Issue a Cut command from the Edit menu (or Command-X). The image disappears from the screen, but it is safely stored temporarily on the Mac's Clipboard.
- Now, go into Show Page.
- Move the MacPaint window to the area next to where you want the segment in the Clipboard to appear, and click "OK."
- Issue the Paste command (or Command-V). The first segment, from the Clipboard, appears in the window, still selected with the marquee or lasso you had originally specified. If you need to adjust the placement of the segment a little, do so now, by dragging it into position with the pointer.
- Now's your chance to undo, if the whole thing doesn't look the way you anticipated.
- View the entire sheet with Show Page. Provided the individual images you wish to shift don't overlap, you can continue to use this procedure to move other images or readjust your move as often as you need.

▲ ▲ ▲ ▲ ▲ ▲ **Aligning Objects**

I'm not very structured in the way I use MacPaint. Instead of carefully mapping out my strategy on a piece of paper beforehand, I usually fly right into the program, and use it as my scratchpad, eventually fine tuning my scribblings with the help of FatBits and liberal applications of Undo.

One of the byproducts of this methodology—one I assume most of us use—is that I am constantly adding elements that must be aligned with previously placed elements. This is especially true of text used for labels on illustrations. I find it difficult to set on an even line blocks of text that are typed at different times, since it is hard to predict whether the text insertion pointer is on the exact same horizontal as some text an inch away. To help me align text or other objects, I use the straight line icon of MacPaint in conjunction with Undo.

Let's say I want to add a text block aligned with a block I've already set.

- After typing the second block, I select it and drag it to the location I want, aligning it to the best of my eye's ability.

■ Just to make sure, however, I select the straight line icon and draw a straight line beginning as close to the bottom of the original text as possible without overlapping any character (excluding descenders). Verifying that the line is indeed a pure, horizontal line, I then draw it under the new text and compare it to the original. As you can see in the following figure, block no. 2 is one pixel too high.

This is Text
Block No. 1.

This is Text
Block No. 2.

■ I immediately undo the straight line. If the new text needs adjustment, I select and move it with the marquee or lasso. I repeat the procedure until the two text blocks rest exactly on the same horizontal row of pixels.

◢ ◢ ◢ ◢ ◢ ◢ **Using the Grid Feature**

I'll bet that the first time you selected the Grid feature from the Goodies menu you expected a backdrop of horizontal and vertical lines to help you keep objects aligned, like the background of MacDraw. But you were disappointed that no such lines appeared. Moreover, you may not have detected any difference in MacPaint with or without the Grid selected. There is a difference, however, and you can use it to your advantage especially if you're not really steady with the mouse.

When you turn on the Grid feature, there are, in fact, invisible lines on the screen. You can detect they are there by watching the pointer very closely as you slowly move the mouse. Notice how the pointer seems to jump from location to location, rather than flow smoothly from pixel to pixel as when the Grid is off. It is actually jumping in 8-pixel increments. The Grid function makes the movement of the pointer more coarse, but also more precise for those who find precise alignments difficult.

The prime advantage of engaging the Grid is to help you use your eye to align objects, rather than use the straight line method described in the last section. The jumps between grid lines are large enough for you to judge whether two objects—one fixed, the other selected and being dragged—are aligned with each other. Not only does the Grid assist in dragging selected images, but also in creating two or more different shapes that need to be aligned with each other. For example, if you need a square and a circle to be side-by-side and of the same height and width, the Grid will help you locate the proper beginning and ending locations of the pointer—thus leaving your eye free to judge the relative sizes of the two shapes, while your hand and mouse control the jumps between grid locations.

Text Tricks

Having the full library of text fonts in MacPaint makes this program a perfect tool for designing informative graphics for business, education, and many other applications. While most of what you can do with text is explained in the MacPaint manual, I have a few words to add that will show you an efficient way to use the Cairo font pictographs, reveal some "hidden characters" in the Mac character set, and how to scrunch text down to sizes that fit your detailed MacPaint pictures.

◢ ◢ ◢ ◢ ◢ ◢ Using the Cairo Font

If you have not yet tried the Cairo font, you're in for a pleasant surprise. It consists entirely of small, ready-made pictures that you can bring into any MacPaint picture (or MacWrite text) by simply pressing a key or two. What a fabulous resource for someone who doesn't want to take the time to create pictures to accent a document or supplement a larger picture.

The Cairo font was designed as an 18-point font. The pictures look best at this size, but you can make them larger very easily, especially in MacPaint, by increasing the font size. It is best to use an even multiple of the 18-point size (either 36- or 72-point) since these increments simply double and quadruple (respectively) the pixels of the original art. You'll probably want to touch up the 36- and 72-point sizes, however, since the extra line thicknesses usually need some smoothing and rounding at these sizes.

In the next figure, I've typed the Option-Shift-A Cairo character in three sizes. Notice how boxy the unretouched 36-point picture looks. A little work with FatBits fills in the diagonals, rounds out the corners, and even lets me add a couple of extra features, like hubcaps, a door outline, and door handle. In the 72-point size, Fat-Bit retouching transforms an almost unrecognizable pile of blocks into a speedy car and driver.

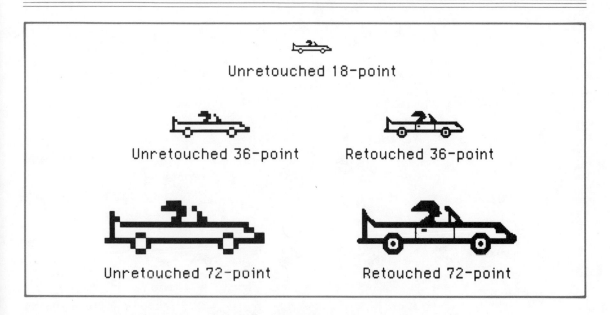

There is perhaps only one difficulty working with the Cairo font: its lack of organization. Since you usually need a character to fill a specific need, it is not easy to look through an alphabetical listing in search of the keyboard equivalent for a particular picture. Therefore, I've subdivided the pictographs of the Cairo font into arbitrary, but I hope meaningful, subject areas. Hereafter, refer to Table 3-1 when you need to locate a Cairo picture.

Table 3-1. Cairo Font Sorted by Category

Arrows and Pointers:

h   p   –   =   +   [

Artist's Tools:

a   i   j

Edibles:

B   C   `   4   5   ! $:

Egypt:

O   U   V

Electronics:

q   r   s   D   ?

Fauna:

c   d   e   z   K   ~   ]   "

Flora:

w   L   X   Y   Z   1   #   ^   *   )

Music:

A   &   .   ,

Mystery Clues:

b   f   k   u   v   M   N   P   S   _   } | <

Ornament:

| 9   0   (

≋   ⊗   ⁄   ✤

People:

m   n   o   2

Shelter and Furnishings:

E   Q   R   T   W   3   %   ;

Solar System:

g   7   8   @

Transportation:

l   t   F   G   H   J   Option-Shift-A

Unclassified:

x   y   6   \   '   /   {   >

◢ ◢ ◢ ◢ ◢ ◢ **Exploring Hidden Characters**

You just saw that the Cairo font holds a warehouse of special graphics characters. You also saw in our discussion about the Key Caps desk accessory that you have a wealth of extra foreign language and currency symbols at your disposal. But what you won't find in any Apple-supplied owner's manual are the extra, secret characters buried deep within the Macintosh character set.

A special key sequence—holding down the Option and Shift keys while touching the accent/tilde key (the key just to the left of the numeral 1 key)—brings these characters to life. The precise character you get depends on the font and font size selected at any given moment. It also depends on what font sizes are installed. A System file loaded with all the sizes of a particular font provides the greatest variety of hidden characters for that font. Table 3-2 is a catalog of all the available characters (up to 24-point sizes) released with the fonts supplied in Finder version 1.1g.

Following each font name and size are 5 characters, created by holding down the Option and Shift keys while pressing the accent/tilde key five times. Let's examine them, font by font.

San Francisco presents simple pictures of an automobile whose size depends on the font size used. The example shown here is from San Francisco's true font size, 18-point (see Chapter 4 for more discussion about true fonts). Other sizes are slightly distorted reductions or enlargements of this picture. Like San Francisco's text characters, this special character makes a humorous adjunct to a personal invitation or similar, casual document.

Toronto's font offers three special characters. Toronto-9 and -18 are three dimensional boxes, which, when linked together in a row, make an interesting pattern. The same goes for the ivy vines of 10-, 12-, and 24-point Toronto. Toronto-10 is an approximation of Toronto-12, so its resolution and clarity is not the greatest. The vine pattern, however, could easily become an ornament for a personal stationery designed with MacPaint and MacWrite together. The Toronto-14 hidden character is the only apple character you'll find. In this case, however, the apple is more like the fruit than the corporate identity of the Mac's developers—there's no bite taken out of this one and no stripes.

Table 3-2. Secret Characters

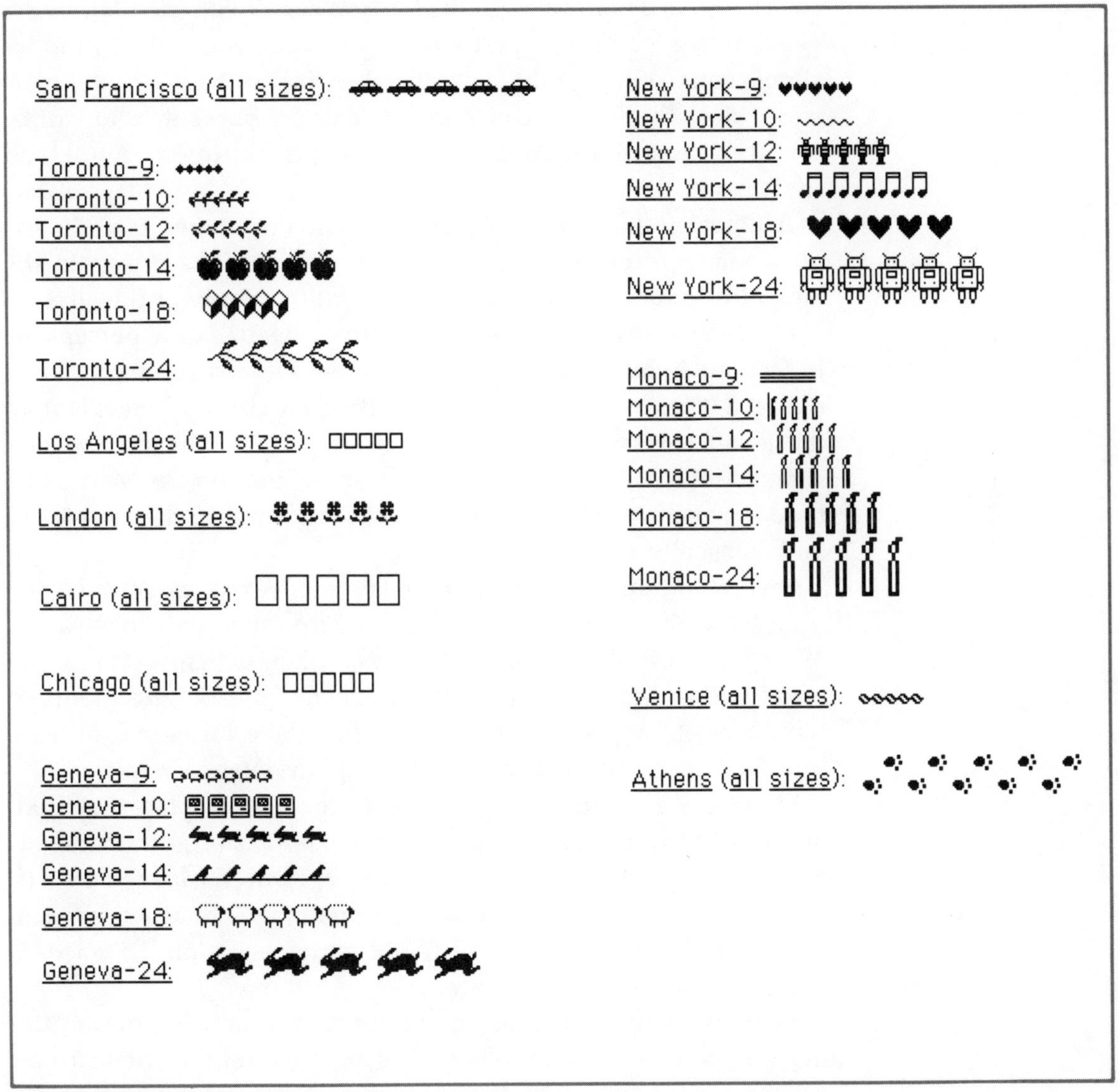

San Francisco (all sizes): 🚗🚗🚗🚗🚗

Toronto-9: ✦✦✦✦✦
Toronto-10: ✦✦✦✦✦
Toronto-12: ✦✦✦✦✦
Toronto-14: 🍎🍎🍎🍎🍎
Toronto-18: ◇◇◇◇
Toronto-24: ❧❧❧❧❧

Los Angeles (all sizes): ☐☐☐☐☐

London (all sizes): ✿✿✿✿✿

Cairo (all sizes): ☐☐☐☐☐

Chicago (all sizes): ☐☐☐☐☐

Geneva-9: ✿✿✿✿✿
Geneva-10: ▦▦▦▦▦
Geneva-12: 🐀🐀🐀🐀🐀
Geneva-14: ◢◢◢◢◢
Geneva-18: 🐑🐑🐑🐑🐑
Geneva-24: 🐢🐢🐢🐢🐢

New York-9: ♥♥♥♥♥
New York-10: ∿∿∿
New York-12: 👾👾👾👾👾
New York-14: ♫♫♫♫♫
New York-18: ♥♥♥♥♥
New York-24: 🤖🤖🤖🤖🤖

Monaco-9: ≡≡≡
Monaco-10: ⌡⌡⌡⌡⌡
Monaco-12: ⌡⌡⌡⌡⌡
Monaco-14: ⌡⌡⌡⌡⌡
Monaco-18: ⌡⌡⌡⌡⌡
Monaco-24: ⌡⌡⌡⌡⌡

Venice (all sizes): ∾∾∾∾∾

Athens (all sizes): 🐾🐾🐾🐾🐾

Los Angeles, Cairo, and Chicago are essentially blank in the special character department (in the fonts released with the Mac Finder version 1.1g). These three fonts, in any size you select, produce simple squares or sightly tall rectangles. Occasionally, if you select a font size other than a true size, some of the boxes in a horizontal row are distorted, with one or two sides of the box being fatter than the others.

A flower is London's only special character. Since London has only one true font size, London-18, that is the one shown in the table. It produces the clearest representation of any of the sizes.

Geneva's special characters range from sheep (barely perceptible in Geneva-9, but kind of fluffy in Geneva-18), to running rabbits (Geneva-12 and -24), to blackbirds sitting on a wire (Geneva-14), to the lovable Macintosh itself (Geneva-10). I can already envision some writers, who do their own correspondence on the Mac, using the Mac symbol at the bottom of each letter where the secretary's initials usually go.

Several different characters populate the New York font. Hearts from New York-9 and -18 will certainly find their way to an inter-office love note. New York-10's waves might actually be more at home within MacPaint in an ocean backdrop. I like the robots of New York-12 and -24, but I'm not sure where I'd ever use them. And New York-14 produces musical eighth notes.

Monaco-9 and -18 are a bit tricky. In the Mac display, they both produce horizontal bars that could become part of a dramatic letterhead design. But in printout on the Imagewriter, Monaco-18 produces lighted candles, as do all the remaining Monaco sizes. You could use the candles for a birthday party invitation; Monaco-12 offers the clearest representation.

Venice actually produces one of the most appealing border designs if you link its special characters together in horizontal strings. Athens, on the other hand, gives you pairs of paw prints (bears?), which are cute and nothing else.

These characters, by the way, are treated just like any other text character. You can bold face them, underline them, make them outlined, shadowed, italicized, or any combination in between. In MacPaint, you can also rotate and invert these characters, just as you would any pictorial drawing.

As future releases of the Finder and more fonts become available, it is quite likely that some changes and enhancements to this special character collection will come along. Someone is also bound to turn up some further "unknown" characters or other screen effects with other bizarre keyboard sequences. The Macintosh is rich in programming surprises, with many designer's trademarks sprinkled throughout, giving exploring hackers much to uncover.

◢ ◢ ◢ ◢ ◢ ◢ **Approximating Tiny Text**

Many times, I set out to create a MacPaint picture that is a replica of another piece of art, or perhaps a representation of an object, both of which have printing of some kind on them. When it's time to re-create the text, however, I often find that I need letters much smaller than the 9-point font size that comes standard on many Macintosh fonts. You may be able to locate a font size smaller than 9-point, but if you can't, it then becomes necessary to shrink one of the available fonts to a suitable size—and suddenly even the Mac's fine graphics resolution seems awkwardly coarse.

Sometimes the situation calls for a long piece of text to be fit into a narrow slot—the height of the characters remains unchanged, but the letters must be skinnier. To do this you can try to shrink the text by selecting it with the marquee and compressing the box by dragging a corner while holding down the Command (⌘) key. But for these kinds of minor width adjustments, I often find that compressing text in this manner tends to distort the letters too much. The reason for this distortion is that as you compress the text's width by one pixel, the program removes only one column of pixels out of a string of text many pixels wide. As you start to squeeze the text, some letters distort right away, while others retain their original widths until they, too, must be squeezed. The result is a sequence of unevenly spaced and ill-proportioned characters. It is, therefore, better in many instances to manually compress text using FatBits instead of the traditional compression technique.

An example of this manual technique is the keyboard replica on the following page, which required a number of textual compressions. In each case, I took the words produced by the Mac and compressed the letters evenly while in FatBits.

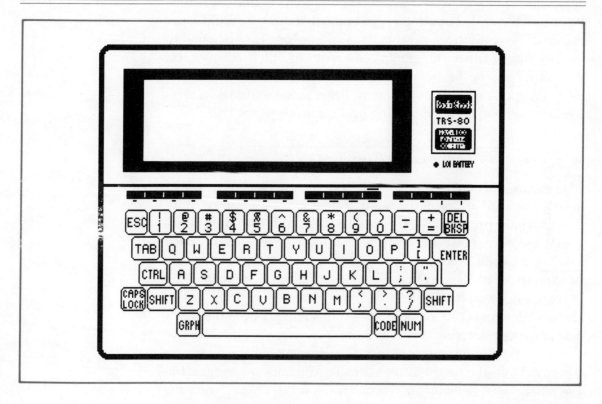

The evolution of the Caps Lock key legend should demonstrate this technique, since it represents a very tight squeeze into a small area.

In a clear work area, I typed "CAPS LOCK" in Monaco-9, the smallest and simplest font in the library. (Some fonts, like New York and Toronto, have extra pixels as ornaments—called serifs in the printing trade—which only make things unnecessarily congested when compressing text.) The resulting text left me with two challenges: to make the letters both narrower and shorter to fit on the key. My first step was to reduce the width of each letter by one pixel in FatBits.

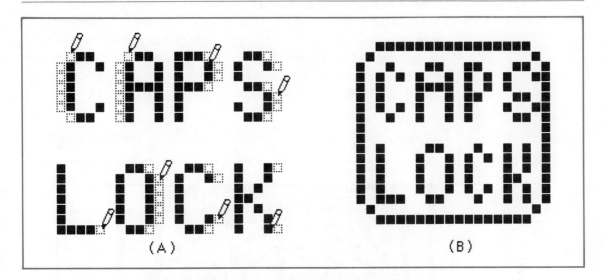

(A)   (B)

The outlined FatBits in the figure (A) above indicate where original bits were erased to make each character one column narrower. After this step, I used the marquee while still in FatBits to select the characters one-by-one and shift them so there was only one pixel of space between them. Through trial and using the Undo option on a couple of letters, I discovered that I could narrow some of them even more without destroying their basic form, as shown in the final form (B).

For example, the letter *L* is clearly an *L* even with only two horizontal pixels at the bottom. Similarly, the letter *C* didn't need to be anywhere near so wide as its original. As long as the general contour of the character is left intact, its integrity remains. Notice how roundedness can be simulated with relatively few pixels on the letter *C*. As you can see from the finished, normal size drawing, the results are quite legible, and yet they fit within the limited space available.

In the same picture, I had to portray some even smaller text in the upper right corner labels. For these words, I used a combination of marquee/command-key compression and FatBits to approximate the minuscule text. Again, I started with Monaco 9-point, the smallest and simplest font in the library.

After typing the text, I placed a marquee around it and dragged a corner while holding down the Command (⌘) key to reduce the width and height of the text so it would fit the box into which I would ultimately place it. Although the finished product was to be in reverse (white letters on black background), the original work was black on white, since it is much easier to conceptualize the end result in that form.

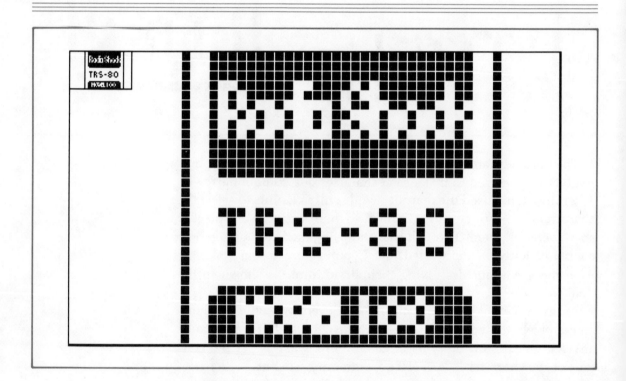

When the text was sized properly, it was time to go into FatBits and clean up the distorted mess. It's all right for such small text if the letters run together—remember that we're only trying to approximate readable text. Rounded letters, like *o* and *c*, usually become squared during the compression process. Their corners need to be rounded wherever possible by removing the corner pixels.

When text is really compressed, it is sometimes not possible to keep each letter a distinct entity. As I clicked pixels on and off, I kept looking at the normal size reproduction of the area in the normal size window of the FatBits screen. It's amazing how a glob of dots in FatBits can look remarkably like real text in normal size.

There is no precise formula to follow in approximating tiny text. If I were to try to reproduce the label in the upper right corner of this illustration three times, each time would come out slightly different. The key, however, is to keep experimenting with turning pixels on and off, checking how the addition or subtraction of each pixel affects the final normal size drawing. Remember, too, that what distinguishes one tiny letter from another are characteristics such as rounded corners and holes in the middle. As you look at a reduced word in the normal size window, look for places where the word becomes unrecognizable. See if you can improve a letter in that spot to make it more readable, even if it means taking space and legibility away from a surrounding letter.

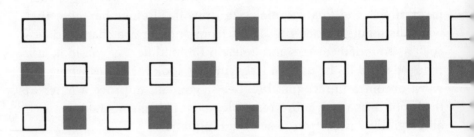

WORD PROCESSING TAKES on a special meaning when used on the Macintosh. Instead of simply storing typed characters and document formatting instructions (how the text is to be laid out on the printed page) as you do with word processing on other computers, Macintosh word processing lets you play a more active role in how the final document will look when it comes off the printer.

Before the Macintosh, you had to have an expensive printer attached to your computer in order to achieve flexibility in the font style. You might need to change print elements, as on daisywheel printers, or be conversant in your printer's special character codes to create different fonts and sizes. Even then, you'd be limited to a handful of sizes and styles. But not so with the Macintosh.

Word processing on the Mac lets you select font styles and sizes that rival those of some professional typesetting machines. You can

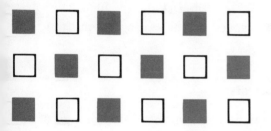

Techniques for Word Processors

select large type for headlines and have it print out on the Image-writer in a quality almost good enough to be used as camera-ready art for printing. And when you print on the LaserWriter, the output is indeed ready for the print shop. Moreover, word processing programs like MacWrite and Microsoft Word allow you to incorporate full-fledged graphics imported from MacPaint or MacDraw right into the document.

Everything in this chapter, except the last section, applies to MacWrite and Microsoft Word (hereafter called Word). Chances are that many of these techniques will also apply to other word processing programs that come out in the future. We'll explore ways to speed up editing, make your documents look more professional, and save extra work all around. For MacWrite users, I've added some special tips on reducing mouse movement.

Faster Editing

The time required to enter text with a word processor on any computer is almost entirely dependent on the speed of the typist. But when it comes time to go back into the document, the editing facilities of a word processing program are what can make the editing job easy or hard, regardless of your typing skills. In this section, you'll learn several techniques to speed up the editing process (and even the text entry process).

◢ ◢ ◢ ◢ ◢ ◢ Keyboard Shortcuts

If there is one kind of program that shows the shortcomings of using a mouse on a personal computer, it's word processing. The primary reason for this is that the keyboard plays such a large role in getting information onto the screen. In MacPaint or MacDraw, on the other hand, you can create a wondrous array of graphic images without ever touching the keyboard. Consequently, those Mac users who cut their word processing teeth on other computers may find the mouse to be distracting at times, especially when you have to jump to the mouse to pull down a menu for a single action, and then return to the keyboard to complete the particular task at hand.

Some of these menu choices, fortunately, have also been retained in MacWrite and Word as keyboard commands—using the Command (⌘) key with one other key. Some of these shortcuts can be rather important and are worth learning if you plan to be a whiz at Mac word processing. A few of the command key combinations are mnemonic (i.e., the letter associated with the command is related to the actual command word) and easy to remember, while many of the ones that are not mnemonic (and not so simple to remember) are used in many other programs, so if you learn them once, you will be able to use them widely.

The three most important Command key shortcuts are the ones for copying, cutting, and pasting. You can see the Command key equivalents for these commands by pulling down the Edit menu in MacWrite.

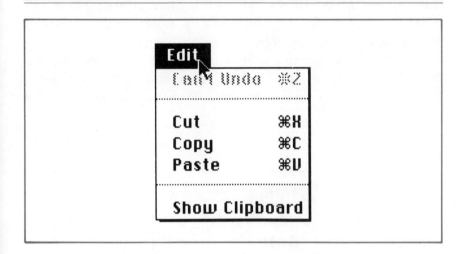

To use the Cut or Copy command, you must first select a piece of text, ranging in length from a single letter to the entire document. Selecting text requires action of the mouse—there's no other way to do it. To select a single word, you can move the pointer to anywhere inside the word and double-click the mouse button. To select more than one word, you need to position the text pointer at one of the ends of the phrase, click, and drag the pointer to the other end of the selected text. I'll have more to say about selecting large chunks of text in the next section.

Keep in mind that whenever you cut or copy a piece of text, that piece is stored on the Clipboard until you cut or copy another piece of text. In other words, the Clipboard holds the most recent text cut or copied from the document. Even if you quit the program, the Clipboard's contents are stored on the disk until the next time you come back to the program. In the case of the Cut command, this saving to the Clipboard is added insurance, just in case you change your mind about deleting the section and wish to restore it long after the Undo command would let you.

It's easy enough to remember that Command-C means Copy. Command-X, for Cut, is not mnemonic, but it's a common saying that to get rid of something you "x it out." I challenge someone to find an easy way to associate Command-V with the Paste command. I couldn't even think of a recognizable brand name of glue that contains the letter *V*. But having the *V* key located right next to the *C*, the Copy command, which, in turn, is next to the *X*, the Cut command, helps me remember this oddball command.

Some MacWrite-specific keyboard shortcuts worth knowing are those that control the Font Style. If you pull down the Style menu, you see a long list of keyboard equivalents to the various font styles available to you.

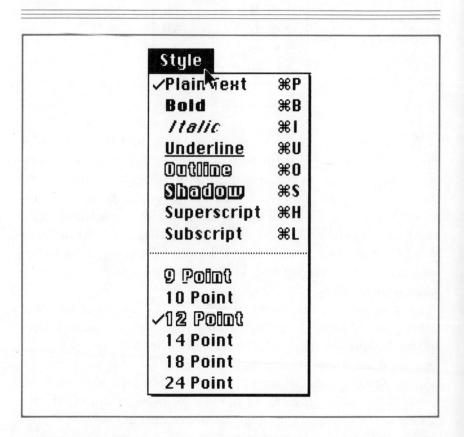

These keyboard shortcuts are most helpful when you are creating text and want the next word or phrase you type to be in a particular style other than the one you're currently using. Therefore, as you're typing away, and you want the next word to be underlined, you would type Command-U, type the word, and then type Command-U again to turn off the underline mode. This on-and-off method is often called a *toggle* command. Each time you invoke the command, the mode is turned on or off—always the opposite of what it was before you issued the command. To revert to plain text after you have invoked a few different styles—e.g., boldface, shadow, and italic simultaneously—instead of turning each one off at the end of the desired phrase, you can issue a Command-P command, which turns off all enhancements.

There are two important notes about underlining text (whether you use the mouse or the Command key sequence). First, you must turn off underlining before typing the space after the last character of the desired text. Failure to do so results in an extra underlined space after the text.

> This text is underlined all the way through.
>
> This text is underlined word by word.

Second, if you want to underline words only—and not the spaces between words—you can't do it by simply invoking the underline before typing the phrase, since it underlines everything, spaces included. To underline a phrase word by word, first type it in Plain text. Then go back and select the first word you want underlined (by double-clicking it with the text pointer in the word). With your left hand (if you're a right-handed mouse user), invoke the underline keyboard command (Command-U) once for the selected word. Go on to the next word. You can keep the Command key pressed while you maneuver and double-click the mouse along the line, and simply press the U key whenever a word is selected, going lickety-split down the sentence. Microsoft Word, on the other hand, makes underlining each word quite a hassle, because there is no keyboard command to invoke after you select a word. Thus you must pull down a menu and select the command for each word in the phrase you want to underline. Microsoft Word has a few command-key shortcuts that you will probably want to use frequently.

You can perform intermediate saves, open a new document (Word allows multiple document windows on the screen at one time), close a document, call up a blank page for a new document, print, and quit the program all from the keyboard. Pull down the File menu to see these mnemonic options.

```
File
  New            ⌘N
  Open...        ⌘O
  Close          ⌘W
  Save           ⌘S
  Save As...
  Page Setup...
  Print...       ⌘P
  Print Merge...
  Printer Setup...
  Quit           ⌘Q
```

▲ ▲ ▲ ▲ ▲ ▲ **Selecting Large Blocks of Text**

One of the perceptual problems many people have in working with a word processor is that unless a document is a short note, it's impossible to see the entire document on the screen at one time. Instead, you look through a tiny window onto a larger piece of electronic paper. If you want to select a paragraph or a large block of a document, and you can't see the beginning and end of the block in one window, there are two shortcuts that will let you select such a large chunk.

The fastest way is to use the Shift-Click method, as outlined in the MacWrite manual.

■ Place the text pointer at the very beginning of the text block.
■ Then use the scroll bar to bring the end of the block into view.

■ Hold down the Shift key while placing the text pointer at the end of the block, and click.

Instantly, the entire chunk of text between the two pointer locations goes into reverse, signifying it is selected. You can scroll through the reversed block with the scroll bars to view anything therein.

But sometimes, the end of your text block is only a few lines below the bottom of the current window. To use the above method would entail more mouse maneuvering than is necessary. What you can do instead is plant the text pointer at the beginning of the text, but hold down the button and drag the pointer to the bottom of the window—actually to *below* the bottom of the window. As you hold the button down, the text scrolls line by line, turning each new line into selected text as it scrolls into the window. When the end of the block comes into view, drag the pointer into the window and position the pointer at the end of the block.

With either method of selecting text, you are not limited to starting your block at the beginning. You can also plant the text pointer at the end of a block and then use either method to find the top of the block.

◢ ◢ ◢ ◢ ◢ ◢ **Deleting Without Cutting**

If you use the Clipboard as a repository for macros (discussed a little later), or for a picture that you imported from MacPaint for use in your document, you must be sure not to upset what you have saved in the Clipboard by performing a Cut operation to delete a word, phrase, or paragraph. To do so would replace the contents of the Clipboard with the Cut text. You need an alternative way of deleting text. In fact, what I'm about to show you is the fastest way to delete text. It requires only one keystroke once you've selected the text to be removed. Moreover, the deletion is still reversible if you find you made a mistake.

The key to this magical deletion method is the Backspace key. You have probably already used it to delete single characters in a word. For example, when you place the text pointer to the right of a letter that shouldn't be there, you simply press the Backspace key, and the letter disappears—at the same time, all the text in the paragraph readjusts itself to reflect the change in character spacing. If you've ever used other word processing programs before, you have probably been doing a lot of backspacing in MacWrite—perhaps over several words—since you think it's faster to delete a few words this way than by going through the select-text-and-cut routine. Admittedly, for erasing a few letters *within* a word, the simple backspace technique is as efficient as you can get. But when deletions are of one full word or more, there is a faster way.

To delete a whole word in MacWrite, you should first select the word by double-clicking it with the text pointer anywhere inside it. Then press the Backspace key twice. The first press of the key deletes the word. The second press deletes the extra space that exists when you removed only the letters of the word (only the letters of the word are selected by the double-clicking method). You can press the Backspace twice very quickly—the Mac accepts both strokes. In Word, you only need to press the Backspace key once, because both the word and the following space are selected by double-clicking a word.

If you find that you made a mistake, and don't want that word deleted, don't worry. You have the failsafe Undo Typing command from the Edit menu (also available as a Command-Z keyboard shortcut).

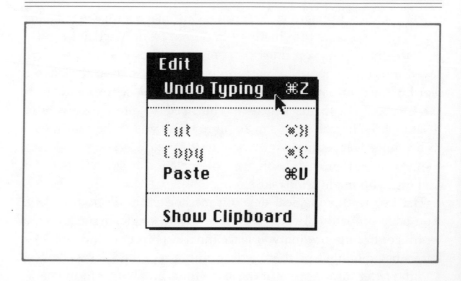

The Mac remembers the keystroke(s) of the Backspace key you made, and restores the text to its original state. All the time you've been deleting and undeleting text, nothing has happened to your Clipboard—its contents are intact.

The backspace method of deletion works with any amount of selected text. I've found, therefore, that it is more efficient to select even a few words at one time with the mouse and then use one press of the Backspace key than to hold down the Backspace key while the letters disappear individually. In fact, the Backspace key method is so much faster (and reversible just the same), that I no longer use the Cut command for deletion of text.

◢ ◢ ◢ ◢ ◢ ◢ Replacing Bad Text with Good

The other side of deleting text is that you often have better words to insert than the ones you took out. I edit my work extensively between first and final drafts, so I am constantly taking out a word or two and inserting something that reads better (I hope). MacWrite and Word have a subtle, yet very powerful function built into them that makes such text replacements even easier than the Backspace deletion method.

If you recall from our discussion in an earlier chapter about renaming documents and other icons on the Mac desktop, all you have to do is select the icon and begin typing the new name. The Mac recognizes that if you are typing letters, you must want to rename the icon, so the old letters are instantly erased to make way for your new name. MacWrite and Word adopt this principle for their text editing as well.

- Type a block of text while in MacWrite or Word.
- Find a word that you want to change.
- Select that word by double-clicking it with the text pointer anywhere inside it.
- Then, without touching anything else, simply start typing the word or words you want to replace the selected word.

Notice that the original word disappears instantly, and the new letters begin to appear in its place. You can type as few or as many letters as you please. The program adjusts the rest of the paragraph to fit whatever you type.

As with the Backspace deletion function, this replacement function is not "destructive" to the original text. Issue the Undo (Command-Z) command, and the original text is restored. In fact you can continue to press Command-Z to compare how the two versions read, and simply leave the text of the preferred version on the screen once you've made up your mind.

No matter how large a section of text you select, this editing feature applies: select the old and start typing the new. All the while, the Clipboard is intact.

These two tips—deleting and replacing text—should speed up your editing tasks substantially, while reducing your dependence on the mouse and pull-down menu.

All About Fonts

While the variety of font styles and sizes is one of Macintosh's and MacWrite's appeals, still it is helpful to understand some fundamental principles of how fonts work in MacWrite and Word. Failure to grasp these principles may result in printed documents that don't have the quality appearance that you expect. I'll be limiting the discussion to printing on the Imagewriter. Font selection on the LaserWriter is a special subject well covered in the February 1985 issue of *Macworld*.

◄ ◄ ◄ ◄ ◄ ◄ Selecting the Right Font and Font Size

As you may recall from our discussion earlier about moving fonts onto the System file, the selection of fonts available to you is largely under your control. The wider the variety of documents your work encompasses, the more fonts you will want to have resident on the disk. The trade-off, of course, is that your available disk space becomes more limited as each font is added to the disk's System file.

Now, just because you may not have every size of, say, the New York font in your MacWrite disk's System file, that doesn't mean that you won't have every size available to you. There is a distinction, however, between what I call *true* fonts (which you have loaded in your System file) and those that force the issue a bit. Let's look at an example.

In the Style menu shown in the following figure, we are looking at the New York font sizes available on a typical MacWrite disk.

```
9 Point
10 Point
✓12 Point
14 Point
18 Point
24 Point
```

Notice that some size numbers are in outline, while others are straight text characters. This is no accident. The outlined sizes indicate those font sizes for which there are fonts installed in the System file. Characters from these true fonts appear on the display and on standard quality printouts as correctly proportioned letters (in the high quality print mode, the Imagewriter overprints and smooths the edges of the pixel patterns).

You can, of course, select a font size for which there is no font in the System file, but the characters in the display or in a printout won't be properly proportioned. This is because, when you select an uninstalled font size, the Mac can only approximate the font in that size. It looks at one of the other sizes for which there is a font installed, and tries to size it as best it can. The result, however, is that some of the letters are distorted, depending on how the Mac has to stretch or squeeze them to fit into a space. In the Seattle-14 printout shown on page 182 as an example, look how one of the two lowercase *p* characters in the word "approximate" is distorted, as the Mac tries to proportionally space an approximate font size.

This is Seattle-10, a true font.

This is Seattle-14, an approximate font.

This is Geneva-14, a true font.

In some cases, this may present a dilemma, because you like a particular font, but there simply is no true font for a size you need. For example, your choice for the Seattle font is restricted to 10-point only (see Chapter 1 for help in extracting the Seattle font from Multiplan). If you need a 14-point headline, you'll only get the approximated Seattle in that size.

In situations like this you might be better off going to another style, like Geneva, which closely approximates the overall style of Seattle but has a true 14-point font that won't appear distorted (as shown in the example).

To prove to yourself how this true and untrue font size affects a particular font, try this experiment in MacWrite:

- Select a font that has only one or two true fonts in the System file (Athens, Chicago, and Los Angeles are good examples).
- Type a few words of text.
- Now select the line of text.
- Pull down the menu with the font sizes and select different sizes to see how the quality of the characters change as you call up true and untrue font sizes.

Microsoft Word protects you to some degree from selecting fonts other than true fonts. When you open the Formats dialog box (in the Character menu) each font in the System file is displayed with its available true fonts. You may, however, type in any font size you wish, an option that is most helpful if you print with the LaserWriter. For Imagewriter printout, however, stick with the true font sizes in the System file.

Another important matter is the accuracy of the font sizes indicated in the font size menu. Unfortunately for some applications—

advertising layouts especially—the font sizes listed are not really accurate relative to what is printed out on the Imagewriter. For example, neither Monaco-9 nor Geneva-9 actually prints out as 9-point type, but rather as 11-point type (1 point = $\frac{1}{72}$ inch).

Moreover, two different fonts of the same font size may have a different amount of space between lines of text—and you can't change font sizes without changing the spacing with them. Monaco-9's standard line spacing—when MacWrite's 6-lines-per-inch feature is not selected—is 11 points from baseline to baseline (thus producing 11-point type on 11-point line spacing, or 11 over 11 as a typesetter would say). Geneva-9, on the other hand, has a spacing of 12 points (thus 11 over 12). The extra one-point spacing on Geneva-9 makes it much easier on the eyes than Monaco-9 when reading a full page of text, but it significantly affects the number of lines per page you can print (I'll discuss lines per page in more detail later). Likewise, Seattle-10's characters print as almost 12-point characters, with a spacing of 13. Generally speaking, then, the actual printed size of a character is two points larger than the size shown in the font table (since the characters are composed of fixed-size dots, this measure may be off by a small fraction of a point). Someone using the Mac for an advertising layout should be particularly aware of this, since it is dangerous to specify type for the typesetter based on the font table sizes only.

```
Now is the time for all good
men to come to the aid of their
country. (Monaco-9)

Now is the time for all good men to come
to the aid of their country. (Geneva-9)

Now is the time for all good
men to come to the aid of their
country. (Seattle-10)
```

In typical text work, I find that a 10-point font (Mac's measure, now) is preferred. When printed, it most closely approximates the size of pica typewriter print, which editors and correspondents expect. The 9-point styles look more like elite. Some people like elite, but I find it too small for extensive reading.

Unfortunately, your choices for true 10-point fonts from the Mac Fonts file is very limited. Seattle-10 is appealing to many, but may not be to everyone's liking because it lacks serifs. New York-10 may be an alternative for some users, since it is a serif font and has acceptable horizontal spacing between letters. Notice, though, that New York-10 is a slightly heavier weight than Seattle-10. Geneva-10, however, is too compressed for straight text: it may be fine when you need to cram information in a table perhaps, but not for long stretches of text.

To help you select the fonts that you might want to have in your MacWrite or Word System file, Table 4-1 shows examples of all the true fonts and sizes, printed in the high quality mode. Experiment with untrue fonts. Occasionally, they are acceptable when you need a headline or small print.

▲ ▲ ▲ ▲ ▲ ▲ **Improving Printing in High Quality Mode**

An important consideration when you are moving fonts to your MacWrite System file is making sure you also move the correct fonts for printing your documents in the high quality mode. This is not quite as straightforward as it seems, since when you print in high quality, the program does not just simply use the font size you've indicated, printing everything twice, instead of once, to make it darker. Instead, it actually starts with a version of the font *twice* the specified size, and prints that font reduced to the appropriate size. Let's use Table 4-1 to illustrate this.

All the fonts printed in the table were printed in high quality from a System file containing every font from the Macintosh Fonts file. If you've ever flipped through the Fonts file, you may have noticed that several font sizes are listed that don't appear in any font size menu—namely Seattle-20, Geneva-20, New York-20, and New York-36. If you intend to print (in high-quality mode) in these fonts at one-half the size, i.e., Seattle-10, Geneva-10, New York-10, and New York-18, you must be sure that these fonts are in your MacWrite disk's System file. What's the big deal, you ask?

Examine closely the printouts of New York-12, New York-14, and New York-18 in Table 4-1. Compare the lowercase *w* in the

Table 4-1.

This is Geneva-9 abcdefgHIJKLMNOP12345
This is Monaco-9 abcdefgHIJKLMNOP12345
This is New York-9 abcdefgHIJKLMNOP12345
This is Toronto-9 abcdefgHIJKLMNOP12345

This is Geneva-10 abcdefgHIJKLMNOP12345
This is New York-10 abcdefgHIJKLMNOP12345
This is Seattle-10 abcdefgHIJKLMNOP12345

This is Chicago-12 abcdefgHIJKLMNOP12345
This is Geneva-12 abcdefgHIJKLMNOP12345
This is Los Angeles-12 abcdefgHIJKLMNOP12345
This is Monaco-12 abcdefgHIJKLMNOP 12345
This is New York-12 abcdefgHIJKLMNOP12345
This is Toronto-12 abcdefgHIJKLMNOP12345

This is Geneva-14 abcdefgHIJKLMNOP12345
This is New York-14 abcdefgHIJKLMNOP12345
This is Toronto-14 abcdefgHIJKLMNOP12345
This is Venice-14 abcdefgHIJKLMNOP12345

This is Athens-18 abcdefgHIJKLMNOP12345
This is Geneva-18 abcdefgHIJKLMNOP12345
This is London-18 abcdefgHIJKLMNOP12345
This is New York-18 abcdefgHIJKLMNOP12345
This is San Francisco-18 abcdefgHIJKLMNOP12345
This is Toronto-18 abcdefgHIJKLMNOP123

This is Geneva-24 abcdefgHIJKLMNOP
This is Los Angeles-24 abcdefgHIJK
This is New York-24 abcdefgHIJKLMN
This is Toronto-24 abcdefgHIJK

word "New" in each size. Notice how the diagonal bars intersect in the 12- and 18-point sizes, font sizes which have corresponding double-sized fonts in the System file. Now look at the approximation made by the printer when it printed the 14-point size. Study the capital *Y* from the word "York" in all three sizes. Notice how in the 12- and 18-point sizes the angled arms are relatively smooth and the two arms are of distinctly different width, while in the 14-point size, the dot pattern is much more noticeable and the two arms are of equal width. The reason for this difference is that when the 24- and 36-point sizes are reduced by one-half, the result is a more finely detailed character.

If all your word processing printing is going to be in high quality mode, you *could* leave the smaller sized fonts, like Seattle-10 and Geneva-10, off the System file, and thus open some disk space on your program disk. The drawback to this, however, is that the characters displayed on the screen in those sizes won't be true fonts anymore, but rather approximate fonts, which are harder to read on the screen. Moreover, if you should want a standard quality printout, you will get the same approximate letters as on the display. The following figure shows what happens to Seattle-10 text when you display or print in standard quality both with and without the Seattle-10 font in the System file. I'd rather look at the true font.

This is a sample of standard-quality printout
of Seattle-10 when only Seattle-10 is installed
in the System File.

This is a sample of standard-quality printout
of Seattle-10 when both Seattle-10 and -20
are installed in the System File.
Notice that there is no difference in this
print quality when we add Seattle-20.

This is a sample of standard-quality printout
of Seattle-10 with only Seattle-20 installed
in the System File.
Without Seattle-10 in the System File,
the Mac only approximates the 10-point
version in standard quality,
producing less readable characters.

When choosing between standard and high quality print, I've found that my choice depends a lot on how new the ribbon is, and what size I'll be printing. With a new ribbon, the characters in 9- and 10-point sizes sometimes run into each other in high quality, while standard quality looks very presentable. But as the ink on the ribbon wears thin, standard quality print begins to look much like an ordinary dot-matrix printer for many situations. Even so, If I'm the only one to be looking at the printout, the standard quality is fine. I don't like draft quality, however, since its tiny characters destroy the page formatting appearance established on the Mac screen.

To sum up, then, when you are assembling the System file for you word processing program disk, be sure to include the double sizes (when available) for each of the fonts you intend to use in high quality printed work.

Work Saving Tips

I'm always looking for ways to do less mouse manipulating and typing on the Mac to improve work flow and my productivity. In word processing, the Mac offers a few shortcuts that are quite useful. In this section, I'll show you how to eliminate typing a frequently used phrase in a document. I'll also demonstrate a way to set up common forms you use in your work so all you have to do is fill in the blanks for things like interoffice memos. And then we'll use our knowledge of MacPaint techniques to devise a letterhead form you can call to the word processing screen in a flash.

◢ ◢ ◢ ◢ ◢ ◢ Using the Clipboard for Macros

In your meanderings through the world of personal computer jargon, you may have encountered the term *macro* without really knowing what it is. A macro is a common function of sophisticated word processing and database programs that lets you store one or more frequently used words or phrases in the computer's memory for instant recall when you need it. In a database program, for example, you might have a place on a form that requires the same response just about every time (but not always). If you assign the common answer to a macro, you can fill out that particular item by pressing one or two keys instead of retyping the full response each time.

Macros in word processing can be equally useful. For example, if you are writing a business report that frequently mentions a long company name—perhaps a foreign language name at that—it is much easier to place the name in the text by recalling the macro instead of typing the entire name, and possibly misspelling it. Word processing programs with space for several macros built into them can also store frequently used items such as closings of letters, standard paragraphs, and so on.

MacWrite doesn't have a macro feature *per se*. But you can use the Clipboard as a holding place for a single macro if you like. And even though Word's glossary functions well as a macro library, you can speed up the inclusion of a single, frequently used macro within a document using this same technique.

- After the first occurrence of the word or phrase you want to become a macro, stop entering text for a moment.
- Select the text to be stored in the Clipboard.
- Copy it (remember the Command-C keyboard shortcut). Now you can proceed to enter text as usual.
- Every time you want to use that word or phrase, simply type Command-V, the keyboard shortcut for the Paste function.

The text stored in the Clipboard will be stored with the font attributes of its first occurrence. Therefore, if you have a word to be emphasized several times in a document, you can store the first occurrence of it, with such things as a special font, size, and style. Then, when you recall it later, you don't have to bother making sure you recreate all the attributes of earlier occurrences—they're already stored in the Clipboard with the word.

▲ ▲ ▲ ▲ ▲ ▲ **Simplified Page Formatting**

You will probably find that most of your word processing work falls into a few standard formats. For example, if you send a lot of memos, then you are constantly typing the MEMORANDUM headline and the Date:/From:/To:/Subject: lines time after time. You might also have to specify the header and footer spacing each time you write a memo. Why not let the Mac simply present you with a preformatted memo blank form each time?

All you need for this work saver is to take the time during one of your memo writings to type out the blank form, complete with header and footer, on an untitled screen. Before you add any specific information about the memo you're going to type, save the blank form with a name something like, "MEMO BLANKS." In other words, what you've done is created an endless stack of blank memo forms which you can fill out every time you need to send a memo. You can save the blank on your storage disk, your word processing disk, or both.

Each time you want to write a memo, then, you click the MEMO BLANKS icon from your desktop. This action automatically loads the word processing program into the Mac, and presents you with a blank memo form to which you can add names, dates, and specifics. Then, to save the completed memo on disk without eliminating your blank memo form, use the Save As... option from the File menu and assign a specific name to this memo. In fact, if memo writing is one of your prime word processing activities, then you can move the MEMO BLANKS icon from the disk window onto the desktop near the storage disk or program disk icon. Then you won't have to open the disk window to get to the memo icon. You'll have it on your desktop the minute you insert the disk.

This concept of creating a blank form and keeping its icon handy for rapid startup isn't limited to memos. It applies to any commonly used page layout, even if the blank layout consists of nothing more than a blank header and blank footer to assure proper top and bottom margins on a multiple-page document. Blank formats such as these also take up very little space on the disk.

◢ ◢ ◢ ◢ ◢ ◢ Creating and Using a Custom Letterhead

In this section, I will show you how to create a letterhead using both MacPaint and your word processing program. When you are finished, you can put the document icon for that letterhead on the desktop of your program disk, and use it like a blank form, as you saw for MEMO BLANKS, above. This exercise brings together many of the techniques you've seen so far, including MacPaint tips. It also illustrates the transfer of a file from one program to another, which will be covered in more depth in the next chapter.

The name of the company I'm going to use is a fictional, Dallas-based company called Digital Readout Slide Rule Company, Inc. I've designed a logo which incorporates both the company name and a sample of the kind of product the company manufactures—a digital slide rule. Follow along on your Mac.

- The first step is to draw the outline for the slide rule, using simple rectangles in MacPaint. If you're using the rulers, draw a rectangle approximately 3 inches by 1/4 inch.
- After drawing the top rectangle, duplicate it, and drag its copy precisely below the original, leaving a space in the middle for the slide—a thinner rectangle.
- To draw the slide, place the pointer directly on the lower line of the uppermost rectangle, about an inch in from the left edge. Drag the new rectangle so it extends beyond the right edge of the two existing rectangles and in such a way that, where the slide meets the other rectangles, their borders precisely overlap.

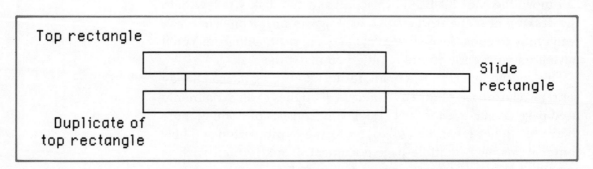

Next, it's time to add the end pieces to the slide rule. The tactic will be to do all the work on one piece and then duplicate it, flip it horizontally, and drag it over to the end.

- Placing the pointer at the upper left corner of the top rectangle of the slide rule, draw a rectangle filled with the tight grey pattern (the same one the Mac uses for the desktop background).

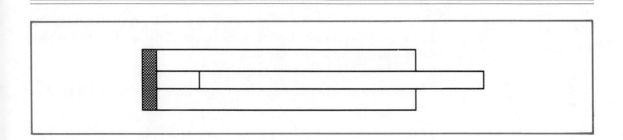

- Make the screw heads by creating black-filled circles in a separate work area.
- With FatBits, erase pixels to create a diagonal line through the screw head.

With a purely horizontal or vertical line on the tight grey background, the screw head lines are too prominent, since they appear too light. The diagonal, on the other hand, gives only a hint of a screw head—which is all you need in this spot.

- To give a little diversity to the heads, duplicate one head and invert it horizontally.
- Then lasso the screwheads one by one and drag them into place on the end pieces.

To create the semicircular blank areas, where you grab the slide with your thumbs, takes some trial and error. The effect is accomplished by using the circle icon with special attributes.

- First, select the dotted line from the line width menu at the lower left corner. This selection draws a filled rectangle or circle without a visible border line.
- Select the filled circle icon and the plain white pattern from the pattern palette below.
- Starting with the pointer to the left and below the upper screwhead, try drawing white circles so that the white of the circle creates the thumb recess. If you don't like the way one attempt works out, undo it and try again until it looks something like the one in the following figure.
- Now that one end piece is completed, duplicate it with the marquee and Option key, and drag the copy to a blank work area.

- There, flip it horizontally and lasso it.
- Drag it to the right end of the slide rule and position it in place. The lasso lets you position it without covering up the lines which extend to the right and the left.

The next step is to draw the slide rule cursor with its digital display.

- Starting with the rectangle icon, draw the basic outline, extending above and below the rule.

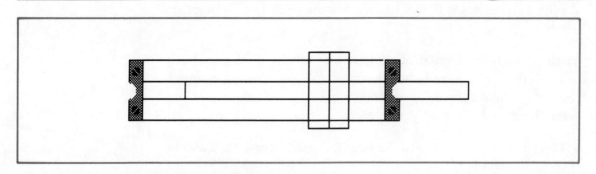

- Using FatBits, doublecheck to make sure that you have made the rectangle extend the same number of pixels above and below the rule.

I recall that slide rule cursors—at least ones on the cheap, plastic slide rules I could afford as a high school student—had decorative ridges in them at the top and bottom, where the two pieces were attached.

- Therefore, select a stripe pattern, and fill in the two small rectangles at each end of the cursor.
- To show that the two cursor end pieces are fastened to a corresponding piece on the other side, use FatBits to create tiny rivets or screws. The stripe pattern and small space don't let you do a circular screwhead, so simply fill in a couple of pixels between stripes. In normal, printed size, the suggestion of the fasteners is all that is needed.

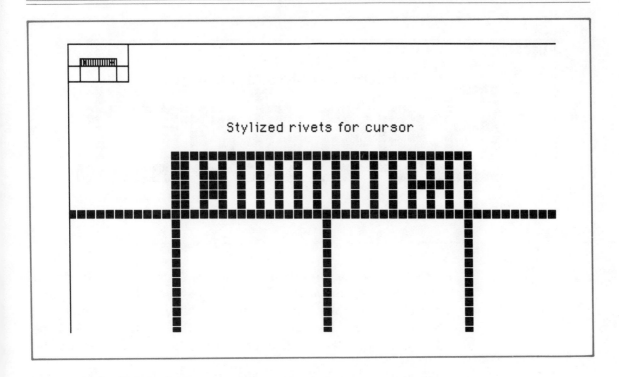

Leave the cursor for a moment, and attend to the text portion of the drawing. We really want some kind of computer-readout-looking font for the first two words of the company name. In this case, the distortion of an untrue font size works in our favor.

Athens-18 looks like a nice heavy, block letter with a little bit of flair to it. The largest font size that fits inside the ruler's rectangles is 12-point. Sure enough, the Mac distorts the letters in 12-point to give a robotic look to most of the letters. Because it is very difficult to envision how to position the text pointer on a MacPaint piece of art, create text first in an open work area. Then lasso each line of text and drag it to its final resting place.

- Type "Digital Readout" in 12-point Athens.
- Use FatBits to round two corners of the capital *R* of "Readout" to make it more recognizable.

- Select the words with the lasso and drag them to the left edge of the top bar on the slide rule.
- For the rest of the company name, use New York-12 in boldface, since it matches the size and weight of the first two words. Type the words "Slide Rule Company, Inc." in an open area on the screen.
- Select the first two words with the lasso and drag them to the left edge of the slide.
- Drag the remaining words to the left edge of the bottom bar.
- Type the text for the founding date, "Est. 1984," in a clear space, but in plain New York-12. You don't want it to be as prominent as the company name. Select and drag it to the right edge of the slide.

For the numbers in the digital display, you'll need to do some special work.

- In a clear area, type the numbers "421.7" in Athens-12, the same robotlike font you used for the first words of the company name.
- Since the numbers don't look particularly like a digital readout, experiment with deleting and adding pixels in FatBits until they look like those in the figure that follows.
- Before dragging the numbers into the cursor (which is the sliding bar in the middle), erase the horizontal lines of the slide and the

middle of the vertical hairline. You're going to cover them up with the digital display.

- Then lasso the numbers and drag them into the middle of the cursor.

To set the digital display off from the rest of the ruler, you should place it in a kind of recess. To do this:

- First create a little box around the digits. Then draw short diagonals from the corners of the box to the sides of the cursor.

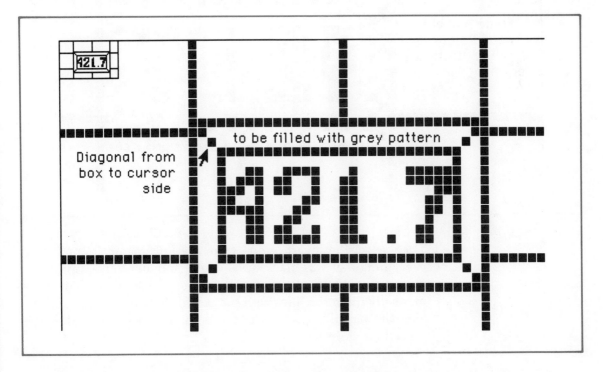

- Where the angled lines meet the cursor side, draw horizontal lines.
- Then, fill each of the tiny trapezoidal areas with the same tight grey pattern as you used on the slide rule end pieces.

The digits still don't pop off the page, so you should put the numbers on a reverse background.

- To do this, stay in FatBits, and carefully place the marquee precisely over the regular rectangle around the digits.

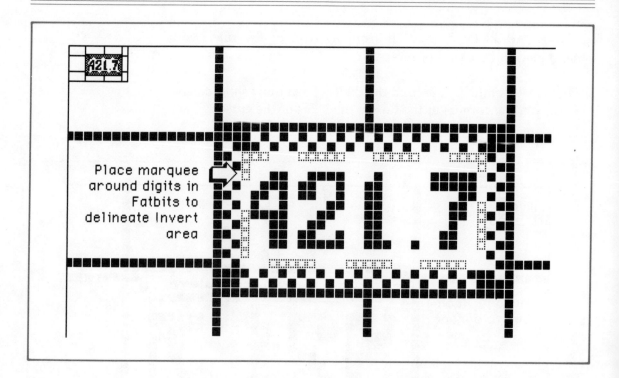

Place marquee
around digits in
Fatbits to
delineate Invert
area

- Then select the Invert option from the Edit menu. Immediately, everything that was black turns white, and vice versa. But it also means that the regular rectangle border is also white. You must manually fill in the lines with the pencil (Shift-clicking and dragging the pencil makes it draw in straight lines and makes this procedure easier).

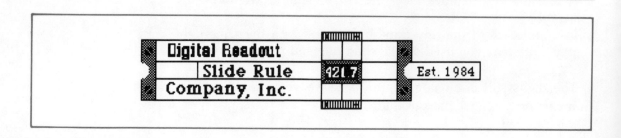

The slide rule still looks flat. It would help to give it some pizazz by adding a modicum of three-dimensionality. Borrow a few techniques used by Macintosh programmers when they create dialog boxes, windows, and the like. You can add shadows to two of the sides of the slide rule, as if a bright light were shining from the upper left corner. When you do this, every raised element on the slide rule should be throwing some kind of shadow. And the depth of the shadow should relate to the perceived thickness of the object throwing it.

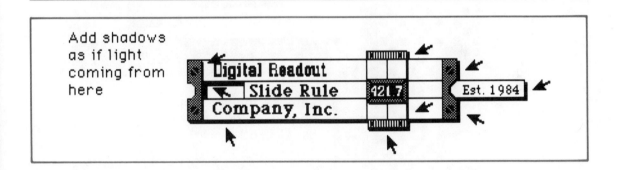

The easiest shadows are of the slide rule outline. Shadow lines are added easily in FatBits by drawing one or two extra lines of pixels along the appropriate sides of the object. Since the theoretical light source is at the upper left, however, the shadow leaves gaps in a few places—at the lower left and upper right corners of the object. The technique for creating these gaps (leaving a few pixels blank) is borrowed directly from many of Mac's internal window drawings.

Shallower shadows should be drawn to the right of the left endpiece, to the right of the cursor, and along the semicircular thumb area of the right endpiece. These are added with FatBits.

The rectangular hole between the bars (caused by the slide being pulled out) should have the deepest shadows, since you want to show the thickness of the whole unit.

- Add three rows of pixels to the top horizontal line of the hole. Add four columns to the left vertical line of the hole for a nice deep touch.

■ With FatBits, remove pixels along a diagonal line linking the corner of the open space to the spot where the end piece and upper slide rule rectangle meet. Without this little touch of white pixels, the depth of the open space would be lost.

Remove three FatBits, and you give this section great depth

■ Now type address and phone number lines in boldfaced New York-12: "P.O. Box 1076/Dallas, Texas 75999/214-555-6240." Make sure the three lines are aligned left by selecting Align Left from the Style menu and pressing the Return key after each line.
■ Then select and drag the text block to the right of the slide rule picture.
■ Use the hand icon to center the entire picture in the window.
■ Select the Align Middle option from the appropriate menu.
■ Place the text insertion pointer about one-quarter inch below the slide rule in the middle of the window.

■ Type the motto "We Bring Nostalgia Up To Speed" in plain New York-12.

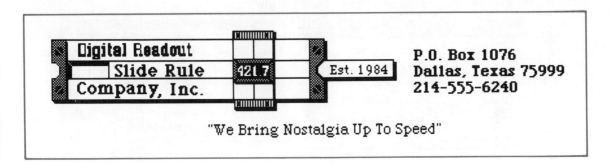

■ Save the picture.

With the letterhead art safely stored on disk, you then need to transfer it to a MacWrite document. We'll be discussing this procedure in more depth in the next chapter, but for now, I'll describe the steps you take. It's really quite simple.

■ First, select the entire letterhead art area with the marquee—notice that since you cannot select an area larger than a MacPaint window, the letterhead must be no larger than one MacPaint window. Extend the marquee a bit below the art area, since you don't want any writing from a future document to be too close to the letterhead area.
■ Then, issue the Copy command. This stores the art in the Clipboard while you close MacPaint and open MacWrite (even if you have to change disks).
■ With MacWrite ready for you, issue the Paste command. The art is instantly brought into the top of the document.
■ To center the art, first select it by moving the text pointer anywhere within the art area and click. A special rectangle surrounds the art. By placing the pointer along the right wall of the rectangle (but not on the black square), you can drag the art (actually, just a representation of the area in which the art resides) horizontally to the center of the page and release the mouse button.

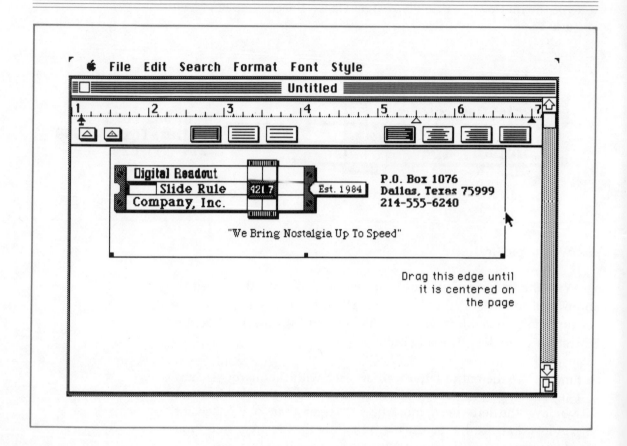

- Now, perform a Save As... operation, naming this document "Letterhead," or whatever will remind you what this document is.
- If most of your MacWrite work is correspondence on letterhead, then I suggest you close MacWrite and drag the icon for the letterhead onto the desktop so that when you close the window to your disk, the letterhead icon remains on the desktop (if you already have the MacWrite icon on the desktop, you can either drag it back into the window, or keep it, as well, on the desktop).

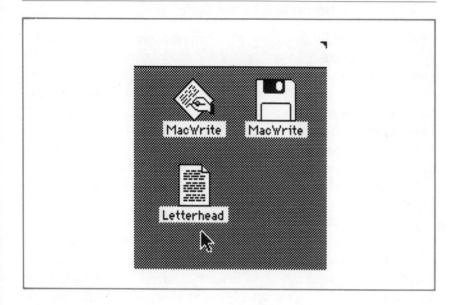

From now on, all you have to do to create a letter on letterhead is to insert your MacWrite disk and select the Letterhead icon. It will automatically load MacWrite into the Mac and get you going. Remember, however, that when you want to save the correspondence on disk (either the MacWrite disk or, preferably, a storage disk), you should perform a Save As. . . command and give the document a new name. If you issue the plain Save command, the blank letterhead on the disk will be replaced by the letter you've just typed. It might not be a bad idea to keep a reserve copy of the letterhead on the MacWrite disk with a different name, just in case you accidentally save an actual letter into the Letterhead file.

MacWrite Tips

We now come to some ideas to help MacWrite aficionados work a little faster when creating and editing documents. In particular, we'll be covering headers and footers and a way to insert rulers into your document without having to pull down the Format menu.

▲ ▲ ▲ ▲ ▲ ▲ **Header and Footer Techniques**

MacWrite offers its users one of the most powerful header/footer arrangements found in any personal computer word processing program. What sets the MacWrite system apart from the others is that once you specify a header and/or a footer for a page, you can have them appear on the screen throughout the body of your text. Most other word processing programs show the header and footer only the first time each appears in the document. And usually, the header and footer are buried within some special formatting code, so the actual text never appears on the screen as it will appear on paper.

If you are working on a document longer than one page—like a report, article, or book chapter—then you must create headers and footers if you want your pages to have adequate top and bottom margins. If you don't specify a header or footer for your page, the program accepts enough lines of text to fill up about ten inches of an 11-inch sheet. This is clearly not enough top and bottom margin for a professionally designed page.

Before you can set off the number of lines for header and footer, however, it helps to know how many lines of text you can put on a page. With other computer word processors, this is usually a total of sixty-six lines—eleven inches at six lines per inch. This measure assumes that your printer prints in a standard six lines per inch mode, which just about all printers do.

There is such a variety of type sizes and fonts that there is no standard for how many printed lines the Imagewriter will produce per page (unless you select the six lines per inch option). Even two fonts with the same point size can print a different number of lines per page because the spacing between lines (leading) may be different. You must evaluate each font and each size. The range of lines per page for typical document font sizes goes from as few as forty-seven for a 12-point New York to as many as sixty-eight for the tightly compacted Monaco-9.

Since MacWrite does not automatically create adequate margins at the top and bottom of a page, you have to do it. Keep in mind, though, that every line you add to a header or footer is subtracted from the total lines of text you can type per page.

- Select Open Header from the Format menu.
- Type your header, starting with the top line (which begins a half-inch below the top of the page). Pull down the page number, date, or time icons as your header style requires.

  I recommend that you type two additional blank spaces after the header to open up some white space between the header and the running text. If you are not using a heading of any kind, you should still put three or four blank lines in the header. These blank lines give you the equivalent of a top-of-page margin.

- Select the Open Footer option from the Format menu (don't close the Header box). If you don't want to have anything in the footer (I prefer to keep my page numbers and all other identifying information in the header rather than the footer), then you still need to indicate some white space to take the place of a bottom margin.
- Press the Return key two or three times.
- Then move the text pointer down to the window containing your document and click.

  The header and footer windows retreat to the background. (You can barely detect they're there, but they are. Look closely at the top right corner of the document window.) The headers and footers should now be displayed in the document. If not, pull down the Format menu again. If the options in the menu read, Display Header and Display Footer, rather than Remove Header and Remove Footer, it means that the header and footer displays had been turned off at some earlier time. Turn them back on now.

  Now scroll through your document pages and inspect how the header and footer look in relation to the page breaks on the screen. If you find that the bottom margin looks too big or too small to your taste, then edit the footer by either backspacing over one of the invisible carriage returns, or inserting another one at the end of the footer.

  Regaining access to the header and footer windows for editing can be hastened if you remember that they are both on the desktop, but just underneath the document window. Move the pointer way over to the right of the document, as far as it will go. If you then place the pointer next to the title bar of the document window, a click of the mouse brings the header window back to the foreground. Move the pointer just below the size box of the header window, again as far right as it will go, and a click of the mouse will open the footer window.

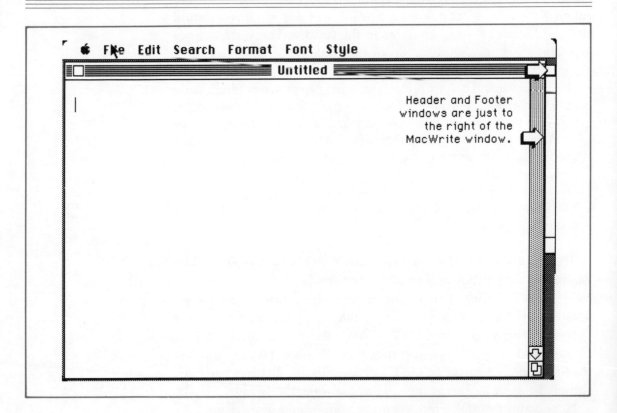

You can display the header and footer boxes by pulling down the Format menu and selecting the appropriate option (Open Header/Open Footer), but I find clicking on the windows themselves at the far right edge of the screen to be faster.

◢ ◢ ◢ ◢ ◢ ◢ **Ruler Shortcut**

Some documents—outlines in particular—call for a large number of frequently inserted rulers. It's a pain to have to reach for the

Format menu just to insert a ruler. But you can put your knowledge of macros to work with rulers, too.

At the top ruler of the document, place the pointer in the upper half of the ruler area, and click the mouse. If you place the pointer correctly, the ruler will be highlighted—if not, move the pointer around and keep clicking until you select the ruler. Copy it into the the Clipboard.

As you come to a section of the document that needs a new ruler, simply paste (Command-V) the ruler into place. You still must use the mouse to set the tabs, alignment, margins, or whatever elements set this section apart from the first one, but at least one mouse manipulation is eliminated.

As with all macros, be sure not to cut or copy anything else into the Clipboard while you need the ruler there. Utilize other deletion techniques learned earlier instead of the Cut command.

This technique should help speed your way through a complexly formatted MacWrite document.

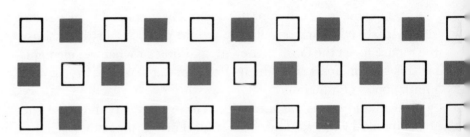

IT DOESN'T TAKE long working with MacPaint and MacWrite to realize that one of the Mac's greatest assets is its ability to pass information from one program to another. There are, however, many principles which you should be fully aware of before dreaming up some great project in the sky . . . only to discover that you can't do what you thought you could.

Principles of Data Transfer

One of these principles is knowing what methods for data transfer are available, and which ones work with the various Mac programs. Other principles are based on more technical matters that may be more difficult to grasp—like the different ways the Mac treats graphics and text—but matters that will help you better understand what's going on inside the Mac. In this section, I'll try to lead you into the depths of the Mac's innards so you can visualize why some programs let you transfer data, while others don't.

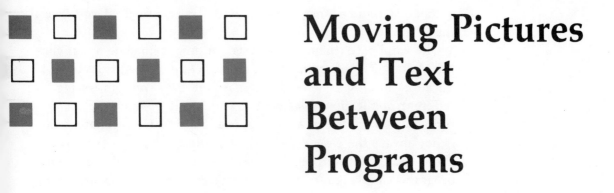

Moving Pictures and Text Between Programs

▲ ▲ ▲ ▲ ▲ ▲ **Basic Concepts**

The Macintosh and many of its software programs have two basic vehicles for transferring information from program to program: the Clipboard and the Scrapbook. As you would expect, each has its advantages, disadvantages, and quirks. When you multiply these variables times the programs for which they do or don't work, you end up with a set of rather confusing guidelines to follow. Practice is the surest way to get the hang of it all.

The Clipboard is both a section of memory and a disk file. In either form, it stores only one block—a character, a paragraph, or a complete picture—at a time, not many pages like the Scrapbook. When you cut or copy only a word or two from a MacWrite document, this small amount of data is placed into the RAM Clipboard inside the Mac. If you change to a MacPaint disk, the contents of the Clipboard memory remain intact during the change of disks. However, the size of the Clipboard memory inside the Mac is finite. If you have copied something very large, it needs help from the disk to store everything you've cut or copied—that's when text or pictures are written to disk in the Clipboard File (if you trashed the original Clipboard File, the Mac creates one to take its place). Then, if you change program disks, and the cut or copied data is bigger than the Clipboard memory, you'll have to perform a disk swap so the Clipboard file is transferred to your current disk. Overall, the system was designed to appear as though the Mac's Clipboard were a constant element that operates across every program you insert into the Mac.

The Clipboard, then, acts just as you might imagine a real clipboard does. It temporarily holds a piece cut or copied from one application until you're ready to paste it back into the same or different application. Ideally, the Clipboard memory is not disturbed when you insert a new application disk. Unfortunately, this is not always the case, especially with those programs that do not allow you to transfer data from other programs in this way. Such programs simply ignore or erase whatever is in the Clipboard memory.

As we've already seen, the Scrapbook, like the Clipboard, is a holding area for pictures or text. But unlike the Clipboard, the Scrapbook has a number of attributes which make it more difficult to use when transferring information from program to program when the two programs are on different disks.

Recall, again, our discussion about the System Folder. One of the files therein is the Scrapbook File. You gain access to the Scrapbook by way of the Macintosh Desk Accessories menu (see Chapter 2). Getting something into the Scrapbook requires more deliberate action than simply cutting or copying something into the Clipboard. In fact, you actually use Clipboard memory in the process of moving data into the Scrapbook. To transfer MacWrite text into the Scrapbook, for example, you first select the text you want, copy it (it automatically goes into the Clipboard), open the Scrapbook from the Desk Accessories menu, and then paste the contents of the Clipboard into the Scrapbook.

But what throws a curve into your planned use of the Scrapbook to transfer data from one program to another is that each program disk maintains its own Scrapbook File. Let's say you paste some text into the MacWrite disk's Scrapbook, eject your MacWrite disk, reset the Mac, insert your MacPaint disk, and start MacPaint. The minute you insert MacPaint, its System Folder for that disk takes over control of the Mac. This folder has its own separate Scrapbook File, which does not contain the text you copied into the Scrapbook File on your MacWrite disk. (The text is, of course, still in the Scrapbook File on the MacWrite disk.)

There is a way around this, but it could be dangerous to your various Scrapbook files. Let's say you have a page from the Scrapbook on one disk that you want to transfer to a second disk—a disk containing a program that does not accept the Clipboard method of data transfer. You can copy the entire Scrapbook File from the first disk to the second. A dialog box warns that doing so will erase the Scrapbook File on the second disk. That's the hitch. If you have some pictures or whatever in the Scrapbook on that second disk, they'll be covered up by the copy of the Scrapbook File from the first disk. You could, of course, copy the valued Scrapbook File from the second disk onto yet another disk (a blank disk, for example) until you're through making the data transfer, and then re-copy the valued file back to the second disk, but that sounds like a lot of disk swapping to me.

I think by now you understand the procedures. Programs that are designed to accept direct data transfers from other programs almost always accept the Clipboard memory style of data transfer. After all, the program designers should be working to make the process easy for you.

There is one more way of transferring information from one program to another, but the programs must be specifically designed for it. It's the case of one program being able to load data directly from storage files created by another program. The first example of this to reach the market was transferring numeric data from a Multiplan spreadsheet to Microsoft Chart for graphing. In this case, however, the programs share a common method of storing information, so related programs can gain access to it. This kind of data treatment is not new. VisiCalc did this years ago with its DIF (Data Interchange Format) files. The pfs: series from Software Publishing practices its own kind of common data file format on the Mac and on other computers. You're likely to see this data transfer methodology in other families of interrelated Mac programs as well.

Programs that don't allow such easy transfer probably have their reasons for making such transfers difficult, if not impossible. And the reasons could include some of the technicalities we're about to discuss. Now's the time to dig a little deeper inside the Mac.

◢ ◢ ◢ ◢ ◢ ◢ Advanced Concepts

To demonstrate the technical reasons why data transfer between some programs doesn't work as expected, let's first consider the differences between MacPaint and MacDraw. Experience with both programs will be helpful, but not essential.

Let's perform the exact same function—drawing a rectangle— with both programs. It's a simple task. In each program, you select the rectangle icon from the menu along the left edge of the screen, plant one corner with the mouse, and drag the pointer to the spot where you want the opposite corner to be. But the instant you release the mouse button, all similarities cease.

In MacPaint, the rectangle instantly becomes merely a pattern of pixels on the screen. You can use FatBits to add or remove pixels from the drawing. You can select any or all of the rectangle's pixels with the lasso and drag them around the window. You can't, however, go back to the corner you pulled and pick up the rectangle creation process where you left off. At most, you can select it with the marquee and attempt to stretch or shrink it. But all you're doing is asking MacPaint to approximate the bit pattern of your first rectangle to fill other proportions. In other words, as far as the Mac is concerned, your rectangle is simply a bit pattern on the screen. The computer tracks only where each individual bit is located. That it happens to look like a rectangle is something only we humans recognize.

Over on our MacDraw screen, however, when we release the mouse button, the program recognizes our shape for what it is: a rectangle. Actually, what the program is tracking is the fact that the shape is indeed a rectangle, with certain attributes regarding the starting point, the location of the opposite corner, what kind of pattern, if any, fills it, how thick the border lines are, etc. In other words, the shape retains its "rectangleness." Therefore, we can now select the rectangle long after we've created it, and stretch or shrink it again—not just as an approximation of the original bit pattern, but as a rectangle to be transformed into a wholly new rectangle with a new list of attributes. If we stretch it, the program simply changes in memory the parameters regarding the locations of the opposite corners. All other parameters remain unchanged. If the original rectangle was filled with a pattern, so will the revised rectangle, and the pattern will not be distorted, but rather adjusted to fill in the new space.

The Macintosh, then, may treat screen displays either as patterns of bits or as shapes with specific parameters or attributes. When programmers design their applications, they choose which method of screen display they want to use—either bit mapping or attributes. Although these two methods are not what you'd call compatible, they aren't totally incompatible either; you can still transfer data between two programs using these two different methods. That's what you've been doing all this time when transferring pictures from the bit-mapped MacPaint to MacWrite, which adheres to the attributes method.

Picture Transfers

The first category of practical transfers we'll discuss is pictures. This involves moving pictures to and from both MacPaint and MacDraw.

◢ ◢ ◢ ◢ ◢ ◢ MacPaint to MacWrite

Perhaps the most commonly used data transfer among novice Mac users is incorporating pictures from MacPaint into MacWrite documents. Even if you've had experience with other personal computers, you've never had this kind of flexibility, nor have you been able to jazz up your word processing documents like this before. MacPaint and MacWrite do not erase each other's Clipboard memory when loading the program, making transfers as simple as the Mac allows. You will, however, have to plan around some limitations when importing pictures into MacWrite documents.

Primarily because MacPaint and MacWrite use two different methods of screen display (bit-mapped objects vs. straight text given attributes of font, size, style, etc.), pictures from MacPaint and words from MacWrite cannot be intermingled in the same horizontal line. In other words, if you import a MacPaint picture, it takes up a horizontal band across the whole width of the page and as far down the page as is needed to display the picture. Therefore, you can't snake your MacWrite text around a MacPaint picture, or insert a smaller picture in a line of text, even if the picture is dragged way over to one margin. If you've seen fancy text and picture layouts, as in some Macintosh user group newsletters, you can be sure that they were either done entirely in MacPaint (unlikely) with the help of a special page layout program, or cut and pasted together the old fashioned way—with scissors and glue.

One way around this dilemma, albeit an inelegant one, is to create both the picture and surrounding text entirely in MacPaint and then transfer that band over to MacWrite. This would assume, of course, that the text of your document is completely finished, and will not change (with the deletion or addition of text, for example) in such a way that it affects the words imported from MacPaint. Adding to the problem, however, is that you won't be able to transfer a MacPaint image that is any wider than the MacPaint window—only about five inches wide, compared to the 6 or 6 1/2-inch width one normally uses for text. In other words, your picture will have wider margins than standard text margins. Perhaps it is best not to tempt Fate, and simply lay out your pages such that any MacPaint pictures stand by themselves. Captions, of course, can be done in either MacPaint or MacWrite.

Once I transfer a picture to MacWrite, I often find that a picture I created in MacPaint is not properly sized for the space I want to devote to it on a MacWrite page. The picture may be too large or too small in proportion to its importance on the document page. After selecting the picture, you can pull one of the corner boxes to stretch the image to fill out the full width of the MacWrite page. By pulling the corner or middle box, you can also stretch it downwards. Rarely does this help the picture's appearance, however, since the stretching procedure adheres to MacPaint's stretching techniques—producing only an approximation of the original picture, since a stretch by its very nature distorts some lines.

One important point to remember when you plan to combine a

MacPaint picture into a MacWrite document is that the printing quality of the two may vary. In MacWrite, the MacPaint picture prints only in the equivalent of the Print Draft selection from the File menu. If you select high quality MacWrite printing, the text entered with MacWrite prints darker and with better resolution than the picture areas. If you need consistent print quality, then you may have to print each element separately (pictures from Mac-Paint, text from MacWrite) and literally paste them together the old fashioned way.

◢ ◢ ◢ ◢ ◢ ◢ MacDraw to MacPaint

When I first saw MacDraw, having spent many hours with Mac-Paint, I was most intrigued by the possibility of creating multiple-page-sized images with MacDraw (MacDraw lets you draw a box, for example, across several pages), and then copying them over to MacPaint for the final touch up with FatBits and other precision tools. Finally, I thought, I won't be constricted by the MacPaint window to create the overall layout of my picture. Well, as I discovered, it's not quite that easy.

As it turns out, the MacPaint window is still the constricting element in moving picture information from MacDraw to MacPaint. If I try to transfer a shape or work area on a MacDraw page that is larger than the MacPaint window, I run into the same problems as when I try to paste a large MacWrite text block into MacPaint. Whatever doesn't fit inside the window doesn't make the transfer.

As a small consolation, at least you can create shapes in Mac-Draw according to a ruler scale that is convenient for you, as long as the drawing itself stays within the size of the MacPaint window. Then you can shift it over to MacPaint for further embellishment.

◢ ◢ ◢ ◢ ◢ ◢ MacPaint to MacDraw

But then, I figured, what if I use MacPaint to create small, detailed shapes—like chairs and desks for an office layout—and then transfer them over to MacDraw to use as elements in a bigger picture? Well, much to my dismay, there is no transfer from MacPaint to MacDraw.

The reason is largely due to the different ways the two programs treat the shapes they create. In order for MacDraw to accept a MacPaint picture, you would need some rather sophisticated software that could look at the MacPaint picture of bits, and find recognizable shapes. It would then have to work backward and figure out what attributes (size, fill pattern, border width, etc.) each shape has. Only then could it pass these shapes and attributes over to the control of MacDraw. That's asking a lot for a piece of personal computer software—at least for the time being.

▲ ▲ ▲ ▲ ▲ ▲ MacDraw to MacWrite

Fortunately, you can transfer MacDraw pictures to a MacWrite document. Both MacDraw and MacWrite use the "attributes" type program. Therefore, MacWrite knows to accept a MacDraw picture larger than the MacWrite window and plant it firmly on a MacWrite page. Use the Clipboard for this transfer.

▲ ▲ ▲ ▲ ▲ ▲ Anything to MacPaint

One of the lesser-used features of the Macintosh lets you make a copy of just about anything on the screen—even business graphics from Lotus Development's Jazz integrated program—and bring it into MacPaint. The only limitation is that what you import to MacPaint cannot be any larger than one MacPaint screen. Here's how to use this feature.

Let's say you've been admiring a screen from a game program, and you'd like to print it out, experiment with it, or further develop a portion of it for artwork you're creating. (Don't forget, however, that material such as this is likely to be copyrighted.) With the desired screen showing in the Mac display, press Command-Shift-3 —all three keys simultaneously. This sends a snapshot of the screen to the current startup disk and labels it Screen 0. Each time you save a screen to the disk, the number increments by one to help you keep them separate (you can rename them, of course) until the disk fills up. When that happens, the Mac beeps the next time you press Command-Shift-3.

The snapshot files you create are MacPaint documents and can be opened with MacPaint. If the disk is a self-starting disk, you must start up the Mac with a different disk—MacPaint would be convenient—eject the startup disk, insert the game disk, and open it to see icons for the Screen files.

To prove for yourself that you can work with these snapshots, try your hand at the above procedure and then double click one of the Screen icons. You'll be prompted for the MacPaint disk (unless you have a second drive with MacPaint already inserted). Depending on the screen image you've selected, you may not see the image in the MacPaint window, but it's on your worksheet. Select Show Page from the Goodies menu, and you'll see that the screen snapshot is located at the upper left corner of the page. Drag either the window to the picture, or the picture into a more central location on the page for further editing.

Now that you have converted the games image to a MacPaint document, you can transfer selections from it (none any larger than the MacPaint window, alas) over to MacWrite. Whenever you're stumped about how to exchange data from one program to another, try the snapshot to MacPaint method.

Text Transfers

Next we'll look closely at how to transfer text among various programs. We'll even import a Multiplan spreadsheet into MacWrite.

◢ ◢ ◢ ◢ ◢ ◢ MacWrite to MacPaint

Moving text from MacWrite to MacPaint is possible, although unnecessary unless you need to bring over a block of text you don't want to retype. Transfers from MacWrite to MacPaint, however, are not quite as smooth as in the reverse direction.

First of all, bear in mind that the MacPaint window is much smaller than the window to a MacWrite document. Therefore, if you try to copy a large chunk of text from MacWrite to the Clipboard, and then paste it from the Clipboard into MacPaint, not all the text will make it into MacPaint. Whatever doesn't fit on the screen after the Paste command does not survive the transfer.

Secondly, no matter what margin and tab settings your MacWrite text adheres to, those settings are not transferred to MacPaint with the text block. Instead, when you paste the text block into MacPaint, the block is reformed to fit into a marquee rectangle. If you let the Mac determine the size of the marquee, it makes a square centered in the window and only large enough to contain the text. You can, however, pre-size the pasted text block into a different proportion (e.g., a long horizontal rectangle) by dragging a marquee on the screen before pasting. As mentioned earlier, however, if the text block is larger than the marquee it gets pasted to, all text not fitting into the marquee won't survive the transfer. Fortunately, you can undo the Paste, resize the marquee, and paste again.

Third, when you import the text into MacPaint, the MacPaint font, font size, and font style in effect at that moment prevail. Recall what we said earlier, MacWrite is an "attributes" kind of program. In other words, it stores the text as bare, ASCII files (standard coding), with certain attributes that only MacWrite converts into the font, size, and style selected. Although these attributes are transferred into the Clipboard along with the text, MacPaint doesn't know how to interpret the attributes. Therefore, even if you have a large, boldfaced heading for a MacWrite paragraph, both the heading and the text will be in the same font, size, and style when they are pasted into MacPaint. Your only opportunity to revise the font attributes are immediately after pasting, but before clicking the mouse to eliminate the marquee.

Unfortunately, when you change the font, size, or style, the entire text block is affected. You can't just boldface a headline and leave the rest in plain text. If you absolutely need a boldfaced headline, then you'll have to retype it in MacPaint's text and position it where needed (after erasing the original headline pasted from MacWrite).

◢ ◢ ◢ ◢ ◢ ◢ Multiplan to MacWrite

There are surely many times when you will want to transfer information from a spreadsheet into a memo, letter, or other presentation prepared with MacWrite. You can do so with Multiplan, provided you follow some guidelines to prevent yourself from getting into what could be real trouble.

When you copy a section of a spreadsheet from Multiplan, it goes into the Clipboard. (As with most other Mac programs, simply select the section and invoke the Copy command from the Edit menu.) Looking into the Clipboard window, all you see is the notation of how many rows and columns are stored there.

	File	**Edit**	**Select**	**Format**	**Options**	**Calculate**		

R7C6	=SUM(R[-4]C-R[-3]C-R[-2]C)

Untitled

	1	2	3	4	5	6
1		January	February	March	April	May
2						
3	Sales	$1500.00	$1250.00	$1309.00	$1410.00	$2600.00
4	Commissions	$75.00	$70.00	$72.00	$75.00	$120.00
5	Cost of Goods	$356.80	$400.56	$539.55	$525.00	$740.08
6						
7	Gross Income	$1068.20	$779.44	$697.45	$810.00	$1739.92
8						
9						
10						

Clipboard

11						
12						
13	7R x 6C					
14						

Quit the program. If the spreadsheet selection is larger than a couple hundred characters, a dialog box appears, advising you that the program is saving a large selection. Depending on the size of the block, it also wants to know if it should store its formatted and/or unformatted values. Save *formatted values* only. Eject the Multiplan disk.

Insert the MacWrite disk and open either MacWrite or a document you've already prepared with a spot for the spreadsheet data. If you have a single-drive Mac, part of the disk swap you make when starting MacWrite is the transfer of the Clipboard File from the Multiplan disk to the MacWrite disk. This transfer occurs only if the data stored on the Clipboard is larger than the memory area set aside in the Mac for it.

Position the text pointer at the left margin of the line in which you wish to paste the spreadsheet info. Then invoke the Paste command. In a couple of seconds, the numbers and titles appear in the space, but probably not in the format you would expect. Here's where some maneuvering comes in.

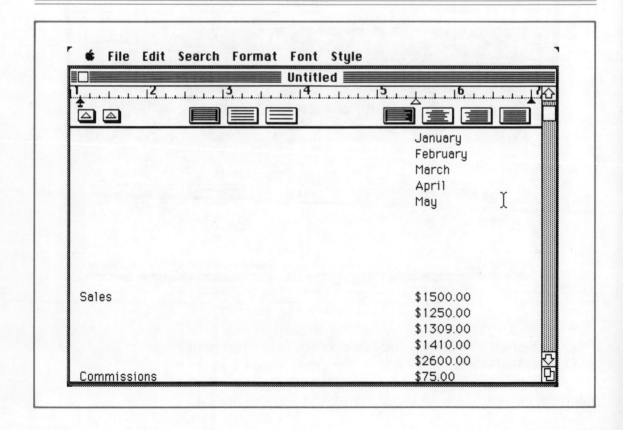

It looks like a mess at this stage, but a close examination of how the information is stacked up should help unravel the numbers and help you put them in the right order without much fuss. Notice that, in this example, all the column titles and numbers are stacked up against the tab marker at the 5½-inch mark. That's a big clue that tabs are important in formatting your spreadsheet data—and indeed the are. Simply by placing tabs at intervals along the ruler, you begin to spread out the columns.

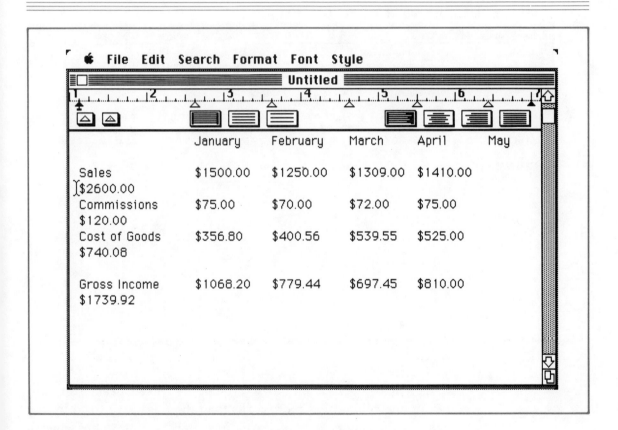

When you have one tab for each—and enough space between tabs to accommodate the titles and numbers in each column—you have your spreadsheet . . . almost.

In the previous figure, you'll notice that I'm out of room to fit the numbers from the last column on the page. The solution is to shrink the font size of everything in the spreadsheet so it all fits. It's almost the same as printing spreadsheets with condensed type on some dot matrix printers, but much better, since the quality of the Imagewriter in high quality mode is superior. Therefore, select the entire spreadsheet, and experiment with fonts and smaller sizes until everything fits. Readjust the tab markers where necessary.

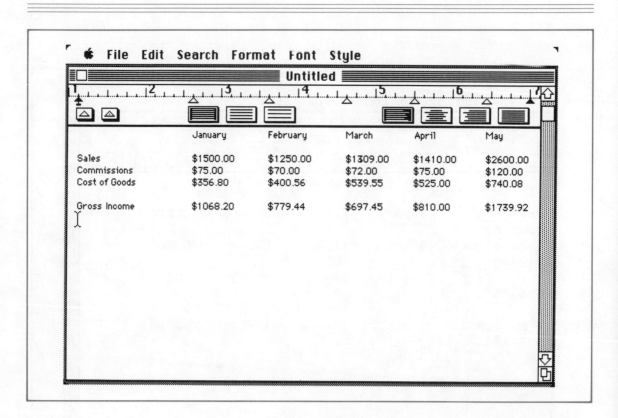

As a final check, scroll down through the spreadsheet. If a number in one column has more digits than there is space for it in the column, the alignment of all the figures after it will be out of whack. If you encounter such a problem, simply go back to the ruler and readjust the tab markers.

It is vitally important to note that there will be only so many columns of a spreadsheet that you'll be able to cram onto a MacWrite page, even at the smallest font size. Therefore, try to plan your

Multiplan-to-MacWrite data exchanges in such a way that you can fit your data sensibly on the page. If you have too many columns, then the information will be better communicated as a separate spreadsheet attached to your memo or presentation—perhaps selecting certain smaller segments of the spreadsheet for insertion into MacWrite for amplification with surrounding MacWrite text.

Fortunately, when you import Multiplan spreadsheets into MacWrite, the titles and numbers become text, just like the text you type in. Therefore, you have complete control over fonts and styles for individual numbers. You might, for example, punch up the positive bottom-line numbers with bold or shadow font styles.

One extra tip for bottom-line numbers. To effect a double underline, you first type an underline (using Shift and the underline key) on the line beneath the final figures. Then select the entire underline and invoke the Underline command from the Style menu. This command underlines the underline, creating a perfect double underline.

As more software arrives for the Macintosh, the permutations of data interchangeability will explode. If you are planning your software purchases around what you hope to exchange from one program to another, be sure you get some proof at the store that such transfers are, in fact, possible. As trite as it may sound, the old phrase "Seeing is believing" applies when it comes to choosing software that lets you successfully exchange data with other programs you use.

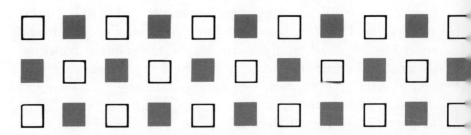

THE MACINTOSH DESIGNERS elected to construct the machine with what in the industry is known as *closed architecture*. What this means is that unlike computers such as the Apple IIe or the IBM Personal Computer, neither you nor non-Apple (third party) peripherals engineers can gain ready access to the "guts" of the computer. More specifically, a part of the computer's circuitry, called the *system bus*, cannot be rapidly tapped into. The system bus is like the spinal chord of the computer. Nearly everything that goes on in the entire computer runs through one or more wires comprising the bus.

In an open architecture machine, like the Apple IIe, the computer's designers bring all the signal lines of the system bus out to a series of connectors on the computer's main circuit board. Anyone with the technical expertise can design plug-in boards that make use of one or more signal lines, depending on the operation the board is to perform. One such board, for example, links the basic Apple IIe to a disk drive. Yet the same connector might also be used for a board that links the computer to a telephone line for telecom-

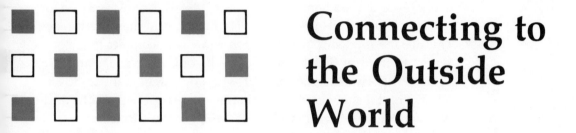

Connecting to
the Outside
World

munications. The latter board simply uses a few different (and a few of the same) signal lines from the system bus.

The purpose of this discussion is to give you an appreciation for what Apple has done in making the Mac a closed system. As it is designed, the Mac has really only two pathways—called serial ports—to connect a variety of peripherals. Sure, there are other connectors on the Mac's rear panel, but they are dedicated for specific purposes—the disk-drive connector is used solely with the external drive, for example. Like the other ports, the two serial ports do have specific legend pictographs above them—printer and modem—but they are not dedicated to those functions only. With the aid of software, you can change the characteristics of those ports so they will work with a variety of accessories (more about this software in a moment). Thus, third-party manufacturers of add-on products for other computers are having to create new products for the Mac that operate not from the system bus, but through one of the serial ports.

This demand for serial ports, however, can cause problems if your needs exceed the number of available ports. Chances are that you will have a printer attached to your Mac at all times. That leaves only one serial port, which you may want to use to connect to a modem today, and directly to another computer tomorrow. But Mac designers had to place a limit on the number of serial ports available on the rear of the Mac. For most users, the two are sufficient. More than likely, the two ports will be used as intended—for a printer and a modem.

This chapter deals with the serial ports. It is to these ports—specifically the modem port—that you can easily connect other computers to transfer files from, say, an IBM PC to the Mac and back again. I'll show you examples of why you might want to do this. Moreover, I'll show you how to connect non-Apple modems to the Mac, and how you can use a modem to obtain (practically) free software for the Mac.

But before we dive into the modem serial port, we'll take two short side trips. One discusses the basics of communications through a serial port. The second covers connecting non-Apple printers to the printer serial port. More specifically, we'll look at the mystery surrounding the use of printers other than those designed for use with the Mac.

■ ■ ■ ■ ■ ■

Serial Communications 101

The minute you start messing around with attaching things to the serial port of any computer, you're bound to get lost within the first sentence or two of the instructions unless you know something about the terminology. I think it's the vocabulary that causes the most frustration for first-time serial communicators.

First, we must distinguish serial communications from another kind, called parallel. Many popular printers on the market require a *Centronics parallel interface* on the computer to which it is connected. Let's take this hairy term apart piece by piece, starting from the last word, interface.

Break the word into two, *inter* and *face*. *Inter* is the common prefix meaning *between*, and *face* is, well, a face. An interface is nothing more than something that acts as a go-between for two dissimilar things. Sometimes an interface is simply a cable that links up two different types of connectors. Other times, an interface requires more electronics working in the background to make the proper conversions so both ends of a link can understand each other.

Parallel means that the information is sent down a cable in rows, like race horses leaving the starting gate. The opposite of parallel, *serial*, means that the horses all come out of one starting gate in single file. As you can imagine, if the horses in both arrangements are running at the same speed, more horses move around the track over time in parallel than in the single-file serial mode. The same goes for computer information, but with the kinds of communications we'll be working with, the increased throughput of a parallel connection isn't of any particular advantage.

Finally, the *Centronics* part is simply the name of an early personal computer printer manufacturer. By virtue of the popularity of this company's products, its particular way of wiring parallel connectors became a standard followed by other manufacturers.

Even though the Mac communicates with peripherals only through a serial interface, I bring up the difference between serial and parallel because you will probably hear of peripherals that run through parallel only. If so, you won't be able to run them directly on the Mac, unless you can find a serial-to-parallel convertor designed for the Mac. Even then, as we'll see with printers in a moment, you may still have some problems.

The next term we must deal with is *parameters*. Let's say you are going to dictate a paragraph to someone over the phone. The person on the receiving end is going to be writing as you speak. The two of you agree on the speed at which you will speak, what the receiver will say to tell you to pause while the writing catches up with the words, what the signal is to continue once the receiver does catch up, and so on. These elements of the exchange are equivalent to communications parameters, or characteristics of the communication.

Now, when two people speak over the phone, the two of them have enough intelligence to automatically adjust to the speed of communication which is most comfortable. Computers aren't so smart. They must be told explicitly what the characteristics of the communications exchange are to be. Both ends of the exchange must have precisely the same parameters as the other for error-free communications to take place.

Inside the Mac, there is special circuitry that converts information such as text characters and bit patterns into a form that can be transmitted through a wire over long distances—long by computer chip standards, that is. We're talking distances of up to twenty-five feet, compared to the few inches data normally traverses on the Mac's main circuit board. Anyway, this circuit also acts as sort of a coach to each character that is to be sent along the wire. The coach conditions each character, making sure its unique identification number (a coded sequence of on and off pulses) has some additional pulses to help the receiver know where a character's ID number begins and ends. These beginning and ending codes are needed because one long stream of ID numbers will be coming down the wire without pause. The coach also establishes how fast the pulses are to race out of the starting gate.

The individual on and off pulses that make up each character's ID number are known in the communications lexicon as *data bits*. In order to have unique sequences of data bits for every letter of the alphabet (upper and lower case letters need separate IDs), numerals, and common punctuation, you need a sequence at least seven bits long. The precise sequence of data bits distinguishes the letter *a* (whose signals are represented in binary arithmetic as 1000001) from the letter *b* (represented as 1000010), for example. And luckily for us, the codes have been standardized among all personal computer and peripheral manufacturers. The standard is called *ASCII* (pronounced ASS-key), for American Standard Code for Information Interchange. Every microcomputer, modem, and printer I've ever come in contact with subscribes to this standard.

The circuitry that coaches the information as it goes out is very flexible. Depending on instructions it gets from the Mac, it can: 1) issue characters in either seven or eight data bit lengths (the former used primarily for text output, the latter for either text or graphics output); 2) set the speed at which the bits go; 3) assign how many and which extra signals are to go along with the characters to assist in detecting transmission errors; and 4) tell both ends of the transfer when to pause or continue. These are the minimum communications parameters which must be established before successful communications can begin. Giving such instructions to the serial port circuitry is called *configuring* the serial port. We've already described one parameter, the number of data bits. Here are the other major parameters.

Foremost is the speed of communications. Serial communications speed is measured in bits per second (bps). A more common term for transfer of speed, however, is *baud* (pronounced bawd). Unfortunately, it is often misused (used when bps is, in fact, the correct term), even by modem and computer manufacturers. The precise definition of baud is rather complex (by all rights, a typical "1200-baud" modem is actually working at 600 baud), but suffice it to say that when someone refers to 1200-baud communications, what is usually meant is a data transfer speed of 1200 bps—bps being the true governing measure of data transfer, regardless of the method of transfer (phone line or direct connection). Common personal computer communication takes place at 300 and 1200 bps for transfer of information over telephone lines (although some new modems on the market are capable of 2400 bps). Communication between the Mac and the Imagewriter through the printer cable is performed at a much faster speed of 9600 bps.

In addition to the data bits sent along the communications line, there is another kind of signal, called a *stop bit*, which acts as a separator between complete characters. A stop bit signals the end of a stream of data bits which, together, should make up a character. Some communications systems prefer two stop bits, while most find one sufficient. Both ends of the communications link, however, must be configured for the same number of stop bits.

The last parameter we'll discuss is called *parity*. The complete explanation of parity goes beyond what you need for successful communications. For now, all you need to know is that if desired, a serial port can send an extra bit along with each character that can help the receiver detect if the character was received correctly. Essentially, the parity bit is a yardstick against which the receiving end can measure the overall content of 1s and 0s among the data bits sent. At most, however, this kind of error checking can only detect errors which may have crept in due to noise or interference along the communications link (like a poor telephone line)—it does nothing to correct the error. Your range of choices for parity error settings are even, odd, or no parity at all. Some serial ports can also be configured to ignore parity bits if encountered, thereby making one setting hold true for all comers.

To sum up, then, before serial communications can take place, the serial port on the Mac must be configured identically to the device to which it is connected—whether it be printer, telephone modem, digitizing pad, or another personal computer. In many cases, this configuration is performed automatically. For example, when you connect an Imagewriter to the Mac's printer port, a special file in the System Folder, called Imagewriter, automatically configures the printer port so it can communicate with the Imagewriter without any fuss. If you're using a modem, on the other hand, you will have to set the parameters yourself using an applications program like MacTerminal, which presents all the possible parameters in menu form for your selection.

Using Other Printers

There are surely many Mac owners who already have a printer from another computer or would like to use a particular printer model other than the ones offered by Apple. To help you determine whether you can use that printer, I'll have to get a bit technical about printers. In the end, however, you'll have a much better understanding of what goes on inside the Mac when it comes to printing, and why most printers not specifically designed for the Mac won't work.

In the graphics area, as when you print a MacPaint document, the Macintosh sends out instructions to a printer to print individual dots in patterns that replicate the pattern of dots on the screen. In addition to this dot information, the Mac also sends long strings of special commands, known as control codes or escape codes, to the printer. A printer command, for example, might instruct the printer to begin printing in bold face, or decrease the spacing between letters for condensed print.

◢ ◢ ◢ ◢ ◢ ◢ **Control and Escape Codes**

The terminology for these codes comes from the convention that printer commands are preceded by the equivalent of a press of either the Control key of a conventional computer keyboard (the Command key on the Mac), or the Escape key (no Mac keyboard equivalent). Even though these keys do not exist on the Mac keyboard, their ASCII code equivalents exist inside the Mac—thereby adhering to the industry standards of characters discussed earlier in this chapter.

Whenever a printer receives either a Control or Escape character, software inside the printer knows to interpret the next character as a command, rather than a printable character. Therefore, if a printer needs a command such as Escape-R, a Mac programmer can put those characters inside a program to instruct the printer to execute the desired command. Unfortunately for us, there is no standard whatsoever governing what most of those printer commands should mean. Escape-N on the Imagewriter, for example, signals the printer to print the following text at a spacing of ten characters per inch. The same command on the Texas Instruments TI-855 printer instructs the printer to enter a bit-image graphics mode.

◢ ◢ ◢ ◢ ◢ ◢ **Printer Driver Software**

What governs the printer commands that come from the Mac is a program called a *printer driver*. This program takes whatever commands come from the applications program (MacWrite, MacPaint, etc.) and makes any necessary conversions of the printer commands so they are correct for the printer attached to the computer. Each printer model needs its own printer driver program if that printer is to ever get the proper commands. The exceptions to this rule are printers designed to emulate a printer for which a printer driver already exists. Some examples are in order.

If you open your System Folder, you see among the files located therein one called Imagewriter. This file is the printer driver that takes instructions from your applications programs and converts them into control and escape codes the Imagewriter understands. Within six months of the Mac's introduction, one third-party printer manufacturer, Okidata, introduced a printer that emulates the Imagewriter for graphics and text. What this means is that rather than try to write a new printer driver for the Mac, Okidata found it easier (or, rather, more within its realm) to manufacture a printer specifically made to accept Imagewriter control and escape codes for both graphics and text.

To use other dot matrix or formed character (i.e., daisywheel or thimble) printers, however, you need specially written printer drivers for the printer you wish to use. Such programs are available, primarily through third-party software and printer companies. But just about every third-party printer driver on the market is designed for formed-character text printers and not dot-matrix graphics printers. Despite their limitations, however, these formed-character printer drivers fill a gap in printing choices originally left open by Apple, since it didn't offer a daisywheel printer for the Mac in its early months.

At this juncture, I should explain why the Imagewrite printer driver won't work with other printers. When you select Draft quality from the Print dialog box in MacWrite, the Imagewriter printer driver sends text to the printer as standard ASCII characters. Both Standard and High Quality, on the other hand, send bit images of your document—signals that, so far, only the Imagewriter and Okidata printers are able to interpret.

The problem, however, is that even in Draft quality, the Imagewriter driver sends an inordinate number of printer control codes (in ASCII) to the Imagewriter—codes which a normal printer cannot interpret. How many codes are there in an Imagewriter document, you ask? Well, take a look at what goes to the printer when you want to print the simple sentence, "The quick brown fox jumps over the lazy dog's back.":

```
^[o^[<^[f^[T26^J^[N^[F0120^[q^O^["^[YThe^[N
^[F0146^[q^O^["^[Yquick^[N^[F0183^[q^O^["
^[Ybrown^[N^[F0225^[q^O^["^[Yfox^[N^[F0249
^[q^O^["^[Yjumps^[N^[F0291^[q^O^["^[Yover
^[N^[F0322^[q^O^["^[Ythe^[N^[F0346^[q^O^["
^[Ylazy^[N^[F0376^[q^O^["^[Ydog's^[N^[F0411
^[q^O^["^[Yback.^[f^[T99^J^J^J^J^J^J^J^J^J
^J^J^J^J^J^[T73^J^Y^O^[z^[T24^[E^[<^["
```

What does all this gibberish mean? Here's an annotated version of the first part:

^[o	—	Escape o, turn on paper error detector
^[<	—	Escape <, turn on bidirectional printing
^[f	—	Escape f, forward line feed
^[T26	—	Escape T 26, distance between lines is to be 26/144"
^J	—	Control-J, advance paper one line (line feed)
^[N	—	Escape N, print in 10 characters per inch (pica)
^[F0120	—	Escape F 120, position the next character 120 dots to the right of the left margin
^[q	—	Escape q, print in 15 characters per inch (condensed)
^O	—	Control-O, turn off double-width headline printing (if on)
^["	—	Escape ", turn off boldface printing (if on)
^[Y	—	Escape Y, turn off underlining (if on)
The	—	Finally, the first word of our sentence!
^[N	—	Escape N, print in pica
^[F0146	—	Escape F 146, place the next character 146 dots to the right of the left margin
^[q	—	Escape q, print in condensed
^["	—	Escape ", turn off boldface printing (if on)
^[Y	—	Escape Y, turn off underlining (if on)
quick	—	And now, the second word of our sentence.

By now you may see a pattern. After the introductory codes, which set up the printer into its basic configuration, the Imagewriter driver issues codes between each word signifying its placement along the line according to its own *dot* measure. It checks for the presence of boldfacing and underlining commands before printing each word. All the Control-Js at the end of the sentence are line feeds to advance the paper to the end of the page.

You can see, therefore, that even if your printer could strip away all the extraneous printer commands, it still could not print your text, because the text coming out from the Imagewriter printer driver does not supply necessary signals, such as spaces between words, left margins, and so on. Even if it did supply those codes, there is an excellent chance that commands for print enhancements like boldfacing and underlining would be different from your printer, making them unusable on your printer.

There is hope, however, if you have a printer for which a driver does not exist. In basic text printing, many printers adhere closely to mainstream printers like Epson, NEC, or Diablo brand printers. If a driver exists for a printer similar to yours, or for a model which your printer emulates, then that driver may work for you. It may not control every feature of your printer, but at least you won't have to invest in an entirely new printer for the Mac.

Printing graphics on printers for which there is no printer driver will be less successful. The precise control over the printer required by the Mac's high resolution graphics means that a lot of control codes need to be sent to the printer throughout the printing of a picture. If the printer is incapable of interpreting every control code accurately, there is no chance your picture will turn out.

I wish there was better news about using non-Apple printers, but such is the price we pay for owning a computer that transcends the state of the art in printing.

Using Non-Apple Modems

A *modem* (pronounced MOE-dem) is a device which converts the on and off pulses of computer-generated characters into audible signals for transmission over telephone lines or other audio media (such as radio). At the transmission end, the modem *modulates* the signals, a process that assigns specific audible tones to the on and off pulses. At the receiving end, the modem *demodulates* the audio and converts the tones back into on and off pulses, which the computer can understand.

Modems come as either direct-connect or acoustic types. The direct-connect type has two jacks on the cabinet that look exactly like the modular phone jacks used these days on all telephone equipment. A cable links one jack to the wall phone outlet, while the other jack is used as the outlet for a regular telephone. In this way, you can use the telephone without having to unplug the modem from the wall jack. An acoustic type of modem features two rubber cups into which you place the handset of a standard desk telephone. A speaker and microphone in the cups convey audible tones to and from the handset.

A direct-connect modem is recommended wherever possible, primarily because there is less chance of extraneous noise accidentally getting into the line. When you travel with a computer, however, you'll find that hotel rooms are loath to have their telephones installed with modular jacks. It seems that the ease of removing the phone from the cable enhances the ease of stealing the telephone. Consequently, most hotel phones are *hard wired* to the wall. In this case, you have little choice but to use an acoustic modem. This should be a major consideration if you plan to telecommunicate and tote your Mac around with you.

To a lesser degree than with printers, modems still present some compatibility problems if you plan to wander from the path prescribed by Apple—the Applemodem. The direct-connect Applemodem—available in 300 baud and dual 300/1200 baud models—comes with an accessory kit containing all the necessary cabling for the Mac. But, there will be many Mac owners who may already own a Hayes direct-connect modem, or perhaps your travels dictate using an acoustic modem. If so, there are a number of cautions to be aware of.

First of all, you'll need to procure or make a cable linking the Mac's modem port to your modem. For this linkup, it's quite possible the cable designed for the Applemodem will work. If not, you may need to build a cable wired for Data Communications Equipment, as described later in this chapter.

The second critical factor is that so-called intelligent modems, like the Hayes Smartmodem, respond to commands from communications software (the applications program that turns your Mac into a communicating computer). Ideally, the modem and software can perform several tasks automatically for you, such as dialing the phone number for a database you wish to tap into, or waking up your computer when an incoming computer call arrives. Dual-speed modems (which operate at both 1200 and 300 baud) also have codes built in that let you change the modem's speed from the program.

Unfortunately, the standards problem gets in the way again, as it does with printers. There are no standards for intelligent modem control codes. While a number of modems adhere to the Hayes code scheme, the Apple modems do not (at least not fully). Therefore, if you use a communications program which does not have compatibility with a Hayes modem, then some of the intelligent features on that modem may not be available to you.

Acoustic modems, unfortunately, simply cannot respond to any *intelligent feature* commands. Typically, you manually dial the desired telephone number and then place the phone handset into the modem's cups. Many of the intelligent modem features of Mac-Terminal won't be usable with an acoustic modem. You will, however, still be able to use all the communications functions, including sending files and pictures to other computers, or saving incoming messages and pictures to the Mac disk.

The Macintosh-to-IBM PC Connection

Although the Macintosh is not *compatible* with other personal computers—it cannot directly run any of the other computers' software—you can still transfer text files from one computer to the other. Where this might come in handy is when you use two different computers in your work—one at the office, another at home. If you have important spreadsheets developed with Multiplan on an IBM PC at the office, you might want to work on them at home or in the field with a Macintosh. Conversely, you may have a word processing document created on the Mac that you want printed out on a computer connected to a laser printer.

To accomplish this kind of flexibility between two computers, you need communications software for each computer, a cable linking the two machines, a serial port on the PC (either the Asynchronous Communications card from IBM or any of the dozens of add-in combination boards from third-party producers with at least one serial port), and a little knowledge about how various programs structure their storage files. You won't, under any circumstances, be able to transfer IBM programs to the Mac or vice versa and expect them to run. That would be like expecting a blind Tibetan monk to convert to Christianity by giving him an English-language Bible. But when you have the same program available on the two machines (each in its own format), or when the files created by a program on one machine can be understood by another program in another machine, then the idea of a file transfer between a Mac and PC makes sense.

As it turns out, cabling the Mac to most computers can be done with a standard cable and specialized adapter. The cable that comes in the Macintosh Accessory Kit for the Imagewriter is properly configured for connection to another computer. Simply disconnect the cable from both the printer and printer port and connect the 9-pin end to the modem port. At the IBM PC end, however, you're going to have a gender problem, that is, your cable is going to have a gender problem.

The 25-pin connector on the Imagewriter cable is a male connector, denoted by the pins facing out. The serial port on the PC, however, requires a female connector (I'll let you draw your own conclusions as to the origin of the connector terminology). You'll have to add what is called a *female gender changer*, which is nothing more than two female connectors wired back to back. Computer supplies houses like UARCO, Inc. (121 North Ninth St., DeKalb, IL 60115), Moore Business Center (P.O. Box 20, Wheeling, IL 60090), and some computer stores carry these little gadgets. At about $30, however, they're not cheap. The alternative is to wire up a custom cable for yourself with a 25-pin female connector at the PC end and a 9-pin male at the Mac end.

Once they are properly connected, here's the procedure you would go through to transfer a file from the PC to the Mac, assuming MacTerminal software on the Mac and PC-Talk III software on the PC. If you're not using these precise programs, you should be able to readily adapt our discussion to your programs, since the procedures are the same, except with different names and screens.

Make sure both computers are on speaking terms, with the same communications parameters:

- Press Alt-P on the PC to get the parameters screen, and choose number four—1200 baud, 8 data bits, 1 stop bit, no parity. That's all you need to worry about on the PC.
- In MacTerminal, pull down the Settings menu and adjust items in the Terminal, Compatibility, and File Transfer settings as follows: set the Terminal Settings for TTY and 80 column line width; set the Compatibility options for 1200 baud, 8 bits per character (data bits), no parity, XON/XOFF handshake, connection to another computer, and the phone port as the connection point; set the File Transfer options to Xmodem as the transfer method, and "Other" as the remote system.
- Now save the settings on the MacTerminal disk by selecting Save As. . . from the File menu and assigning a name like "PC-to-

Mac." Hereafter, you'll be able to get into these settings by opening the icon with this name.

- At this point, the two computers should be communicating with each other. Type a few characters on each keyboard, and look for those characters to appear on the display screen of the other computer.
- If the characters are garbled, there is something amiss in the parameters department. Double-check the settings on both computers to make sure they are identical.
- If you get nothing on the screen at all, then something is rotten in the cabling department. Double-check that the cable is firmly connected to the modem port on the Mac (not the printer port) and to the communications port on the PC.

Now it's time to perform a file transfer. The method we'll use is the Xmodem protocol. This file transfer scheme is fairly recent, but very popular for transferring files between computers over the phone line.

Without getting too technical, I'll mention that the Xmodem transfer does a bit of error detection during transfer. Data is sent in 128-character blocks. The receiving computer sends each block back to the originating computer, where the block is compared against what was just transmitted. If there is a discrepancy, the block is sent again. The net effect of these extra steps is that accurate data transfer is assured. While it is unlikely that data errors will occur between two directly-linked computers, MacTerminal's quirks in other modes make Xmodem file transfer the easiest to accomplish.

The first file transfer we'll do is from the PC to the Mac.

- Place the disk with the file to be transferred in one of your PC disk drives.
- Select Receive A File. . . from the Mac File menu. Respond to the dialog box by typing in the name you want to give the document on your Mac disk. The Mac should be ready to receive.
- On the PC keyboard, press Alt-T (transmit a file).
- Type in the name of the file on the PC disk you want to send, making sure you type in the disk drive designation if other than the current drive and the "=x" Xmodem designation after the file name (e.g., b: filename = x).

The PC disk whirs for a second, and PC-Talk starts sending blocks one at a time. As each is received and verified, the MacTerminal block counter on the screen increments by one. Both computers will pause occasionally as one writes data to the disk, while the other fetches more to send.

When the end of the file is reached at the PC, the PC-Talk program beeps to let you know it's through. The Mac file automatically closes, returning you to the regular communications mode.

That's all there is to it. You may then want to copy the file to another disk for use with an application program, like MacWrite or Word.

Now, let's transfer a file from the Mac to the PC. Assuming all the parameters are still set from our earlier experiment, it's time to reverse the procedure.

- First, press Alt-R (receive a file) on the PC, and type in a name for the file soon to reside on a PC disk. Be sure to add the "=x" Xmodem designation.
- Go over to the Mac and select the Send a File. . . option from the File menu.
- Use the scroll bars to locate the name of the file you wish to transmit, select it, and click the Send button. After a couple of seconds, MacTerminal's Xmodem transfer indicator starts moving from 0 to 100 percent completion. On the PC-Talk screen, each received block is noted and verified.
- When the file finishes, both transfer routines end automatically. Your file is ready to use.

The Macintosh-to-Model 100 Connection

I bring up the Radio Shack TRS-80 Model 100 computer in this chapter because it has become a portable computer that is rather popular with writers and reporters. Many use this battery-powered, lap computer to compose on the fly, and then return to the office to transfer the text to a more powerful word processing program on a desktop computer. There's no reason you can't use the Macintosh for this desktop task.

Connecting the Model 100 to the Mac is about the simplest of any computer-to-computer links. The Imagewriter cable is an exact fit for the Mac modem port to Model 100 serial port link. Without any modification or gender changes, this cable joins the two computers in holy communication.

On the Mac end, you'll still need a telecommunications program. We'll use MacTerminal in our example. Inside the Model 100 is a built-in telecommunications program, which normally works very easily in computer-to-computer transfers, but exhibits a few problems when sending data to MacTerminal. For the moment, however, we'll use it to make sure our cabling works properly.

- From the Model 100's main menu, select the TELCOM program.
- Press F3 (Stat) to set the Model 100's communications parameters. We may as well be consistent with the parameters we've been using in this chapter: 1200 baud, 8 data bits, 1 stop bit, and XON/XOFF enabled. Set the Model 100 to Ignore Parity. Therefore, the complete Stat command line should read: 58I1E (5 is the Model 100 code for 1200 baud). Press ⟨ENTER⟩ to set those parameters in motion.
- Then press F4 (Term) to go into terminal mode.
- Select the various MacTerminal settings (from the Settings menu) as described for the Mac-to-IBM communication, above, but do not select Xmodem file transfer.
- Save these settings by selecting Save As. . . from the File menu. Give the file a name like "Mac-to-M100." Hereafter, you'll be able to get into these settings by simply opening the icon with this name.

At this point, you should be able to tap a few keys from each keyboard and have letters appear on the opposite computer's display. One note: pressing the Return key on the Mac keyboard does not advance the cursor to the next line of the Model 100 screen, as you might expect. Likewise, the Model 100 Enter key doesn't advance the cursor to the next line of the MacTerminal screen, either. Each computer needs an explicit linefeed command from the other to advance the cursor. To test this out, press Command-J (hold down the Command key and press the J key) a few times on the Mac keyboard, and Control-J on the Model 100 keyboard. This key sequence sends the linefeed signal through the modem port to the Model 100. Notice how the cursors advance down the screen.

MacTerminal is very unorthodox in the way it captures text from its screen for storage (downloading) to a disk file. In fact, its method is so unlike the way most communications programmers would expect it to work that you really cannot use MacTerminal and the Model 100's TELCOM program together to transfer data from the portable to the Mac. You can, however, make such a transfer with the help of a short BASIC program, which you can type into your Model 100 and save in memory (Save "TOMAC") for use at any time:

```
10 REM    **    M100-to-MAC File Transfer Program
20 REM    ** for the TRS-80 Model 100 Portable Computer
100 CLEAR:CLS:MAXFILES=2
110 LF$=CHR$(10)+CHR$(13)
120 FILES
130 PRINT@245,"";:INPUT".DO File To Send";F$:F$=F$+".DO"
140 OPENF$FORINPUTAS1
150 OPEN"COM:58n1e"FOROUTPUTAS2
160 C$=INPUT$(1,1)
170 IFEOF(1)THENPRINT#2,LF$:PRINT#2,CHR$(7):GOTO1000
180 IF C$<>CHR$(10)THENPRINT#2,C$;ELSEPRINT#2,LF$;
190 GOTO160
1000 CLOSE:BEEP
1010 CLS:PRINT@125,F$;" Transfer Complete"
1020 PRINT@245,"Transfer Another? (Y/N)"
1030 Q$=INKEY$:IFQ$=""THEN1030
1040 IFQ$="Y"ORQ$="y"THEN100
1050 MENU
```

This program operates in lieu of the TELCOM program and adds some important control codes to the data being transferred to the Mac.

You must also make one change to the Terminal settings on MacTerminal to use this special Model 100 program. Select "Auto Wraparound" on the Terminal Settings dialog box.

To transfer text from the Model 100 to the Mac:

- Exit the TELCOM program if you used it to test your cable and parameters.
- Run the program given above on the Model 100 by moving the menu pointer to the program name and pressing the Enter key. A list of files, including all text files, in the portable computer will appear on the LCD screen.
- Type the name of the file you want to send from the Model 100 to the Mac. Don't type the ".DO" extension, because the program does that for you.
- The text will appear on the MacTerminal screen during the transfer.
- When the transfer is complete, both computers will beep.
- Perform a Save As. . . on the Mac, and give the downloaded file a name when prompted.

Once the file is transferred, Quit MacTerminal and go into MacWrite or Word. You will find that, unfortunately, the Auto Wraparound feature has added hard carriage returns (the equivalent of a press of the Return key) at the end of every line as received on the 80-column MacTerminal screen. This means that, when viewing the document in MacWrite, for example, your paragraphs will be all chopped up—as if you had originally typed the document and pressed the Return key every 80 characters. Before you can edit your document, you will have to manually remove the extra carriage returns by placing the text insertion pointer at the *left* margin of the long lines and pressing the Backspace key. It's quite a nuisance, to be sure.

Fortunately, most other Mac telecommunications programs let you use the Model 100's TELCOM program without these hassles. If you plan to do a lot of this kind of transfer, you should investigate other Mac software, including a program called MacTEP (Macintosh Terminal Emulator Program), which is available from most Mac user groups and the CompuServe Special Interest Group devoted to Apple computers (called MAUG, for Micronetworked Apple Users Group—for more about this organization, see "Communications for Free Software" later in this chapter).

In case you have a MacWrite/Word document that you want to take with you for editing while on the run, you can transfer documents to the Model 100 using the Model 100's built-in TELCOM program. Here's how:

- Save your document on the Mac as a Text Only file. You must always do this in order to transmit it to the Model 100.
- Connect the two computers through their respective serial ports.
- Enter the TELCOM program on the Model 100, and configure the status line to read 58I1E.
- Press F2 (Down) on the Model 100, and type in the name of the file you want for the incoming text.
- On the Mac, select Send File from the File menu, and choose the appropriate file from the list presented in the dialog box.
- When the transfer is complete, press F2 again on the Model 100 to close the file.
- If you find that some characters were lost in the transfer (quite possible if the original file has lots of blank lines at the beginning), then repeat the above procedures, but change the speed of MacTerminal (Compatibility setting) to 300 baud, and the Model 100 TELCOM status to 38I1E.

After your trip, you can bring the Model 100 back to your Mac, and retransfer the document for further editing or printing on the Imagewriter. All your previous formatting and enhancements, however, will not have survived the transfer process. You'll have to go back through and add the underlinings, line centerings, and other formatting you had in mind.

The Macintosh-to-Apple II Connection

Linking up a Mac to an Apple II is very similar to what we discussed for the IBM PC and Model 100. The needed software and hardware elements are the same—communications software on both ends, an available serial port on the Apple II, and a cable to bring the two together.

Cabling an Apple IIe is essentially the same as an IBM PC, if it has the optional serial adapter card that provides a 25-pin serial connector. The connector on the serial card, however, is a female type, so you can use the Imagewriter printer cable as your serial link (connected to the modem port on the Mac).

Cabling for the Apple IIc is a little different, since the serial port is built into the IIc and the connector is a completely different type, called a DIN connector. The last part of this chapter describes how to construct such a serial cable.

The same rules about setting up communications software on both ends apply as they do for other link ups. Text files from the Apple II to the Mac must be in ASCII for MacWrite or Word to interpret them. Applewriter documents are stored in ASCII, so no conversion is necessary. AppleWorks files, however, must first be printed to an ASCII file—it is that ASCII file which is then transferred to the Mac. In the opposite direction, a Text Only file from MacWrite/Word is readable by AppleWorks and Applewriter. If your Apple II word processing software is other than these two, check for ASCII compatibility before getting too involved with file transfers.

■ ■ ■ ■ ■ ■ _____

File Compatibility

Where most dreams of file transfer shatter is in the realization that files can be strange animals when mixing them with different programs—even on the same computer. If all word processing documents were stored as ASCII character files, there would be no compatibility problems. But programs like MacWrite on the Mac and WordStar on the PC store their documents as specially coded files which only those programs (or those very similar to them) can successfully load into memory. On the plus side, however, are programs like Multiplan, which place a strong emphasis on being compatible with the same program running on other computers. Therefore, if you have a Multiplan spreadsheet stored in a particular way on a Mac disk, you can transfer it to an IBM PC disk file, which can in turn be read successfully by Multiplan running on the PC.

The trick, then, is knowing ahead of time which files can be transferred and which ones cannot. I can present some guidelines here for text kinds of programs (word processing and database programs), but they are only guidelines. The entire subject of file transfer among different computers and different programs is a complex one. Often, the only way to determine compatibility is to actually try a transfer to see if everything works. That's a tall order to accomplish at a computer store, to be sure, but with any luck, your dealer should be understanding enough to let you try the link up. Above all, don't just take the dealer's word for it that such-and-such a program on the PC is fully compatible with so-and-so a program on the Mac. It's tough enough to be compatible between PC compatibles, much less between a PC and a Mac. Seeing is believing. Bring your cables to the store, if you need to.

First of all, if you are intent on transferring word processing files from another computer to the Mac for use with MacWrite or Word, you should know ahead of time that both of these programs do accept straight ASCII files. That means that the files on the PC must be stored as ASCII files, with no other formatting commands or extraneous characters included. Often, a PC word processing program that normally stores its text in a coded format also gives you the option of making a copy of the document in ASCII form (sometimes called a DOS file). If so, then your transfer should be a success. Be aware, however, that any text enhancements you have in the text (boldface, underlining, etc.) will not be transferred along with the text. Even if they were—as some programs store beginning and ending markers for these enhanced sections—MacWrite and Word won't know what to do with them. They'll simply interpret any extra characters as actual text characters, and you'll have to go through the text and remove them manually.

Since WordStar is such a popular word processing program on computers other than the Mac, I should say a few things about it. It is possible to store WordStar documents as text files—but it means knowing beforehand that you want the document to be an ASCII file only (called a *nondocument file* in WordStar lingo). Doing so, however, means that you lose all the power of WordStar to format text on the screen, display page breaks, count page numbers, and so on. Once you create a file as a Document File, there's no turning back. The program automatically inserts carriage returns at the end of each line where the lines word wrap. These carriage returns are sent along with the text when transferred over to the Mac. It's a good idea to eliminate these carriage returns from the file before sending it by replacing the ASCII equivalent of the carriage return (^M) with nothing. Unfortunately, you have to do this on a line-by-line basis; to do this to the entire file would also erase valid carriage returns between paragraphs. If you leave them in the file during transfer, MacWrite and Word, of course, interpret these carriage returns as true carriage returns, thereby eliminating any hope of reformatting paragraphs without first deleting each and every word-wrapped carriage return—what a waste of time.

If you investigate some of the IBM PC user group dial-up bulletin boards (*PC World* magazine lists several such bulletin boards in each issue), you may find programs (which you can download) that convert WordStar files to ASCII files. So far, however, I haven't seen one that successfully removes the soft carriage returns of word wrapping. Therefore, until someone comes up with a better solution, WordStar files will be very difficult to work with on the Mac.

Transferring MacWrite and Word documents to the IBM PC is much easier. Both programs have a Save option that lets you store a copy of the document as a Text Only file—Mac terminology for ASCII file. This option converts your beautifully formatted and enhanced MacWrite or Word document into unadorned text blocks, each paragraph looking like one long sentence. WordStar accepts ASCII text in this form and converts it to a true WordStar file. You'll have to go back through the document and realign the paragraphs (the ^Q^Q^B quick reformat command will do it for the entire document unattended), and add enhancements like boldface and centered lines, but you'll save a lot of retyping in the end.

Transferring files from a database program contains the same perils that a spreadsheet transfer holds. In other words, the programs on both computers must store information—the way it groups records, separates items in each record, and so on—in exactly the same formats. If the storage formats of both programs aren't identical, the transfer from one computer to the other won't be of any use to you.

One kind of transfer you won't have any trouble with is moving files from Macintosh to Macintosh via modem. In fact it is only with the Mac that you can communicate a picture from MacPaint, for example, and have it reproduced on another computer. Until such time as another computer manufacturer makes a Macintosh-compatible computer, no other computer will be able to use graphics files transmitted from the Mac.

Communications for Free Software

One final note about communicating on the Mac. Aside from all the other productive things telecommunicating is good for, you can use your Macintosh, communications software, and modem to retrieve tons of practically free software from CompuServe and Mac user group bulletin boards. Before we see exactly what these services may cost, let's examine what's available, and how easy it is to get it.

CompuServe, one of the largest consumer-oriented databases in the country, has a Special Interest Group (now called a Forum) devoted to Apple computers. Of course, before the Mac was introduced, the Forum was used exclusively for exchanging messages, news, and programs related to the Apple II and Apple III. But not long after the Macintosh was in general circulation, this Forum exploded with contributors offering all kinds of interesting software and help for the perplexed (the Mac portion may eventually break off into its own Forum). Most of the programs placed on the system during the first half of 1984 were written with Microsoft BASIC, the only readily available programming language for the general public. Soon, however, programs appeared in Forth and MacPascal, as these languages reached the market. In most cases, a program you download from CompuServe requires that you own a copy of the language in which the program is written. A few programs, however, are in machine code and run by themselves (although they need to be converted by a "binary-to-hexadecimal" utility program available from MAUG and user groups). To gain access to these programs from CompuServe, you must first subscribe to Compu-Serve. Many computer stores have a CompuServe starter kit which contains a temporary account number and password, which you use until your application goes through and you become a full-fledged subscriber. Then you need to join the Apple Forum, which is called Micronetworked Apple User's Group, or MAUG for short. To join—it costs nothing to join—simply go to the CompuServe "page" on which the Forum starts (all services are listed by "page number," as if you were browsing through an electronic book).

■ From the command level (the ! prompt) type: "GO PCS-51".

- You are prompted on screen to leave a message for the System Operator (SYSOP) that you want to join.
- Within a couple of days, your name will be added to the MAUG roster, and you'll have access to every service therein.

You'll probably want to read through the messages, since frequently you'll see queries from newcomers who are looking for help, as well as advice from more experienced Mac users on the Forum. But the real meat is in the data library part of the Forum. To gain access to it:

- From the MAUG function menu, type "DL".
- You'll be prompted for a data library number to access. As of this writing, databases number four and eight are the ones containing the bulk of Mac programs, but consult the general information files noted at sign-on for more detailed and up-to-date information.
- The best way to acquaint yourself with all the programs in the database is to select the Browse option from the data library menu. This presents a listing of each program (starting with the most recent addition), complete with program name, author, date of submission, and synopsis of what the program is.
- Either make notes about program names that interest you, or download the information to disk as it comes in.
- If you saw a program you'd like to have, when you are finished browsing return to the data library menu.
- Type "DOW" plus the full name of the file you wish to download. If you are presented with a list of transfer protocols, select Xmodem.
- Be sure you have Xmodem file transfer selected from the File Transfer dialog box of MacTerminal.
- Start the Receive A File. . . procedure for MacTerminal (or the equivalent procedure if you are using a different communications program).
- When the transfer is complete, press the Return key to get back to the MAUG data library command level.
- Repeat the procedure for any other programs you want to transfer (although the first time, it may be wise to try just one program to make sure you have the hang of it before running up connect charges).

To try your program:

- Exit from the data library by typing "OFF". That clears you from the Forum and logs you off CompuServe in one move.
- Quit MacTerminal and load in a word processing program.
- Open the newly downloaded file and check the beginning and end of the file for extraneous lines which might throw the program off if the language disk encounters them. Usually, you'll want the first line of a program to be at the very top of the document. At the end, some CompuServe prompts usually sneak their way onto your document, so delete them.
- Next, quit your word processing program and load your language disk.
- Open the new program file.

If all went well in the transfer, you should be the proud owner of a new piece of running software.

Self-running programs, MacPaint pictures, text fonts, some BASIC programs, and text files downloaded over the phone aren't usable until you run them through a binary-to-hexadecimal conversion program. Most user groups and MAUG have such utilities which run under MS-BASIC, MacForth, and other languages. When you sign onto MAUG, read the general information files for the latest information on these "BINHEX" programs.

As this book goes to press, an expanded version of MAUG is to be available through a different telecommunications network, called Delphi. Like CompuServe, Delphi is accessible through local telephone numbers around the country. The plans call for the Macintosh part of Delphi's MAUG to be divided into two groups, one for Mac developers, one for Mac users. The CompuServe and Delphi MAUGs will probably share the same libraries of public-domain software for downloading, but the message and conference areas will be different. For more information about the current status and costs for MAUG on Delphi, write to Delphi at General Videotext Corporation, 3 Blackstone Street, Cambridge, MA 02139.

Several Macintosh users' groups around the country also offer program library services like MAUG's, but only to their members. You must first join the group to get the phone number to the bulletin board and a password. If one of these groups is in your community, then the cost won't be much. But if you have to call long distance, your connect charges might get high if you log on frequently. CompuServe and Delphi, at least, offer local telephone numbers in hundreds of cities across the country, reducing the phone cost substantially.

Signing up for CompuServe is free, although the introduction kits at the computer store cost around $20. After that, the only charges you'll have are connect-time charges. During evenings and weekends, connect time is under $8 per hour.

Macintosh user groups can cost $35 to $50 per year to join, and usually include a monthly newsletter for the fee. Some clubs even offer monthly program disks to its members, which can save on the long-distance charges, to be sure. To find out more about Mac user groups, read *Macworld* magazine (555 De Haro St., San Francisco, CA 94107). Also, you can put a query on the CompuServe Forum, and someone will surely know if there's a group near you.

Making the Physical Connection

Even though there are cables around to do most of the serial port connection jobs you might have for the Mac, you may still need to build a cable for special equipment. If so, it's time to learn about the pins that make up the Macintosh serial port. Both serial ports are identical as far as the actual pins on the rear panel connectors go. Therefore, what I say in this section goes for both ports.

First of all, the 9-pin connectors on the back of the Mac are designed according to a particular serial communications standard called RS-422 (the RS stands for Recommended Standard, and the number is one assigned by an industry standards committee). As of yet, this standard is not as widely used as is a simpler serial communications standard called RS-232C. Most serial communications, serial printers (including the Imagewriter), modems, and other personal computers subscribe to the more popular RS-232C standard. Although not RS-232C ports per se, the Mac serial ports, however, do support RS-232C when the cable connectors are wired in a particular way.

It turns out that the odd-numbered pins on the 9-pin connectors are the ones used for RS-232C communications. The pins contain signals as follows:

PIN	SIGNAL DESIGNATION
1	Frame Ground
3	Signal Ground
5	Receive Data (from the Mac to the device)
7	Data Terminal Ready (signal from the Mac that it is ready to send data)
9	Send Data (to the Mac from the device)

The devices to which you will be connecting the Mac have a different kind of connector on them—a long, 25-pin connector called a DB-25. Of those 25 connections, however, you need to concern yourself about only five of them—the same signal lines coming from the Mac serial port (some of the other pins are used for other devices subscribing to the RS-232C interface, but not for what you'll be doing with the Mac).

How you link the signals between the Mac 9-pin connector and the 25-pin connector, however, depends on what kind of device you're hooking up with. And, frankly, this is where things might get a bit confusing. A serial device, you see, is configured either as Data Terminal Equipment (DTE) or Data Communications Equipment (DCE). The distinction is this: DTE is like the Mac, a printer, or another personal computer you're communicating with, which either transmits or receives data; DCE is a device like a modem, which acts merely as an intermediary between two pieces of Data Terminal Equipment. In other words, if you have two computers hooked up directly to each other, they are both considered Data Terminal Equipment, because each unit is at an ultimate end of the link. But if the two computers are linked via a modem (one modem per computer, with the modems communicating over a telephone line), each modem is considered Data Communications Equipment.

It's a weird distinction, to be sure. And the only difference in the connections is how the send data and receive data lines—pins 2 and 3 of the 25-pin connector—are wired. Let's see how this affects wiring a cable that will link up a Mac to another computer (like an IBM PC) or to a non-Apple modem, as we build such a cable, wire by wire.

A word of caution: *Making cables for computers is no simple task, espe-*

cially if you've never used a soldering iron before. Even if you have soldering experience (built any Heathkits lately?), the close quarters of 9- and 25-pin connectors can make for some frustrating hours. Therefore, if you cannot locate prewired cables, then I strongly suggest you try to locate a friend who is experienced at soldering electronic components. And, while there are such things on the market as solderless connectors, they won't work when you don't have the same connectors and connections at each end—as is the case with making Mac serial cables.

For parts, you can go to any Radio Shack outlet and look for the 9-pin male connector (part number 276-1537) and the 25-pin connector (part number 276-1547 male or 276-1548 female, depending on the connector requirements on your serial device). For cable, you can use either the flat ribbon cable (part number 278-772 for a five foot section of 25-conductor cable) or round cable available from some computer supply retailers and mail order firms in 9- or 12-conductor sizes. In the case of the Radio Shack ribbon cable, simply tear off the needed length of only five conductors; for round cable, snip away unused conductors at each end, leaving the five you need (they're color coded to help you know which is which).

Working with these connectors is no easy task because the pin numbers on the connectors are very hard to see. Moreover, when you look at drawings of the connectors in the manuals you can never be quite sure if the picture you're looking at is of the connector on the device or the connector on the cable to attach to the device. Fortunately, the numbers of the pins are the same on both, so always go by the numbers—even if you need a magnifying glass to see them. The numbers are usually raised characters on the plastic insulating material around the pins. Look very closely in good light, and you'll find them.

I'm going to assume that you're going the Radio Shack ribbon cable route, since it is the least expensive and most accessible. Prepare both ends of the cable before you start wiring. Separate the individual wires, so each wire at each end has about one inch free. Use a wire stripper to remove about $\frac{1}{16}$ inch of insulation from the end of each wire. If individual strands of wire from any line are sticking out in disarray, twist them so they are tightly wound, as one wire.

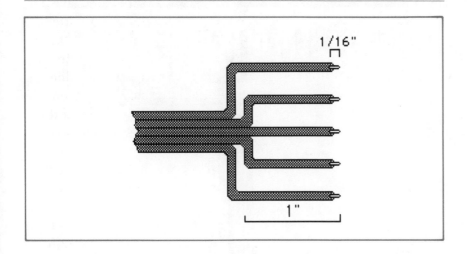

Next, use the soldering iron to *tin* each wire. This means heating the wire with the iron tip and dabbing a small amount of solder on each end. This serves to hold the individual strands in place and provides each wire with enough solder to hold it in place during an upcoming critical step.

Start with the 9-pin connector. Stick the tinned end of either of the outside wires of the ribbon cable into the hole of the solder lug of pin 1. Verify that you have the correct pin before you do anything else. When you are sure you have the correct pin, hold the wire in the hole with a pair of needle-nose pliers (you may have to brace the plug side of the connector against something heavy to keep it from sliding around the table during soldering), and apply the soldering iron to the juncture of the wire and the solder lug. Within a couple of seconds, the solder from the tinned wire will flow onto the inside of the solder lug, holding the lead in place temporarily. Remove the soldering iron tip from the connection.

At the other end of the cable, perform the same solder operation *with the same outside wire of the ribbon cable* to pin 1 of the 25-pin connector (again, verify that you indeed have pin 1 before soldering). Now, solder the next available wire (adjacent to the one used for the pin 1 connection) to pin 7 of the 9-pin connector. With the following illustration as your guide, continue to solder the rest of the connections on both connectors.

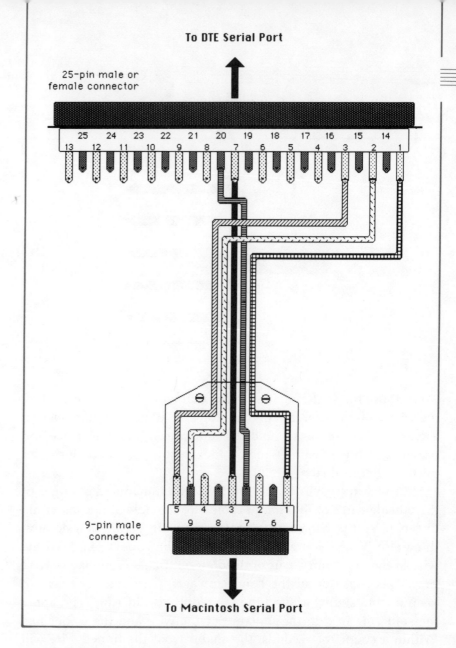

To DTE Serial Port

25-pin male or
female connector

9-pin male
connector

To Macintosh Serial Port

The key connections to watch out for are the way you wire pins 2 and 3 of the 25-pin connector.

As you can see in the illustration, pin 2 is connected to pin 9 of the Mac connector, while pin 3 is wired to pin 5 of the Mac connector. This order is for a Data Terminal Equipment connection—if you're using the cable to attach to a serial printer or directly to another computer. If you're using the cable for connection to a modem or other Data Communications Equipment, then you want to reverse the connections at pins 2 and 3 of the 25-pin connector, that is, pin 2 should be wired to the Mac's pin 5, while pin 3 goes with the Mac's pin 9.

When you're through making the initial connections, it's time to go back and firmly solder each joint. Reheat each connection and add just a small dab of solder to fill up the hole in each solder lug. Do not let solder flow between connections or between a solder lug and the metal frame of the connector. Allowing either to happen may prevent you from establishing proper communications between the Mac and the device.

If you need to make a cable for the Apple IIc, here's how the connections should go from the 9-pin Mac connector to the 5-pin IIc connector:

MAC PIN	SIGNAL	IIC PIN
1	Ground	3
3	Ground	3
5	Receive Data	4
7	Data Terminal Ready	1
9	Send Data	2

If you find yourself getting involved with a serial device having a connector other than a DB-25 or DIN-type—such as the Centronics type printer connector—use your newly found knowledge about the signals emanating from the Mac's serial ports. The signal descriptions and signal directions should be standard across the range of serial devices, so simply match up the signals between the two devices when wiring cables.

Finally, I also recommend that you finish off the job by attaching the hoods available for the two kinds of connectors we've been discussing here. Radio Shack carries them. For the 9-pin Mac connector, the hood is part number 276-1539; for the 25-pin connector, the hood is part number 276-1549. The hoods give you something firm to grab onto when plugging and unplugging the cables, while taking pressure off the solder joints by clamping the wire to the hood. Both hoods also come with screws that let you secure the plugs to the connectors on the Mac and your serial device so they won't jiggle loose.

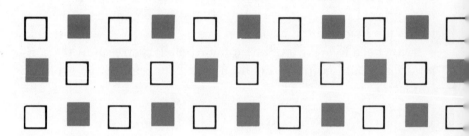

ONE OF THE truly fun aspects of a new computer, especially one with the built-in capabilities of the Mac, is looking at new software programs as they reach the market. Since the Mac environment is so different from that of any other personal computer, no amount of experience with a CP/M, MS-DOS, or Apple II/III computer is going to make you an instant expert on what makes a good Mac program and what does not.

In the early days of the IBM PC, dozens of programs that had proven successful in the CP/M environment were *ported over*— quickly translated—to the PC environment. This was relatively easy, since the environments of the two types of computers (both the technical environment and the way the computer interacted

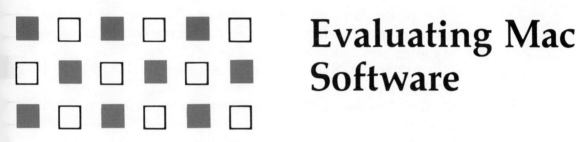

Evaluating Mac Software

with the end user) were very much the same. MS-DOS computers were, in many ways, fashioned after CP/M computers, but with the ability to accommodate more memory.

But with the Macintosh, software developers will not be able to simply adapt an already successful program to the Mac environment without violating the underlying tenets that went into the heart and soul of the machine. To create a program that does not use pull-down menus is blasphemous on the Mac. And there's much more to making a good Mac program than that. Such is the topic of this chapter—things to look for in software when you mouse around with new programs at the store.

◢ ◢ ◢ ◢ ◢ ◢ Editing Conventions

For a computer like the Mac to be labeled as truly "easy to use," it is important that the software offer a level of consistency in its most basic features. It is through consistency of functions that you will build confidence in the computer and its software. You'll always know what to press or where to look for the command that performs the elemental function you need. This is especially necessary in editing functions.

By editing, I'm talking about ways you select text, delete text, insert text, and replace text. Built into the Mac operating environment, as demonstrated in the way you edit folder, document, and disk names on the desktop, is a convention centered around the text insertion pointer and the mouse button. The ability to select an entire word by double-clicking the mouse button with the pointer anywhere on the word, or to select a block of text and immediately replace it with freshly typed text are important editing functions that should be consistent from program to program. Whether the program be a word processing, spreadsheet, or graphics program, if text is involved, you should have the exact same editing operations available on all of them.

Here's a checklist of editing features to try out:

1. Place the text pointer anywhere in a word and press the Backspace key. The letter to the left of the pointer should disappear, and the word close up around that space.
2. Double-click the mouse button with the pointer in the same word. The entire word should be selected (highlighted). Without pressing the mouse button start typing a new word. The first word should disappear and the new letters appear in its place.
3. At this point, you should have an Undo command available—preferably in the Edit pull-down menu. Invoking this command—it should also have the command-key equivalent of Command-Z—should restore the original word, less the one letter you backspaced over in step 1.

4. Finally, select one word as in step 2, invoke the Cut command (preferably with the Command-X keyboard equivalent), move the cursor to the end of the document, and paste it (Command-V).

If the program passes this minimum editing test, it will be consistent with programs like MacWrite, MacPaint, and many others already on the market. At the same time, however, don't let yourself be limited by these commands. If a program comes up with a logical and practical extension of these commands, then study them closely to see if they make sense to you. For example, Microsoft Word lets you select a line of text by positioning the pointer anywhere in the left margin next to the line and clicking the mouse button; double-clicking in the margin selects the entire paragraph. These conventions make sense to me as logical shortcuts, so I rate those editing enhancements good ones.

◢ ◢ ◢ ◢ ◢ ◢ Keyboard Commands

Another important point to check for in a new program is the availability of keyboard command equivalents for many of the commands in the pull-down menus. This can get out of hand, as we'll see, but it is better to have them than not to have them, and wish you did.

Keyboard command equivalents—with the exception of uniform commands like Cut, Copy, Paste, and Undo—are rarely consistent from program to program. One programmer's name for a particular function is different from another's, as one's concept of what is easy to remember differs from another's. For example, in MacPaint, you can select three ways of entering text in relation to the text pointer: Aligned Left, Middle, or Right. The keyboard equivalents, as shown in the Style menu, are Command-L, Command-M, and Command-R respectively. In this case, the programmer went with mnemonic keyboard commands—the command letter is the same as the first letter of the key word of the command. But if you then go over to Multiplan and want to align your column headings to the left, middle, or right of a column, the keyboard commands are Command-F, Command-G, and Command-H respectively. In this layout, the programmer found three keys in a row, both physically and alphabetically. I'm more likely to remember the MacPaint way of doing it, but if I use the Multiplan functions enough, sooner or later they'll become second nature.

A point I want to make about keyboard shortcuts is that you shouldn't feel obligated to use the mouse when a keyboard shortcut you've mastered is handy. If you're typing away on a MacWrite document and you wish to boldface a word, it is much more productive for you to issue the keyboard command than to take a hand away from the keyboard to pull down a menu with the mouse. By the same token, you should not feel pressured into mastering the keyboard commands immediately. It is more important that you become familiar and comfortable with the flow of a program, using the mouse to explore all the menus. Once you've established a work pattern with the program, then keep a lookout on the menus as you pull them down for keyboard equivalents. Slowly work the keyboard commands into your work pattern, provided they fit logically into improving your productivity with the program. The goal, after all, is to accomplish more work in less time.

When looking at a new piece of Mac software, then, make it one of your first tasks to pull down all the primary menus, which appear across the top of the screen of the program once you've started it. Notice how many commands have keyboard equivalents. The more the merrier.

◢ ◢ ◢ ◢ ◢ ◢ Mouse and Keyboard Work Flow

Testing a new piece of software for the next criterion may take some time, depending on the complexity of the program. What you should look for is the flow of keyboard and mouse input such that the steps for often-performed procedures involve either a string of mouse maneuvers or a string of keyboard maneuvers. Avoid programs that force you to hop from keyboard to mouse to keyboard to accomplish certain operations. Let's look at some bad and good examples.

Some of the worst instances of ergonomic gymnastics are in a word processing program like MacWrite. Specifically, the motions needed to select a word that is to be replaced by another typed from the keyboard places inordinate demands on the hand. Let's say you're typing some text and realize that you want to substitute a better word for one you left back in the last line. You must take one hand away from the keyboard to move the text insertion pointer to the errant word and double-click it to select it. Then you have to come back to the keyboard to type in the new word. After that, you must reposition the text pointer to the end of the document or wherever else you want to perform further work.

Since a word processing program is so keyboard intensive (due to its text entry demands), anytime there are mouse manipulations involved, such movements should be strung together to keep your mouse hand active for a few commands or pointings before releasing the hand for the keyboard. Keyboard command equivalents help reduce the need for mouse manipulations for a single command while entering text. Therefore, programs with many keyboard command equivalents will likely earn a high mark in keeping your hands on the keys when it is most productive.

In contrast to the above example is Multiplan. This program not only groups mouse movements together nicely, you also use the mouse to establish a nice work flow with the keyboard. If you wish to enter figures in two or more columns down a page, you can use the mouse to select the block of cells into which your entries are intended. The program knows that whenever a block such as this is selected, text entry from the keyboard is to proceed in an orderly fashion, left to right, across each succeeding row. Each time you press the Enter key following a keyboard entry of figures or labels, the cursor advances to the next appropriate cell in the sequence— thereby eliminating the need to pick up your hand to move the mouse to select the next cell.

My favorite programs, however, such as graphics programs like MacPaint and MacDraw, are those that work almost entirely in a single entry medium—in both these cases, the mouse. Except for the entry of text blocks, there is practically no need to bring the mouse hand into contact with the keyboard. You still need the keyboard occasionally for a press of the Shift, Command, or Option keys in conjunction with the mouse button, but all that can be done with one hand on the mouse, the other on the keyboard.

◢ ◢ ◢ ◢ ◢ ◢ **Mouse Shortcuts**

You should also seek out those programs that are designed with shortcuts built in such that you don't have to move the mouse pointer across the entire screen just to perform a single function. While the mouse is a relatively simple control to use, it is still desirable to keep mouse movement and particularly the need for precision mouse movement to a minimum. MacPaint, Multiplan, and Microsoft Word feature some wonderful mouse shortcuts worth noting as examples of things to look for in new programs.

In MacPaint, for example, getting into FatBits by double-clicking the pencil icon represents a saving over having to open a pull-down menu to select the FatBits option. Similarly, the ability to get out of FatBits by simply clicking the pointer anywhere inside the normal-size drawing window is an ideal example of saving both lateral movement to the pencil icon or to the pull-down Goodies menu. And finally, while in FatBits, the shortcut of combining the Option key with the pencil icon selection, turning the pencil pointer into the hand for dragging the picture around, is pure design genius when it comes to reducing the potential back-and-forth motion between selecting the pencil and hand icons alternately.

In Multiplan, a mouse shortcut helps speed scrolling in any direction through a spreadsheet. By dragging the pointer to any side of the window, the spreadsheet scrolls before your eyes. This sure beats the precision necessary to shift the spreadsheet the correct amount with the scroll bars.

And in Microsoft Word, a noteworthy mouse shortcut is the one that selects complete paragraphs. Instead of carefully positioning the text pointer at one end of the paragraph and dragging the selected area to the opposite end, all you need to do is bring the text pointer anywhere in the margin to the left of the paragraph and click the mouse button. Instantly, the entire paragraph is selected for a further operation.

It may not be so easy finding mouse shortcuts while exploring a fresh piece of software in a store. In some cases, the shortcut may not even be covered in the program's manual. Only by working with the program on a daily basis will some of them surface. At best, you can look to the program and its manuals and hope somewhere in the table of contents or index there is a listing under "mouse shortcuts."

◢ ◢ ◢ ◢ ◢ ◢ Minimum Typing Requirement

We noted in Chapter 2 that with a single disk drive system, you will be more likely to perform these all-important periodic saves of your current document if you temporarily transfer a copy of that document to your program disk. With that arrangement, you won't have to bother swapping disks to make frequent save operations. But no matter how many drives you have, you should also maintain a backup storage disk for your documents, saving each updated document to that disk after safely saving the document to your regular storage disk. On a well-designed Mac program, all this document transferring should be handled from within the program without typing a single character.

To illustrate how a program should handle this, use MacPaint or MacWrite (and a storage disk) to follow along these steps:

1. Start up the Mac with your program disk, eject the disk, and insert a storage disk with some documents on it.
2. Open a document icon.
3. Obey the dialog boxes for swapping disks between the storage disk and the appropriate program disk.
4. Once you are in the program, with your document on the screen, perform a Save As. . . command from the File menu.
5. On a well-designed program, the name of the document will already be shown in the document name blank, highlighted in reverse.

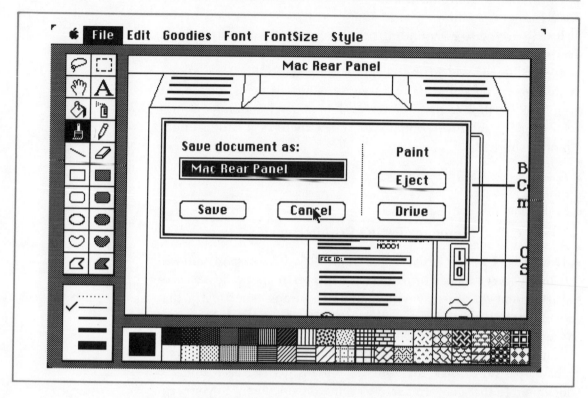

6. To save the document to the current disk (the program disk will also be preselected for you), either click the Save box or press the Return key on the keyboard.

Step 5 is the key one. By having the name of the current document already in the dialog box, you are spared the need of thinking of what the name of the document is, and retyping it. As long as that document name is in the box, you can eject and insert disks all day long, making copy after copy on each disk.

In a dual-drive system, this will save time if you also maintain a backup storage disk (as I recommend). When you are through with your session, perform a Save As. . . command, select your external drive, eject the main storage disk, insert the backup, and either click the Save box or press the Return key on the keyboard.

Of course, if you wish to change the name of the document on any of the copies you make, you can do it by simply typing the desired name when the dialog box is displayed. Since the original name is already selected (highlighted), the program should let you start typing the new name immediately, while the old name disappears—provided the program is following the editing conventions described earlier in this chapter.

The test in the store, then, should go something like this.

- Start up the application and enter some kind of saveable data in the program (numbers in a spreadsheet, words in a word processing program, a data entry form in a database program, etc.).
- Perform a Save As. . . command.
- Assign a document name (your name or "test") and save the document.
- Make one more entry or edit onto the document currently on the screen.
- Again issue the Save As. . . command.
- The dialog box should appear with your original document name highlighted. If so, the program passes the minimum typing test.
- Try to rename the document by typing another document name. If the old one disappears and the new letters you type appear in the box, the program will probably pass the editing conventions test as well.

▲ ▲ ▲ ▲ ▲ ▲ **Minimum Human Memory Requirement**

As long as we're using the Mac's powers to help reduce our typing requirements, we should expect the Mac to help us reduce our reliance on memory for things we shouldn't have to keep track of—such as document names. To illustrate, I will use examples of one way it should be and one way it most definitely should not be.

For my good example, I can take any of the Apple brand Mac software. When I issue the Open command from the File menu (from within an application), a dialog box appears on the screen complete with a scrollable, alphabetical directory of documents that can be opened from the application. To open any document, all I need to do is bring its name into the little window and double-click the pointer over it (I can also select the name and click the Open box, but that takes more mouse movement than is necessary). At most, you may have to decipher your own document names if you didn't adhere to the guidelines detailed in Chapter 2.

In any case, this is the way to go when it comes to opening a document from within an application.

An example of the worst-case possibility in opening a document comes from Microsoft BASIC (the original version, 1.00). When you select the Open option from the File menu, you are presented with this dialog box.

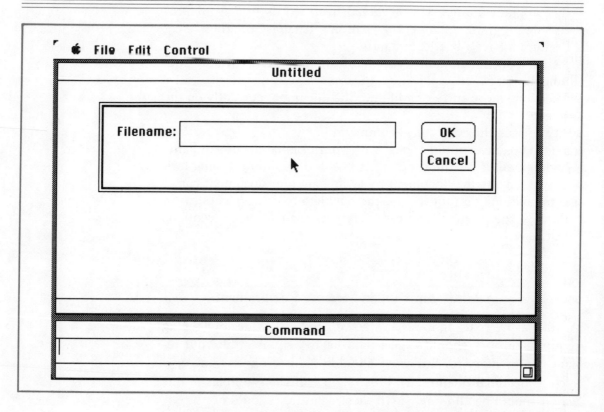

All it does is ask you to type in the program name you wish to load into memory. Unless you cancel, return to BASIC and type the Files command (which displays a list of all files on the disk), you probably won't remember the precise program name you need. This method violates both the minimum typing and minimum human memory requirements for sound Mac programming. But that doesn't mean that some future programmers will avoid such a waste of Mac power. Be on the lookout for these signs of sloppy programming.

▲ ▲ ▲ ▲ ▲ ▲ **Other Evaluation Tips**

Beyond the special requirements Macintosh software should have, there are other principles to follow when shopping for software, regardless of the computer. Of particular importance are the software's manual and its intuitive operation.

The software manual is frequently the downfall of a great program. There are a number of reasons for this, ranging from last minute changes in the program that cannot be reflected in the printed documentation, to a predominantly engineering focus on the part of the software developer. It is also difficult to judge some manuals while thumbing through them at the store. On quick perusal, the original Multiplan manual for the Macintosh version seemed to have everything a good manual should have: screen illustrations, a lengthy reference section for experienced users, and an index. But when a novice user tries to learn to use the program from the manual, it is clear that there are some gaps and incomplete descriptions of key points.

One thing you should search for in the manual is a separate section devoted to a tutorial. Even though the Mac is much simpler to use than most personal computers, the software coming out for it is very sophisticated. It takes a certain amount of hand holding for the use and application of these programs to sink in for the first-time user. The tutorial should not only lead you step by step through the basic operation of the program, but it should also provide an example of using the program in a real-world situation. I understand a program much more quickly when I see precisely how the program works with examples of the kind of work I do.

Intuitive operation of a program is a little easier to determine while sitting in front of the program running on a store Mac. Actually, it's something we all look for in a program—we'd rather be able to sit down, turn on the computer, and start using the program without ever cracking the manual.

If you know the general category into which a progam falls—financial modeling, word processing, database, graphics, etc.—then a truly intuitive program should provide enough information on screen and in the pull-down menus to lead you through a rudimentary application of the program.

When you first try a program, take a moment to look at the opening screen. Programmers will be using the Mac's high resolution graphics more and more to portray an explicit visual environment that replicates something you might find on a nonelectronic desktop—like the Habadex phone directory. Ask yourself if the onscreen metaphor is self-evident.

Next, pull down each menu and study the options in each. Are they grouped logically according to the name at the top of the menu? Do the options, themselves, make sense to you in the context of the program? Or are they ambiguous? I foresee Mac menu specialists evolving soon, whose sole purpose is to squeeze the meaning of a command description into fewer than ten characters so it will fit inside a menu column.

Select those menu options followed by three periods (such as Save As . . .) to study the dialog boxes which follow. Not only should they offer you many options (including the Cancel option), but the options should be clearly labeled so you can understand them. Now, don't expect to understand *every* option, especially in a program designed for a specialty you're not trained in. It is perfectly normal for a program designer to build into a professional program the terminology that a professional works with daily. That is a logical extension of the metaphor to the real-world work environment the Mac can depict.

Finally, try to work with the program without studying the manual. You might not get too far, but the further you get, the more intuitive the program will be for you. That means that even after you've studied the manual, you will be able to find your way out of difficulty by searching for a menu choice, rather than tearing through the manual for help.

I've worked with a lot of different computers over the years, and have torn the wrappers off hundreds of program packages. But today, when I'm presented with a batch of new software for several machines, I invariably reach for the Mac software first. Perhaps it's because I know that I'll probably be able to get something out of it without cracking the manual. Or maybe it's because programs for other computers are looking all the same, while a new Mac software program is almost an odyssey to a software designer's imagination. Whatever the reason behind my enthusiasm for new Mac software, however, I must temper it—as should you.

Now that Mac software is far more diverse and plentiful than in its early days, it is very important for us all, as software consumers, to be very critical and selective in our choices. Put a prospective program through its paces with precisely the kind of work you do, whether it be college coursework or a board of directors presentation. Shun programs that are all show and no substance. Embrace those that do the job elegantly and productively. The more we demand of software developers, the more they will respond in the future by pushing the state of the Mac programming art to its limits.

We'll all benefit from that.

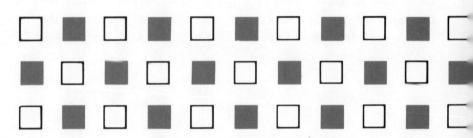

THIS DISCUSSION IS for experienced computer users—those who come to the Macintosh after struggling their way up the ladders of knowledge by learning CP/M on their Osborne 1 or learning MS-DOS on an IBM PC or compatible. I come from the second group. I cut my hard-core computing teeth on an IBM PC, fighting my way through the buggy and feature-less PC-DOS 1.00 (IBM's version of MS-DOS), the upgraded DOS 1.1, and learning all the vagaries of the substantially improved DOS 2.0/2.1 series. I recognized that the quickest way to become comfortable with life on a PC was to become comfortable with the operating system—memorizing its commands and nuances, conceiving of new methods to utilize batch files for ease of use.

Then came Macintosh. It was, according to Apple, for "the rest of us." That is to say, for those who have *not* dug their way into the guts of an operating system. Boy, were they right! I had become so enmeshed in a traditional operating system that the knowledge of keyboard commands, filename restrictions, disk drive names, and diskette formatting choices actually inhibited my feeling comfortable with the Macintosh. In talking to other converts from MS-DOS and CP/M computers, it seems that the more you know about an old-fashioned disk operating system, the more

APPENDIX

Unlearning CP/M and MS-DOS

difficult a time you have warming up to the Mac. You must literally "unlearn" everything you know about an operating system to feel at home on the Mac desktop.

◢ ◢ ◢ ◢ ◢ ◢ Who's in Charge?

I think the main difference between DOS and the Mac operating environment is that with DOS you must continually be on your toes, always in firm control over the destiny of files, filenames, and disk drives. This means that in your mind, you are doing a lot of double-checking about the commands you're issuing. DOS forces you to do the thinking for the computer. The Mac, on the other hand, does most of the thinking for you. The vague, jargon-filled, housekeeping tasks of DOS are performed automatically for you by the Mac operating environment. In return, experienced DOS users feel like they've lost control over the Mac because they don't have the feeling of direct access to the functions that comprise DOS. Let's take a look at some examples.

When you buy a box of 5¼ inch disks, you know that you'll be ahead of the game if you format the whole box at one sitting. That way, you won't run the risk of running out of blank disks and having to stop your application to format a new disk. If you've mastered DOS, you know that you can specify a few ways to format a disk: as single or double-sided, as an 8- or 9-sectored disk, with or without DOS copied to it, and in whatever disk drive is available. That's the power you have over these disks. After each formatting, the disk is checked, and you get a readout of the space available on the disk before proceeding.

But with the Mac, a DOS junkie gets nervous with a new box of disks to discover that there is no menu choice for formatting disks. Cold sweat runs down the back. You're so accustomed to issuing commands, and responding to a prompt to insert the blank disk that it seems entirely unnatural to do it otherwise.

Actually, the Macintosh way of initializing disks makes more sense. Simply insert a blank disk as you need it, even before a critical Save operation. The Mac operating environment recognizes that it is not yet initialized, and asks you whether you indeed want to initialize it. If so, you simply click the OK response and type in the name for the disk when prompted. You don't have to quit the program you are working on. You don't have to worry about whether the blank disk is in drive A: or B:, or whether the FORMAT program is on your current program disk. You don't have to remember which of the several possible parameters you want.

How about erasing a disk file to open up space on the disk? With DOS, you issue the ERASE command with the filename to be deleted, and then instantly issue a CHKDSK command to see how much space is now available on the disk. On the Mac, however, you can drag an unwanted file to the Trash and watch it disappear from the desktop. But to your surprise, the amount of available disk space displayed in the disk window does not change. That's because the file isn't fully removed from the disk until you either empty the Trash (from the Special menu) or eject the disk. The minute you choose Empty Trash, the disk space listing is updated.

Of course, this may seem like a frustrating, extra step in an otherwise straightforward operation. But what's happening here is that the file in reality is untouched until you perform a deliberate, second act of deletion (Empty Trash). It's a safeguard built into the Mac operating environment to let you recover from what might otherwise be a tragic error. Once you ERASE an MS-DOS file, only the help of a Norton Utilities program will let you laboriously recover the accidentally erased data on the disk—a slip of the digit while performing the ERASE command might accidentally rub out the wrong file. But with the Mac, you always have a second chance to dig that file out of the Trash and put it back on your desktop.

And then there are cases in which there is no equivalent in the Mac operating environment for a DOS command. One DOS command I sorely missed when experimenting with the Mac was the TYPE command, which displays the contents of any file on the screen without starting up any applications program. Taking that power away from me felt like burdening me with ball and chain. But I realized that more often than not, I used the TYPE command to see what the cryptic file name meant without loading the program disk. But the Mac gives you more room to name and describe the contents of a file than you'll ever use. So why bother looking at a raw data file?

◢ ◢ ◢ ◢ ◢ ◢ Letting Go

After working with the Mac for quite a while, I realized that the only way to feel comfortable with the strange environment was to roll with it. Each time I thought I was losing control, I stopped to examine the operation I thought I wanted to do, and how the Mac handles the operation. I discovered that in most cases, the Mac did an excellent, and a much more automatic, job of those functions than MS-DOS ever could. I also discovered that I no longer had to keep track of a lot of disk and file nonsense that MS-DOS insisted I remember to prevent making a DOS mistake.

The Macintosh operating environment, I've concluded, has been carefully crafted to take into account the possibility that its users will not be inclined to remember things about disks and files—therefore the environment had to be made much more forgiving and more anticipatory in its actions. It reaches out to the user, instead of sitting back with a smug A> prompt. It removes from the user the burden of memorizing commands, specifying file names and gibberish parameters, and creating all kinds of tricks to try to make the operating system as automatic as possible.

The final point, I guess, is that the Mac's operating system is so well integrated into its overall onscreen presence that there is barely any recognizable operating system in effect. You're not at an operating system level one minute, and at an applications level the next. You're either surveying your entire computing work area (the desktop) or focused more closely on one job (the application). If something akin to an operating system function needs doing along the way, the Mac alerts you and guides you ever so gently through whatever the procedure is.

That, in conclusion, is the essence of unlearning MS-DOS or CP/M when moving over to the Mac. Simply forget everything you learned about personal computers, and let the Mac lead you through it all.

INDEX

ABOUT THE AUTHOR

DANNY GOODMAN is a contributing editor to *Macworld, PC World,* and *Creative Computing* magazines. He is the author of numerous books, including *Going Places with the New Apple IIc* and *The Simon & Schuster Guide to the TRS-80 Model 100.* Danny Goodman appears frequently as a commentator on personal computers and electronics on the Public Broadcasting Service television series *The New Tech Times.* His articles on computers and electronics have appeared in *Playboy, Better Homes & Gardens, Chicago, Consumers Digest,* and many others.